Tiger Girl (Hu Nü)

A Creative Memoir

LIEN CHAO

We acknowledge the support of the Canada Council for the Arts for our publishing program. We also acknowledge support from the Ontario Arts Council.

Cover art: *Hu Nü*, 17" x 9" x 8.5", Bronze, 1997, by Peng Ma

Illustrations by Peng Ma, 2001

National Library of Canada Cataloguing in Publication Data

Chao, Lien, 1950-
 Tiger girl = Hu nü : a creative memoir

ISBN 0-920661-92-0 (bound).—ISBN 0-920661-93-9 (pbk.)

 1. Women—China—Social conditions. 2. China—Social conditions—1949-1976. 3. China—Social conditions—1976-
I. Title. II. Title: Hu nü.

HQ1767.C435 2001   305.4'0951   C2001-903765-1

Printed in Canada by Coach House Printing

TSAR Publications
P. O. Box 6996, Station A
Toronto, Ontario M5W 1X7
Canada

www.candesign.com/tsarbooks

In memory of my mother, Hu Liubo (1916–2001),

whose stories led me to tell our stories.

Part One

—————

My First Birthday

Like most people, I don't remember my birth, nor my first few birthdays. For the missing pieces in my life, I rely on my mother for reference. My father doesn't gossip, nor does he tell stories about the past. My mother, on the other hand, not only tells stories, but also enjoys mimicking the voices of the characters. She dramatizes the details and adds her own comments at the dénouement.

In September 1984, when I was about to leave China for Canada to pursue my graduate studies, my mother gave me a fading black-and-white photograph. "This picture was taken when you were one year old," she said. Reminiscing, she then told me the story of my journey. According to her, I was fated to go to a remote place as distant as Canada. She said my fate was decided when I was a year old.

Born in the Year of the Tiger, I was the eldest daughter of my parents and the eldest grandchild of the Hu family. My grandparents lived in a village in the southeastern part of China. According to tradition, grandparents named their grandchildren, so mine did their job by giving me the name "Nü," which, as I later found out meant "female," stating the obvious fact that I was a girl. It was hardly a personal name. However, because our family name "Hu" had the same sound as the word "tiger" except for a slightly different tone, my name "Hu Nü" became significant to me. I can't imagine myself with another name. I am not just an ordinary Chinese girl—-I am a Tiger Girl.

Looking at the faint black-and-white picture, I simply couldn't visualize myself that young. In the photograph, I had a short haircut, I looked more like a baby boy than a girl. A Chinese girl in the 1950s usually had a silk ribbon decorating her hair, even if her hair was short. "Why didn't I have a colourful ribbon on my hair, Mama?" I asked, without lifting my eye from the photo.

"It would please your grandparents when you looked more like a boy than a girl," she said. She then told me about my first birthday at my grandparents' home. It was the day when my destination was revealed.

"When your daughter grows up, she will leave you and go far away from home," my grandmother told her son and daughter-in-law with the voice of a family authority. She was sixty years old with six grown-up children, five sons and one daughter. Her grey hair was combed neatly backwards and rolled into a black fish net pinned behind her head, the skin on her face was tight and shiny.

According to the custom of the village, which holds still today, the elders, usually the grandparents, sit at the top end of the table, sons and daughters-in-law sit along the two sides of the table, and grandchildren are supposed to sit at the opposite side of the elders. The top of the table faces the door and faces away from the ancestors' photographs above the altar. That day since my mother had me on her lap and I was the first grandchild, we were made to sit at the end of the table, facing my grandparents and our ancestors' framed photographs.

"So how do you know?" asked my mother, the daughter-in-law, who was then in her late twenties.

Grandmother was not used to direct questions from her family. She was surprised that her city-born daughter-in-law actually dared to challenge her. Calming herself down, she pointed her finger at me. "Just look at the way she is holding her chopsticks, how many babies can hold chopsticks at the far ends? That is an indication of her future life in a faraway land."

Sitting comfortably on my mother's lap, I was playing with a pair of chopsticks, holding them at the top ends and dipping them in a small wooden bowl. Everyone at the table, except my mother, was convinced as they turned to look at me.

In the village where my grandparents lived, if a daughter-in-law contradicted her mother-in-law, she was condemned by public opinion. Although my mother didn't believe in fate, she didn't want to upset the old woman. Without looking at her mother-in-law, she responded, "If Hu Nü has to go far away from home when she grows up, that's all right with me." After a pause, she added as if talking to herself, "Maybe she would be even better off."

"But, you don't want her to go too far away, do you? You don't want to lose sight of her to . . . ," Grandmother, who had never left her village, couldn't come up with the name of a distant place. Yet the unknown place had given her an indescribable maternal pain. "Then, you won't see her much . . . , " her voice dropped low.

"Something, you know, something can be done," the older woman resumed her tone looking at her grown-up children at the table. "We can stop her from going that far." She regained her certainty as soon as her mind returned to the village.

Putting down his chopsticks, Grandfather thought it was time that he stated his opinion in this important family matter. "What's the point of bringing up a daughter for someone else far away? You can never have her do filial duties. And that's why you have children in the first place." He looked at his wife, she nodded; he turned to his sons sitting at the sides of the table, they were all silent. The older couple now waited for their eldest son and daughter-in-law to respond.

"What do you suggest, Mother?" my father, the eldest son, asked his parents.

"We are not suggesting anything new or different, why don't you just follow the tradition of the village?" Grandmother asked, trying to sound reasonable. She and her husband took it as their responsibility to advise their son and daughter-in-law. In fact, they had been waiting patiently for an entire year to tell the young couple what should have been done as soon as their daughter was born.

My mother was holding her breath. She didn't know the customs of her husband's village. Her husband remained silent, he was brought up to obey his parents unconditionally. After a short pause, the older woman barked: "Give this baby girl away! Give her to cousin Yu-lin's family as a child bride. They have three sons. One of the boys will marry her when she grows up." The old woman paused, watching her son and daughter-in-law.

"Maybe, in addition, you should pay Yu-lin fifty yuan compensation," added Grandfather thoughtfully. "His family will treat your daughter as their own."

Letting out a sigh of relief, Grandmother smiled. "Then, you see, you two are immediately free to have a son next year."

Dead silence fell over the table.

But Mother's ears echoed with the words she had just heard. "Give this baby away! Give her to cousin Yu-lin's family as a child bride." She hugged me tightly to her chest as if someone were about to snatch me away from her that very moment. Father stopped eating, there was a lump in his throat; he couldn't swallow or speak. Actually, he preferred sons to daughters, what could a daughter achieve in life except get married and have children? But, as the first university graduate in his family, he felt that giving away his first-born as a child-bride was not appropriate.

Grandmother took the silence of the young couple as consent. She went on to elaborate her plan. "This way, your daughter will not go far away from home, because we will kow that she will be married here in the village."

Mother heaved a sigh and felt she was choking. Her mother-in-law stopped talking. Taking this opportunity, the young couple asked to be excused from the table. They left the village without packing.

For the two hours my parents walked swiftly and silently on the country road towards the railway station. The sticky clay path pulled them back.

All these years, my parents had never said a word about my first birthday until I was about to leave China. In fact they had never talked about it again between themselves until their second daughter was born. But to this day, my mother still vividly remembers what happened on my first birthday. She remembers I was unusually quiet that day. She said sometimes a child can grow up suddenly under the circumstances. I did that, she said, on my first birthday in my grandparents' village.

"Let's Swap the Babies!"

"What was Grandmother's name?" Hu Nü asked her mother, curious about the old lady who had wanted to give her away as a child bride. Mother looked at Father, indicating he should answer the question. It took Father a few minutes to recollect his thoughts; finally with his eyes fixed on his daughter, he said, "Her last name was Chen."

"What was her personal name?" Hu Nü asked.

Father was hesitant. After a pause, "she didn't have one," he answered quietly.

"What?"

"She didn't have one."

"But why?"

"People didn't think they needed to name their daughters at that time. Sooner or later she would be someone else." Father sighed, his eyes shifting away to the blank wall. The sad look on his face only reminded Hu Nü of his deep depression which surfaced from time to time. She knew she had touched a sensitive nerve by reminding him that he had no sons but four daughters.

Mother said it was lucky that her mother-in-law died in 1952 before the birth of her second granddaughter in 1953, her third one in 1959, and the fourth one in 1963. "Had your grandmother lived long enough to see all of you," she said, "she would have died of a broken heart, and she would have had your father divorce me as a sonless daughter-in-law a long time ago."

Mother likes talking about the births of her grown-up daughters on their birthdays. It was Mei's birthday. They knew Mother would tell a story about her birth. Mei was the second daughter of the Hus, born in 1953, in Beijing. At the time Father was working for the Chinese Railway Ministry; the Hu family was living in a one-bedroom apartment in the Railway Ministry Residence. They were looking forward to having another child, because with two children, they would be qualified to apply for a two-bedroom apartment. It was glorious to have more children. Ever since the Korean war, the Chinese government encouraged women of reproductive age to have more children and thus help build up a strong China.

Another time, Mother said: "There was this mother; she already had six children, and she was pregnant again. This time she had quadruplets."

"Wow!" Her grownup daughters cheered.

"Well," Mother continued, "the newspapers published big headlines `Heroic Mother,' 'Our National Pride,' and photographs of the mother with her four babies who looked like four piglets clinging to her bosom."

"Shortly after the quadruplets were born, the state and national organizations stepped in to help," Mother continued. "Beijing municipal government offered to support one baby; China's Children's Aid Society would take care of another; the Chinese National Women's Association would adopt a third one, so the parents would only have to raise one baby as in a normal situation." Mother looked around at her four grown-up daughters at the table.

"But this made three babies orphans," Mei protested.

"They had no choice, and after all, the Party was trying to help," Mother answered. However ridiculous the heroic mother's story was, this was how the Chinese population doubled in two decades, before birth control was imposed in the 1970s. "Anyway," Mother said, "the heroic mother's story was but a historical backdrop for Mei's birth".

When Mei was born, Father was at work in another city. Realizing her time was coming, Mother put a washing basin in a fish-net bag and walked to Beijing Railway hospital, where her family had medical coverage.

At birth, Mei weighed nine pounds and five ounces, an extraordinarily big baby with a chubby face, big round eyes, and oily black hair covering her soft head. The nurses in the labour room immediately fell in love with this big baby. They passed her around and everyone congratulated Mother for her successful delivery of a healthy baby. For a while, Mother was relieved, but shortly afterwards she began worrying about her husband's response to another daughter.

Half an hour after Mei was born, next to Mother in the same labour room an older woman in her earlier fifties gave birth to a healthy baby boy. The nurses congratulated her, but the woman burst out crying. She had already had four sons and she really didn't want to have another boy. She told the nurses her life story: she and her husband joined the revolution in the early 1940s; their sons were born during the war and raised by relatives. Upon liberation, her family was reunited, but the boys were not close to the parents. Now before her biological clock ran out, she and her husband wanted to have a daughter. The nurses listened to her with sympathy; they tried to console her, after all, she was a revolutionary cadre who was supposed to have unusual courage.

Suddenly the woman suppressed her sobbing as she looked around Mother, who had already been moved to a wheeled stretcher. The nurse was about to take her to her ward. Mother was resting quietly with her baby wrapped up in a bundle beside her pillow, and she was thinking what her husband would say upon hearing the news of another daughter.

"Comrade," the revolutionary cadre called softly, raising herself from the bed with her arms. Mother tried to open her eyes, wondering who was talking to her. "Comrade, let me ask you something, how many children did you already have?"

"One," my mother murmured.

"A boy or a girl?"

"A girl."

"Oh, how wonderful! This is going to work out just fine." The revolutionary cadre sat up in her bed excitedly. "Now listen, I have a proposal, which will benefit both of us and our families. Let's swap the babies! You have my son and I have your daughter! Nobody will ever know this except you and I. Let's do it now before the sexes of the babies get out of this room." She was so excited that she was nearly out of breath. "If you agree," she paused, "I will tell the nurses to keep it a secret." The older woman looked anxiously at the younger one.

"Let's swap the babies!"

"Let's swap the babies!"

Mother felt her heart racing. She heard a drum beating inside her head. Stretching her arm out and quickly pulling it back, she held her baby tightly.

"Do you agree? You can certainly trust me that I would give your daughter, of course, it would be my daughter then, the best upbringing in China. We have professional nurses, she will go to the best kindergarten in Beijing, and later the best school. My husband and I will be able to satisfy all her needs, financially and politically. Come on, comrade, I am pretty sure your husband would be much happier to have a son than another daughter."

Mother's heart pounded faster and the drumming inside her head suddenly became unbearable. The room was spinning with echoes of the woman's voice, "Let's swap the babies!" She felt anxious at the mention of her husband's likely reaction towards another daughter. How could this woman know her husband so well?

"Let's swap the babies!"

"Let's swap the babies!"

She repeated the sentence inside her head to feel its weight. The volume of the echoing voice started to increase and became louder and louder. How can any mother ever say that? Mother was ashamed of herself for being tempted by such a crime, even if the idea sounded mutually beneficial.

"Comrade, comrade," the woman started to beg, "you have to decide now, we don't have the whole day to ponder over it. My husband is outside in the waiting room. The nurse is going to tell him the sex of the baby now. What if I pay you two thousand *yuan* compensation for your pregnancy?"

"Compensation?" This time Mother felt a churning pain in her heart as if she were stabbed. She had heard the words before.

"Compensation money," she gasped, remembering what her father-in-law had suggested to her and her husband two years ago at their elder daughter's first birthday. If giving away baby girls as child-brides was a crime according to the government, what about swapping babies? What about this revolutionary cadre who would pay compensation money to swap her son for a daughter?

"No!"

"No!"

"No!" Mother said the word three times. She didn't want to hear any more about trading her child. Her loud voice startled everyone in the labour room, echoing down the long hallway to the waiting room behind the glass door. With a deep sigh of relief, she closed her eyes, exhausted. The face of the revolutionary cadre turned pale and stony. Collapsing on her bed, she cried again. A nurse started pushing Mother out of the labour room and another went to inform the husband of the other woman in the waiting room.

Two days after Mei was born, nurses at the maternity ward were wondering why nobody came to visit Mother; in fact, there was not even a single telephone call inquiring about the sex of the baby. On the evening of the third day, the duty nurse was delighted to hear finally somebody asking about the woman. Before she found out about the caller, she started giving away the exciting news: "A beautiful and healthy baby girl. She weighed nine pounds and five . . ." Before she could finish her sentence, the nurse heard a click, the other party had hung up. For a while she didn't know what to say, she felt deeply insulted. Should she tell the patient about the caller? If this was the patient's husband, the nurse thought, the patient should definitely be prepared before returning home.

At eight o'clock that night, half an hour before the hospital's closing time, Father showed up in the maternity ward, which was shared by seven other women. Putting down a bundle of green bananas on the little cupboard next to his wife's bed, he sat down in a chair. She didn't need to mention the phone call, she could read the disappointment written all over his face.

"How are you?" he asked her brusquely, and his sight quickly swept across her pillow.

"Fine," she answered firmly.

He didn't ask for the baby, but she thought she would mention it. "It is too late to see the baby tonight, the babies' room closes at seven."

Talking about babies, the other women started to interrupt: "Oh, you are one lucky man, your wife has given you such a gorgeous baby!"

"Wait until you see her pink round face, her big bright eyes and her thick black hair! She is every parent's dream baby!"

"Oh, you lucky man!"

Looking around, Father didn't know what to say. He felt something in his throat moving up and down, it was hard for him to swallow. "I'll come early tomorrow to see the baby," he said, standing up to leave "I've brought you some bananas."

Their hands covering up their mouths, the women tried to suppress their giggles. As soon as Father left the room, they burst out laughing. They laughed loudly for such a long time that their overstretched, post-labour abdomen muscles hurt.

"How could any man in the world bring green bananas to his wife right after her labour?" they asked.

According to Chinese custom, after labour, women should eat only warm food. In order to have milk for the baby, they are supposed to have protein-based soups, with fish or meat or the most popular, pig feet. Women are expected to recuperate for a month after giving birth. During that month, they are not supposed to do any physical work, or to touch cold water, or to read intensively, or to go out of the house, or to have sex.

When the women in Mother's ward heard Father was an architect by profession, they called him a bookworm who knew little about real life.

Mother stayed in the hospital for a week. On the day she and her baby were discharged from the hospital, the green bananas had just started to turn yellow.

"It's not her fault that she was born a girl!"

Following Father's job transfer in 1959, my family moved from Beijing to Wuhan. We moved into a bachelor apartment on the second floor of a small building. Next door to us lived the Mas, whom we called the horses behind their backs, because *ma* means "horse" in Chinese. The Mas were a three-generation family living in a one bedroom apartment: father, mother, two sons and their paternal grandmother. I remember the months when Mrs Ma and my mother were both pregnant. The two women often compared notes, for example, about the babies' first kicks and the shapes of their abdomens. I learned that a rounded belly usually signalled a girl, while a more protruding belly a boy. Knowing my parents were hoping for a boy, Mrs Ma confirmed that my mother's belly looked quite sharp from outside. My mother appreciated Mrs Ma's kindness; in return, she said Mrs Ma's belly was almost perfectly rounded.

Summer was a season of sweating for people in Wuhan, one of China's famous three furnaces. People in the building wore as few clothes as they could possibly manage without being embarrassed. It gave me a daily opportunity to observe the shapes of both women's abdomens. I saw the very opposite of what they each might be hoping for. It seemed to me that my mother was going to have another girl and Mrs Ma another boy, but my observation was kept a secret, because a girl was not supposed to gossip about such matters.

As their due dates approached, almost all the neighbours said the same thing, that my mother was going to have a boy, and my father was really happy. I was truly confused; how could adults fail to see what was so obvious in front of their eyes? The shape of my mother's belly was like an extra-large basketball hidden under her loose shirt.

Mrs Ma was due first, at the end of June. To nobody's surprise, she had a boy. All neighbours were happy for the Mas. On the day the baby came home, our narrow staircase was crowded with visitors going up and going down. All day long Grandmother Ma, whom we called "Ma Nainai"in Chinese, was busy serving brown sugar tea. Usually Ma Nainai wore no top on a hot day, because the only two grown-up men, her son and my father, didn't come home until the evening. During the day, she was not embarrassed at all walking around the second floor with her flat dry breasts hanging in front of her bony chest. But that day when her daughter-in-law came back from the hospital with her baby grandson, Ma Nainai wore a dark green silk shirt. I heard her mumbling through her toothless mouth, *dou-zi-duo-fu*, "more sons more happiness." How could Ma Nainai suddenly become so sarcastic? Though toothless, her words bit deeply into the flesh of the Hus.

Mother went to the hospital when Father was at work and we were all at school. She must have realized her time was coming, and she managed to cut up a sweet yellow-skinned pumpkin and put the slices inside a wok to cook. It would be our dinner that day. Then she took a washing basin and walked to the hospital by herself. July 23, 1959 was the hottest day of summer that year. And in Wuhan, the thermometre went up to 43°C. It was also the year that China suffered from starvation due to the failure of the "Great Leap Forward." People were told that an unprecedented three-year natural disaster hit the country and in addition to natural disasters, the Soviet Union had suddenly withdrawn its technological aid from China. My family was surviving mainly on vegetables, pumpkins in summer and turnips in winter. The government allowed us seven *jins* (1 *jin* equals 500 g) of rice per person per month. The rest of the rationed food consisted of half *jin* of meat, a quarter *jin* of oil, two pieces of tofu, and fifteen to twenty *jin*, depending on whether one was a child or an adult, of mouldy dried yam, rough corn flour processed with the husks and probably even the core inside, or other types of stale grains. Many people, including Mother, developed liver problems from eating mouldy grains.

Coming back from school that afternoon, my sister and I saw sweet nutty pumpkin slices simmering in the wok on top of the coal stove. We each had a few pieces. It didn't even occur to me to ask Ma Nainai where Mother went. We went outside to play with other kids until Father came home in the evening.

Father looked anxious. He didn't have time to eat his pumpkin. Putting down his briefcase, without talking to us, he left immediately for the hospital.

It didn't take him long to return from the hospital. The anxious look on his face was replaced by the familiar expression of personal sorrow and even self-disgust that I was afraid to see. His dark face showed a lack of emotion, his eyes avoided the questioning eyes of Ma Nainai in the kitchen. The pumpkin slices had gone cold and lost its luxurious golden colour and sweet fragrance. Father ate a piece with a glass of cold water from the pitcher. From his face I could tell that they had another daughter, and I, another sister.

That night, lying inside my mosquito net, I felt unusually hot and suffocated. For hours I heard Father fanning himself. The palm tree hand fan flapped rhythmically, the sound interrupted only by his deep sighs and when the fan occasionally fell from his hand. I lay sweating and awake, my eyes fixed on the ceiling of the mosquito net. Gazing hard through the cloak of hazy darkness around the bed, I could see the shapes of things in the room. I also heard the deep fog horns of ships on the Yangtze River a kilometre away. The usually busy ferry was resting inside the harbour, but the bigger ships on longer journeys upstream to Chongqing or downstream to Shanghai didn't retire at night. They stopped at Wuhan Harbour for supplies. The sleeping city was so used to the fog horns that most people never heard them at all, except for those who suffered insomnia. That night I heard the fog horns for the first time in my life as they accompanied Father's sighs. I promised myself that I would live to prove to Father that some daughters could be as good as sons, if not better.

Two days later Mother came home from the hospital with a tiny baby girl wrapped inside a single layer of a flowery cotton sheet. My baby sister already showed signs of extraordinary beauty. Her big bright eyes, thick shiny black hair, and especially her tiny cherry mouth evoked admiration. All female visitors complimented Mother on her baby's delicate mouth. Mother thought a good brain would be more important to her daughter's future than the size of her mouth, but she was still happy to see her neighbours' enthusiasm for her baby. However, since the baby's birth, she had not heard a single response from her husband. It seemed as if he hadn't even noticed they had another daughter. He was simply preoccupied with an unusually busy schedule. Most people worked six days a week, her husband worked on Sundays as well. Normal people in Wuhan had a siesta after lunch and then went to the office or workshop late in the afternoon for a cold drink provided by the government. Her husband was different; being the chief architect he always had too much work. She thought perhaps this was how he managed not to think about his third daughter.

It was a sticky, breathlessly hot evening. We had our dinner and bath before Father came home from work. Usually the rest of the evening before nine was our playtime. We lived within a short walking distance of the Yangtze River, and we liked the riverside. On both sides of river, a long dike had been constructed in 1954 after an unusually severe flood. The dikes are three and half metres high. They look like small pyramids: their inner sides are built with huge stones, and the outer sides facing the street are covered with weeds all year around. Big cement stairs are constructed at each street intersection, so people can go up to the top of the dikes. There is a narrow path at the top which is also covered with weeds. Wuhan people like their river dikes. They go there almost every evening. Climbing up the stairs and facing the cool breeze from the river, everyone lets out a deep sigh of relief. There is the river; when it is not surging, it lies far away from the bank. People even live inside the banks. You can always hear the river, its deep echoing sound is part of an eternal background.

Mei and I loved to chase each other in the tall grass on top of the dikes. Sometimes, we tried to roll down the slope towards the street. We knew just when to stop, before we could fall off the slope and hit the street. This was considered a boys' game, but I wanted to be better than the boys. Sometimes we caught grasshoppers, locusts, and fireflies and put them inside a small bottle. Then we watched them jumping on each other. I was fascinated by fireflies, they never gave up, not even inside the confinement of a small bottle. They made a glow of light before they died.

There were always a lot of people sleeping on the sidewalks of the streets. This is a peculiar summer custom in Wuhan. In late June and the whole month of July, the temperature rises as the day proceeds, and it can reach its peak of above 40°. Usually, there is no wind. Humidity and heat drive people outside for relief. Residents pull out their beds to sleep outside, some even with mosquito nets. My parents found it hard to appreciate this local custom of sleeping beside neighbours. No matter how hot it was, we had to sleep inside our bachelor apartment.

My parents had a proper double bed with a wooden head board, an end board and a traditional flex-woven matress. Mei and I each had a single bed made of a wooden board between two wooden benches. Our apartment was actually one large rectangular room seven metres long by four metres wide. In order to create some privacy, my mother put an off-white cotton curtain in the middle of the room, so that we had two rooms instead of one large room. My parents' bed was in the inner room, and behind the curtain in the outer room were our single beds side by side. The rest of the furniture we had were a bookcase, two desks, a round dinner table and four chairs.

Before Mother had her third daughter, she made the desk in their part of room into a baby's bed. She said it was too hot to have the baby sleeping with them. She put a cotton padding on the desk and even sewed a little mosquito net to hang over it. Although it didn't quite look like a cradle, it was my baby sister's bed for two years.

I would never forget what happened later one night after Mei and I came back from playing on the riverbank. It was about ten o'clock when we walked into our apartment. Our parents were still sitting at the dinner table facing each other. I could tell that they had had a drink, because there were two small Chinese wine glasses on the table. I felt my mouth watering. At dinner, Mother gave us each some of the pork-turnip dish which we ate slowly to enjoy its taste. Pork was rationed in 1959. In order to make it last Mother bought half a *jin* at a time, which was about the size of a chicken breast. She sliced it into smaller pieces and cooked it with vegetables. So we seemed to have more meaty dishes than other people. But we never had a dish of real meat as the Mas did. As Muslims, they were given twice more rationed beef each month than the portion of pork we received. The dish we had that night tasted so delicious that both Mei and I wanted more. But we knew that pork was rationed for Mother's postpartum nutrition, we should let her eat it, so our baby sister could have more milk.

Mei and I climbed inside our mosquito nets to sleep. I heard Father standing up from the table and asking his wife to save the rest of the food for the next day. He then went inside their part of the room behind the curtain. He put down the wooden bathtub. Ordinary Chinese families didn't have the Western style bathtub and shower in their apartments. Instead, every family had at least one or two portable wooden bathtubs, which could contain five to ten litres of water. Before Mother put the cotton curtain in the middle of the room, the rest of us had to go outside when someone was having a bath. Now with the curtain in the middle of the room, Mei and I got used to the noise of water splashing and towel rubbing when my parents took their baths one by one at night while we were in bed.

I must have fallen asleep already when I heard the baby crying. Mother was still busy with the dishes in the kitchen. I heard her footsteps rushing back to the apartment from the corridor, I closed my eyes again. She put down the leftover food she had just reheated. Nobody had a refrigerator at that time, but we knew every leftover dish had to be reboiled and then left to cool off at night. I heard Mother put down the dishes on the table and rush into the inner apartment. The curtain was disturbed as she pushed through, ripples spreading out on the sheet from where she entered. She changed a diaper, I heard the baby sucking her breast.

"Isn't it better to stay inside mother's belly than coming out into the world?" She was talking to the baby, "You wouldn't have to suffer this heat if you were not born." Was Mother complaining for the baby or herself? I wondered. But I knew she hadn't had time to take a bath yet.

Father seemed to have finished his bath, since the washing noise had stopped. I heard him fanning himself to cool off. Mother put down the baby on her little bed, the desk. But as soon as she touched the bed, the baby woke up and started to cry again. Mother picked her up and fed her again with her other breast. This time she didn't talk. She was waiting for the baby to fall asleep so that she could finish her chores and take a bath. It was getting late. After about five minutes, she put the baby back to bed; by then Father had already emptied the bath tub, he was ready for bed. Mother would have to go to the kitchen to get her bath water. Just as she had left the room, and before the ripples on the curtain settled down, the baby started to cry again. I heard Father stirring in bed, I thought he was going to pick her up and at least talk to her until Mother came. But he was grumpy about something. The baby didn't stop crying, her voice got louder. My eyes were wide open, gazing at the curtain between my parents' bed and mine. Suddenly, I heard Father getting up; his feet searched the floor for his slippers. The next thing I heard was the baby bawling because Father was whipping her with his belt. Against the light in their room through the curtain, I could see the silhouette of Father's arm raising up in the air with his belt and then coming down on the baby.

"Mama! Mama! Father is beating the baby!" I screamed at the top of my lungs. The baby's howling became a sobbing, there were pauses between her cries, as if she was choking. Mother was running; her slippers flapping rapidly on the old wooden floor. I sat up in bed inside my mosquito net like a statue not knowing what to do. Mother rushed inside the room, almost pulling down the curtain with her. She started screaming as soon as she saw what was happening.

"It's not her fault that she was born a girl! It's nobody's fault that the weather is hot! You must be crazy to beat a baby! You are a hypocrite, an animal to beat a baby!"

Father didn't say a word. He simply went back to bed. The baby was still sobbing, so was Mother. She picked her up, sat down in the chair beside the desk and fed her. Gently patting her, she said, "Don't forgive him when you grow up."

I lay down quietly. Soon enough, I heard Father snoring.

In those hot days, both the Mas and my family slept with our apartment doors open for ventilation. The next morning, Mother said the leftover pork-turnip she had reheated and left on the table to cool off was eaten up by a wild cat at night. She said she was too tired to remember covering it up. Mei and I felt awfully sorry for letting a street cat enjoy such a delicious meat dish.

The Story of Shuixian

Growing up, we heard more stories about Ping's birth than anybody else. In fact Mother said the reason she decided to have the fourth child was strictly because of what had happened to her when she gave birth to her third daughter. Ping was born on July 23, 1959, the hottest day in the Chinese lunar calendar year. The temperature rose up to 43° in the afternoon. When she was ready, two nurses moved Mother on a stretcher to Maternity Ward 4. There were eight beds in the ward, most of them unoccupied. It seemed that other women had planned their pregnancy with more common sense to avoid the heat of the year. The nurses covered my mother with a hospital blanket and left her there to rest. The bed was between two windows facing west. The fierce afternoon sun cast its powerful beam through the curtainless windows across the room to the door. Exhausted and dehydrated, Mother was dozing off in the sunshine.

Half an hour passed, maybe even longer, Mother seemed to sense the physical state of her body. She felt as if somebody was pounding her head, there was a painful buzzing inside. She decided not to open her eyes. But the extreme bright sunshine penetrated her eyelids and cut through her flesh; she wanted so much to rest her exhausted body, but she couldn't.

Mother was dreaming of fetching water from a well. She was a child, more than twenty years ago, back at her hometown in Hangzhou. After all these years she still remembered how to throw the empty pail at the end of a long rope down into the deep well. As soon as the bottom of the pail touched the surface of the water five metres below the ground, she gave the rope a quick yank, then a pull, then another quick twist. Now she felt the weight of the pail in her hand as it started to sink; she knew it was time to pull up the rope. She was so thirsty, she put her face into the fresh cool water in the pail and started to drink. She drank until she had enough of it. She poured the rest of the pail down her bare legs and down her feet. A heavenly treat!

Mother woke up. Remembering the soothing cool drink from the well, she felt her throat burning like a furnace, and so was her head. Remembering the nurse had said something about ringing the bell if she needed assistance, she stretched out her arm. She pressed the button, and for a while she thought she heard the the bell ringing. But nobody came; she pressed down the button again, this time with her thumb. She noticed it was not a brass bell that would make the crystal clear "ding-dong" sound. This was only a plastic button; when pressed, a little red light started to flick for a few seconds like a firefly at night. She pressed the button again, and kept her thumb on for at least five minutes. Nothing happened, the flickering red light died out as soon as she let go her thumb. Meanwhile she felt the weight of her head increasing and the pounding pain inside sent her an urgent signal. She decided to get up.

Mother struggled to sit up in bed, pushing the blanket off. On the straw sheet and pillow case there was a wet shadow shaped by her sweat. She was actually sitting in the wet stain. She moved to the edge of the bed and got up. Under the wet straw sheet there was a thick cotton mattress on a wire bed. Mother used all her strength to pull the mattress off the bed and threw it on the floor. She was out of breath; she tried to lick her dry lips, but she didn't seem to have any saliva left in her mouth. Looking around for water, she saw another woman sleeping on a corner bed opposite her side. Mother decided not to disturb her; she would go to the washroom by herself.

In the corridor, she didn't run into anyone, not even a nurse or a doctor. The whole hospital was having a siesta. There was nobody in the washroom either. Mother went in, turned on the tap, washed her hands and face with the clear cold water. She then scooped the water to her mouth, very much like the way she had done in her dream a while ago. She could feel cold water running down her hot throat into her stomach. It was so soothing that she thought it would be really nice if she could have a shower at this point. Looking around the washroom, behind the toilet cubicle there was a metre high cold water tap, under which the janitors usually rinsed the mops and chamber pots. Mother remembered she was not supposed to touch cold water for a whole month after labour, but she had already drunk plenty of unboiled cold water. Should she have a cold shower, since there was no hot water? She hesitated for a few minutes, wondering whether she should risk health problems in her old age because of washing in cold water. Traditional Chinese doctors believe that after labour women are extremely vulnerable; improper activities, such as washing in cold water or going out without wrapping up one's head, can cause back pain, arthritis, migrant headaches, cracking skin, and other problems. If the problem was a postpartum condition, it could only be cured during the next postpartum recuperation.

Mother recalled the ward, her bed, the curtainless windows from which came in the unbearable heat. She felt the pounding headache come on again, she decided she would have a cold shower. She locked the door of the washroom gently and went over to turn on the tap. Peeling off the hospital robe from her back, and using her hands, she threw water onto her body. It was immediately comforting. She stepped over, and let water come straight on her body from the waist down along her legs to her feet. She imagined herself fetching water from the well twenty years ago back at her home in Hangzhou. She always liked to play with water!

Someone was knocking on the door. This kind of shared washroom was generally not supposed to be locked from inside. She quickly wrapped herself up with a towel and went over to open the door. It was a nurse.

"What are you doing here? Oh, my God, you are washing yourself in cold water! Don't you want to live any more?! Did you know you could catch the deadly puerperal fever? Having a cold shower right after labour, this is insane!" The nurse went on and on, scolding her patient as if she were her inexperienced daughter-in-law. Mother felt ashamed of herself for lacking common sense, and especially for being caught by a much younger woman. She apologized for her inappropriate behaviour, then made a gentle complaint about the suffocating heat in her ward. She said she knew she was about to have a sunstroke if she didn't get up to drink some water and cool herself. She also made another soft complaint about the emergency bell which didn't seem to work in her room. The nurse didn't say anything.

Back in her ward, Mother felt more comfortable. She put the straw sheet back on the bed and wiped it with a towel. She changed into her own clean clothes, a loose silk top and a pair of loose cotton shorts. She took some *rendang*, a Chinese herbal pill for sunstroke and heat-related headache. Then she sat on a chair outside the ward and fanned herself with a palm-leaf fan she had brought from home.

It was time for visitors. Mother was wondering what time her two daughters would return home from school and if they would be able to find the pumpkin slices in the wok. What about her husband? He normally came home around eight in the evening. He would be even more disappointed now to find out that he had a third daughter. She remembered Mrs Ma saying her belly was pointed, a sign for a boy. She had known Mrs Ma was lying to her, as she had done to Mrs Ma. She wished her husband would come home later than usual that evening. Maybe he wouldn't have time to come to the hospital before closing time, or at least he wouldn't have to stay for long.

While Mother was preoccupied with her own thoughts, she saw a young man hurrying down the corridor with a basket of food in his hand. He looked like a visitor, somebody's husband. From his manner, Mother guessed he was a first-time father. By the time a couple had two or three children, they would have slowed down. The young man looked only in his twenties, he was sweaty and excited. He smiled at Mother and then went straight into Ward 4. By then

Mother remembered there was another woman in the same ward. She seemed to have been under the hospital blanket for quite some time. Mother thought she should have offered the woman a glass of water after she came back from the washroom. Anyway, she was glad to see the woman's husband here.

The young man tiptoed to the corner bed, putting down the basket on the cupboard carefully. Bending over, he gently patted the woman underneath the blanket. "Shuixian . . . Shuixian . . . are you sleeping? Time for dinner, I'm here . . ." the man paused waiting for a response. Looking at the hospital blanket suspiciously, he started pulling it down quickly. "Shuixian, wake up, I'm here! Shuixian . . . what happened? What has happened to you? Shuixian, my wife . . . Shuixian! Wake up! Wake up!" The young man was rocking the woman, there was no response from the limp body.

"Nurse! Nurse! Nurse!" The young man screamed.

"Nurse! Nurse! Nurse! Emergency! Ward 4!" Mother yelled simultaneously. Her heart was beating like a drum. She tried not to think about the worst. She rushed down the corridor to the office . The young man pressed the emergency bell. The little red light started to blink.

A group of nurses rushed in with emergency rescue equipment. A doctor followed them. The team started checking the woman's heartbeat and blood pressure; a nurse gave her an injection, the doctor began artificial respiration. The empty and quiet Ward 4 became a battle field. Heat and tension hung in the air. Sweat was streaming down everyone's face. The young husband was standing by, clenching his fists nervously.

Ten minutes passed, the rescue team suddenly slowed down and stopped. A deadly silence fell over the bed. The nurses looked around at the young husband with sadness in their eyes, when the doctor stepped forward and said in a hoarse voice: "I am very sorry. She had a heat stroke. She passed away."

"A heat stroke?" The young man burst out shouting. "But, this is a hospital! How could a patient die of heat stroke in the hospital? This is ridiculous! I want my wife back! I want my wife . . . Somebody has to pay for her life! Shuixian . . . you can't be gone like this . . ." He choked over his own unbearable anger and sudden loss. A white sheet was pulled over the woman's body. The young husband jumped up and threw away the sheet on the floor. Kneeing down, he held his wife's head inside his arm, wailing like a child.

"Shuixian, what a lovely name . . ." Mother murmured to herself, all the time she was standing by the door, praying silently to the Buddha of the Eternal Mercy to save the young woman's life. By the time the doctor was leaving the ward, Mother had collapsed on the chair. "Shuixian, what a lovely name . . . a water fairy, and a daffodil, you shouldn't have to die so young." Tears were streaming down Mother's cheeks.

We heard about Shuixian's story many times on Ping's birthdays. Shuixian had given birth to a boy. The baby boy stayed in the hospital for two months before his grandmother from a northern village came to take him home.

Mother Wanted Another Child

After Ping's birth, Mother developed arthritis and back pain. She spent a lot of time in bed because of the excruciating pain in her lower back and her legs. She nicknamed her problem "a lazy disease," because as soon as she touched the bed, the pain went away. Her doctor prescribed hundreds of vitamin B1 and B12 injections. Eventually she got out of her bed. Mother believed that the pain was caused by her having washed in cold water after Ping's birth. However, she didn't regret it. Had she slept through that day, or had she not dared to wash herself in cold water, she could have easily become the second Shuixian in Ward 4. Since she believed that health problems related to inappropriate postpartum activities couldn't be easily cured, except in another labour, Mother decided to have another child for her own need.

By then it was getting almost too embarrassing for Hu Nü to listen to the gossip between her mother and Mrs Ma, and especially to

Ma Nainai's daily observation of Mother's abdomen. Father had no interest at all in having another child. He became indifferent to his wife's pregnancy. On the other hand, Father and Hu Nü became good friends. They spent a lot of time together on Sunday morning solving difficult mathematical problems. He bought her teach-yourself math books, collections of past mathematics contests for elementary and high school students. Hu Nü enjoyed working on them in her spare time. She could see that Father was trying to raise her as the son he never had. She wanted to meet his expectations, so that she could prove to him that daughters could be as successful as sons, and perhaps even more.

This time Mother seemed to have gone through her pregnancy faster than before because it was winter time. She didn't have to show it. In 1963, China had already recovered from the Great Leap Forward. Although most of the food, such as grain, meat, fish, eggs, and sugar was still rationed, there was plenty of everything in the black market. Before her due date, Mother bought a lot of food, including a few live fish which she raised in a basin underneath Hu Nü's bed.

It was the seventh day after the Chinese New Year in 1963. If she were born seven days earlier, she would be a little Tiger, but, she was born in the Year of the Rabbit. That morning, Mother told Hu Nü to call a tricycle, a kind of a rickshaw on wheels. She had to go to the hospital. "Hu Nü, remember, you are going to bring me some fish soup this afternoon," Mother said as she went downstairs, a washing basin in her hand.

It was the first and only time in her life that she was expected to kill a living thing. All morning after Mother left, Hu Nü was troubled by the thought of making fish soup: first she had to kill the fish, then scale it, cut it up, wash and drain the pieces. Then she had to fry and boil it for forty minutes on low heat until the colour of the soup turned milky white. Several times Hu Nü pulled out the basin from underneath her bed to look at the fish. There were five of them, called *ji*, a kind of fresh-water carp. It is believed in Wuhan that carp soup is most nutritious, and helps produce milk in women after labour. Since Mother had bought the fish one week before her due time, Hu Nü got to know every fish in the basin, because she changed water for them every day. She knew eventually Mother would eat them all, but she couldn't really argue with her to save the fish. Right now she only wished she didn't have to kill them on the chopping board.

After lunch, it was time for her task. Hu Nü knew she could always ask Ma Nanai for help, but somehow she didn't want to. She pulled out the basin, closing her eyes before stretching her hands into the basin. Fish felt so slippery between her fingers, but somehow she managed to catch one. She threw it inside the basket beside her. The fish was flapping up and down, water was all over the floor, so were fish scales. Hu Nü was scared as a murderer. She quickly ran to the kitchen, left the basket on the sink, and went back to the apartment. Half an hour later, Hu Nü went back to the kitchen to take a look, a limp fish was lying in the basket. She let it slide out of the basket on the cutting board: its red eye was glistening. She hesitated, forgetting what the next step was in making fish soup.

Ma Nainai came back from shopping. She was surprised to see Hu Nü holding a knife over a dead fish. "You're supposed to make a soup out of a live fish, not a dead fish, your mother paid a lot of money for these live fish! She could have saved her money if she knew she would get dead fish soup!" Hu Nü didn't defend herself, and was relieved to hand over the knife to Ma Nainai. Ma Nainai made a nice soup for Mother. Hu Nü took it to the hospital in the late afternoon. She didn't tell Mother the fish was already dead before Ma Nainai scaled it. Mother said the soup was delicious, it was worth buying the live fish.

Early on a cold February morning, Mother came home with a tiny baby girl wrapped in a small woolen blanket. Without central heating, the apartment was almost as cold as the outside. No neighbours came to visit. By 1964 there was plenty of food in the market, nobody was interested in a cup of brown sugar tea for visiting a woman who had just given birth to her fourth daughter. Ma Nainai was the only visitor. Over a cup of hot brown sugar tea, she said to Mother, "Congratulations, another thousand *jin*!"

Hu Nü had heard this saying before. A couple who had a baby girl was congratulated for gaining a thousand *jin*. Hu Nü asked Mother what people said to those who had male babies. Mother thought for a while, then said, "There isn't any particular phrase for having male babies."

"You say congratulations for gaining ten thousand *jin*," to everybody's surprise, Father snapped back without a second thought.

"Ten-thousand *jin* ? I have never heard such a saying," Mother replied. Hu Nü looked at her parents, regretting her question. She was not totally shocked that Father still believed boys were ten times better than girls. But her father should have seen his daughter doing better than most boys at school. In fact, in her application for high school, Hu Nü put down Wuhan No.2 High School as her first choice. No.2 High School was historically an elite high school for boys only. She heard that the school was going to admit some exceptional female students for the first time as an experiment. She made up her mind she was going there. Most smart girls from her school applied for Wuhan No.16 High School, an elite high school for girls. But Hu Nü didn't even put No. 16 down in her application. She only wanted to go to No.2 High School.

After Mother gave birth to her youngest daughter, she took better rest, and consequently she recovered from her previous health problems. Mother knew her husband didn't want another daughter. In fact it looked like he didn't even notice they had another daughter. He kept a busy schedule as usual. He made trips to other cities every month. Whenever he was at home, Mother asked Hu Nü to watch her youngest sister so she didn't cry. When the little one was two years old, she learned to play outside.

At age fourteen, Hu Nü thought she had already known what it meant to be a mother in China. As for her own childhood, she wouldn't know how different it would be had she not been the eldest daughter.

Chamber Pot on the Table

In the following years, Ping became a hot topic for neighbourhood gossip. Her melon-seed-shaped face, her big black eyes, and her tiny cherry mouth seemed to catch ever-growing interest in the neighbourhood. Every day when the Hu girls passed by the big yard, they heard neighbours talking about Ping's beauty while pointing their fingers at the rest of them for lacking such. Soon enough Ping believed herself superior among the four, especially to Ning who was four years younger. Ping demanded attention from their parents; it didn't take her long to get an upper hand over Father. He would back her up even when she was obviously wrong. Hu Nü wondered whether this was his way of dealing with his own guilt for hitting her with a belt when she was one week old.

Like other apartment buildings in the big yard, Building No. 7 was originally designed for single-family dwelling. There was a large kitchen, a dining room, and a sitting room on the ground floor, and there were three bedrooms on the second floor. There used to be a proper washroom with a toilet, a urinal, and a stoneware bath tub on each floor. After the Hus moved into the building in 1959, Mother and Ma Nainai converted the upstairs washroom into a kitchen by asking the district housing department to remove the washroom fixtures. However, the two women didn't realize that with a dozen people living upstairs, every morning each family had to empty at least a chamber pot from the previous night. Without a toilet upstairs, they had to carry their chamber pots downstairs in the morning.

During the day when Father was not home, if the washroom downstairs was occupied, women in the Hu family would urinate in the chamber pots inside their own apartment. Soon enough a chamber pot was filled up; then the girls would start the usual argument about who used it first and how many times each person had used it. Most of the time, either Mother or Hu Nü would take the chamber pot downstairs to clean it. But they did become used to seeing a chamber pot in the corner of the apartment with its strong presence. Mother cautioned her daughters that the chamber pot had to be cleaned before Father came home from work. They observed this rule for years, except once.

It was evening, Father would soon come home. Hu Nü made sure the chamber pot was emptied and cleaned. She started her homework, so did Mei who was in Grade Six. Ping was playing with Ning on the dinner table. Mother was in the kitchen getting dinner ready. From the staircase finally came the familiar footsteps.

"Baba is back! Who is going to open the door?" Hu Nü asked.

"I will!" said Ping. When the door swung open, she jumped up and put her arms around Father's neck. Father gave her a big lift into the air and put her down on the floor, laughing loudly.

Mother was calling from the kitchen; she timed her cooking so well that dinner could be brought in as soon as her husband came back from work. Hu Nü ran into the kitchen to help.

Moments later, when she came back from the kitchen with a hot serving dish in her hands, the atmosphere in the apartment had completely changed. In the middle of the dinner table, where she would have placed the dish, Father slammed down the chamber pot. There was a light yellow liquid at its bottom. Father's face had changed colour. The loving, cheerful daddy standing in the door frame five minutes before was replaced by a furious madman. Before Hu Nü could understand what had happened, she heard Father shouting at Ning, his youngest daughter, who was only four years old.

"Empty the chamber pot! Empty the chamber pot now!"

Ning was scared to death. She trembled as if she were cold. Ever since she could remember, she had been afraid of Father. She was told to stay out of his presence to avoid annoying him. Mother hushed her and told her to go downstairs and or outside to play whenever Father was home. Ning couldn't remember if she had ever looked at Father in the face.

The four-year-old was sobbing, as she stretched out her short arms and went on tiptoes. She pulled the chamber pot from the centre of the table to the edge, and managed to lift it up and put it down on the floor.

"I didn't do it." Though Ning's voice was low, it surprised Father that she actually dared to talk back.

"Go empty the chamber pot!" He shouted again.

"Did you hear her, damn it! She didn't do it!" Ping burst out. "Why do you always pick on her?" Ping was seven years old, she could swear like a true Wuhanese in the streets.

"Who did it then?" Father's voice softened instantly.

"I did! I pissed in it! What's a chamber pot for, eh, if it's not for pissing?" Her two elder sisters exchanged a look. They were glad Ping dared to challenge Father's authority. He didn't say anything, but went inside the parents' part of the room.

Hu Nü quickly took the chamber pot downstairs to have it cleaned.

Women in the Hu family continued to use their chamber pot for another ten years, until sometime in 1977, when the Hus were finally assigned a two-and-half bedroom apartment with a washroom and a kitchen. This was the first apartment ever assigned to them by the Railway Institute of Architectural Design in Wuhan, where Father had worked as its chief architect for almost twenty years.

At twenty, Ning graduated from Beijing Medical University as an obstetrician in 1983. Father went to Beijing to attend his youngest daughter's graduation. He apologized to her for making her empty the chamber pot when she was four years old. Upon reconciliation, Ning made great efforts to call him Father again for the first time since he put the chamber pot on the table in front of her.

A Doll in the Closet

Not far away from the big yard, there was a department store adjacent to the vegetable and meat market where we shopped daily. Whenever Mother asked me to run errands in the market, I always went to the department store. To a growing teenager's curious eyes, the store contained treasures: rolls of beautifully printed cotton, silk, and other man-made fabric in tall glass cabinets; beauty soaps, toothpastes, face and hand creams displayed inside glass counters; women's personal hygiene products wrapped up in soft white tissue paper and displayed discreetly at a corner section; tennis shoes, cotton shoes, and rubber boots laid out in pairs inside the shoe counter. It seemed to me that the department store was connected to every stage of my life and my needs. I bought my first bras there after I joined the track and field team in high school. I also bought my sanitary belts from the store when my menstruation started. These products for grown-up women were boxed. Customers were not allowed to open them unless they had paid first. Once opened, they could not be returned. Other girls and women seemed to know their sizes, but it took me several purchases to find out mine. However, whenever I remember the department store, I remember my sisters standing spellbound in front of the toy counters.

My parents had never bought us a doll or a stuffed animal to cuddle. Perhaps they were not necessary for me, since as far back as I can remember I was helping Mother raise my three younger sisters. My sisters wanted me to play with them all the time. Who would need to play with dolls then? But Ping and Ning were different, they envied other kids for their dolls. To quench these desires, we would go to the department store to look at the dolls inside their glass counters. I would read the labels to them, telling what each doll could do. Ping liked big dolls whose eyes could open and close. They cost about five *yuan*, which was very expensive. Ning was fascinated by dolls that were well dressed, it did not matter if they were male or female. As long as the dolls had layers of clothes, from underwear on, she liked them. The shop assistants knew we were only window shopping; they carried on their gossip without paying attention to us.

Chinese New Year of 1966 was the last Spring Festival my family spent together before the Cultural Revolution. At the time, Mother and other women in the neighbourhood had organized a small shoe factory by moving their sewing machines from their homes into a workshop on the street, and they started taking work from the nearby shoe factory. Working ten hours a day, six days a week, these women could earn twenty *yuan* a month, which was about one-eighth of my father's salary as a chief architect. Women in the workshop also organized a savings club. Each month one member would collect an agreed amount, for example five *yuan*, from the rest of the members. So if there were ten people, it would take ten months for the ten to go around, and each month a woman collecting 50 *yuan*. However small this amount of saving, it was the first time these women had planned their own finances, saving towards something more than their daily food. In two years, Mother herself bought a five-drawer dresser with her first club savings, then a full-length cabinet with her second club savings. The Mas were surprised to see our new furniture arriving, because it was the first time that my family had ever bought any decent furniture since moving into the apartment.

With Mother's twenty *yuan* a month, our family life started to have variety. Besides the three meals a day, Mother would open her locked cabinet and give us a candy and one or two cookies in the afternoon. Father didn't believe in giving children snacks in addition to three meals. Both our parents grew up in wartime China; they considered us children pretty lucky with no bombers flying over our heads. But Father was still a much more restrictive parent than Mother.

Every family was preparing for the most important holiday of the year, the Spring Festival; plenty of food was brought home in baskets and bags. Children were talking about their new clothes, new shoes, new toys. Besides shopping for the festival, the Chinese have another custom of giving their house a thorough cleaning. During the weekends before the holidays, therefore, people were busy dusting their rooms and washing sheets and duvets.

On Sunday morning, Mother asked me to change the sheets on my sisters' beds. She gave me the keys to her cabinet. I was eager to see what was hidden behind the locked cabinet doors, so were my younger sisters. They all gathered around me, waiting to see Mother's secret treasures. As I opened the cabinet doors, I saw bags of candies, sugar-coated peanuts, melon seeds, and other goodies for the holidays. I quickly pulled out the sheets from the shelves and threw them at my sisters for their beds. And then, something else fell out among the sheets. It was a doll!

Wow! It was a beautiful doll!

"What's that? Let me have a look!" As soon as I realized I had pulled out something that Mother had hidden, I wanted to put it back. But it was too late Ping had already grabbed the doll with both her hands. It was a golden-haired male doll with big blue eyes that could open and close, an adorable handsome face and a sailor's blue and white outfit and black leather shoes. "Wow . . . I can't believe my eyes . . ." Ping was stunned by what she held in her hands.

Ning was jumping up and down, making an unusual amount of noise on the floor. "Let me look at the shoes, are they real?"

Mei, who was usually self-occupied, started to fight with Ping, trying to snatch the doll from her. "Give it to Ning, she is the youngest, she should play with the doll!" We were so excited and noisy that none of us noticed Father coming out from the inside section of the apartment.

It took him a few moments to assess the situation. Before we realized he was standing behind us, he had seized the doll from Ping. Dashing it against the wall, he said firmly, "No dolls in this house!"

We heard a crack, our hearts sank. The plaster head of the doll was broken. Ping and Ning burst out crying. They ran over to pick up the damaged doll from the floor. They hugged it together and they hugged each other.

"You're not our father! We don't need a father like you!" Ping cursed. "Why didn't you die!" She stamped her feet. The apartment was filled with cries and screams.

Mother ran in from the kitchen, her hands were covered with soap bubbles. She saw immediately what was going on. Tears ran down her cheeks, she wiped them off with her rolled-up sleeves.

"You didn't have to be so cruel to the girls. I bought the doll with my club savings. It is a surprise for them." She took the doll from her two younger daughters, and without looking at her husband, she said to us: "Mama will fix up the poor doll—you know, once Mama was a nurse for the Red Cross. I know how to treat injury."

Father went inside.

On New Year's Eve, Mother put a bandage over the doll's cracked skull, she made a little winter hat for him, which had two ear-muffs hanging down the sides to cover his scars. With Mother's home-made hat, the sailor doll looked more than a sailor. He looked somewhat like a northern trapper with his head wrapped against winter cold. My sisters named the doll "Tom"; they believed it was a good name for a golden-haired sailor from the West.

Shortly after we had Tom, in the early summer of 1966 the Great Cultural Revolution broke out. The movement began with the Red Guards destroying artifacts and commercial products that could be termed bourgeois or feudal. Traditional dolls with beautiful dresses and the blond-haired ones were all sentenced to be destroyed by the Red Guards. Some Red Guards went to Ning's kindergarten, searching for bourgeois toys. They destroyed dozens of dolls by smashing their skulls on the wall, pulling off their limbs, and burning their remains and garments in a bonfire.

From the beginning of the Cultural Revolution, for at least two or three years there were no dolls in our local department store. Instead, Chairman Mao's busts, painted golden or silver, made from the same kind of plaster as the dolls' heads, stood inside the glass counters of the store. Later, dolls of the People's Liberation Army, male and female Red Guards, and workers and farmers came into the toy market for the next generation of children, those born during the Cultural Revolution.

Tom was the only doll that my family ever had. After what happened in Ning's kindergarten in the summer of 1966, my sisters asked Mother to hide Tom permanently inside her locked cabinet.

Part Two

The Politics of Class Struggle

There is a lot of rainfall between May and June in Wuhan. It rains almost everyday; people wear a tired look, dragging their rubber boots, umbrellas, and raincoats. The Yangtze River starts to surge. After the rainy season, the temperature shoots straight up. Soon residents move their bamboo beds outside at night. There is hardly any time for people to enjoy themselves before the heat comes upon the city in July and August.

June of 1966 was the last month before Hu Nü's graduation from junior high school. Like thousands of other graduates, she was busy preparing for a city-wide senior high school entrance examination. Then came one quiet afternoon when her life suddenly changed.

Mr Soo, the home-room teacher, walked in for a regular weekly class meeting. Putting down a pile of senior high school application forms on the teacher's podium, turning around with a usual dramatic manner, he wrote on the blackboard, "Chairman Mao's Class Struggle Theory." Pausing and putting the piece of chalk in the chalk box, he said slowly, Chairman Mao's Class Struggle Theory, his eyes sweeping across the classroom. Students from the "Red" family backgrounds straightened up their backs proudly. Hu Nü immediately felt pressure descending from the ceiling.

"What is Chairman Mao's Class Struggle Theory?" Mr Soo asked. "To summarize it in one sentence: schools should open their doors to the offsprings from the working-class, poor peasant, revolutionary cadre, and revolutionary soldier families." Mr Soo paused again, to give his students time to reflect what was coming from above. "We need to change the senior high school admission policy that has been based largely on academic performance, especially in elite high schools like Wuhan No. 2 High School. If we let the academic-record-oriented tradition continue to dominate our school admission policy, it will only prolong the historical unfairness, which has produced the current low ratio of students from good families in higher education." He finished his sentence with a determined hand gesture sweeping through the air. Hu Nü thought her teacher was imitating the great leader Chairman Mao from the documentary movies. "Now let's divide up the class into four groups for discussion." Mr Soo made another sweeping hand gesture.

Group discussion was part of the mass movement that was invented and implemented by the Communist Party to reinforce its policies down to the grass roots. In group discussions, everyone was expected to make a public statement. Those who spoke were believed to be more progressive than those who did not. Sometimes people competed with each other to speak first and get over the pressure, other times they waited to the end to see if they could be exempted. In Hu Nü's class, each group had twelve students; though small-scale, it was a carefully planned grouping with equal numbers of male and female students, who came from a mixed family backgrounds. In her group, most students came from the "Red" families. She and another female student came from "Grey" families of the petty bourgeois class, which meant that their fathers were intellectuals. Two other students came from the most unfortunate "Black" families: the bourgeois class, whose fathers were property or factory owners before liberation.

Students moved their chairs to form a circle. Those from the "Red" families started talking about how Chairman Mao understood them. Tien Ming, who failed most of her maths tests throughout the school year, raised her voice: "Both my parents shed their blood in the battlefields against the Japanese. They were wounded and disabled for the rest of their lives. Without them, there wouldn't be new China." The rest of the group looked at each other. Tien Ming's sentiments were justifiable. After all, her parents were the generation who had founded new China and made it different from the old days.

"But you see, here is the unfairness. How can we expect students like Tien Ming, whose parents did not have much education, to compete for admission into an elite high school with students from the Grey or Black families, whose parents had higher education?" Wei Dong, our group leader, asked the question. "Students from Grey or Black families get help from their parents all the time, while we don't. That's not fair. It's not fair to base school admission on academic performance. And now Chairman Mao himself wants to have this changed." Tears shining in his eyes, Wei Dong rose up from his seat and raised his arm, "Long live Chairman Mao's class policies!" Following Wei Dong, Tien Ming stood up and shouted, "Long live Chairman Mao's class policies!" Looking around the classroom, Hu Nü saw her classmates in other groups standing up and raising their arms as well, shouting "Long live Chairman Mao!" "Long live Chairman Mao's class policies!"

At another group discussion, the two male students from the bourgeois families made a public confession. They said they felt guilty for their parents, who were both rich and well-educated before liberation. Therefore, to help unload their parents' double guilt, they had decided to give up applying for senior high school. They would only apply for technical schools. The class gave them a warm applause. Yaochi, whose father was a school teacher and therefore belonged to the same petty bourgeois class as Hu Nü, said she was not interested in going to senior high school. Her family couldn't afford it; ever since her father passed away, she was expected to find a job and help her mother raise her two younger brothers.

After her classmates had spoken, Hu Nü knew she was expected to say something. She felt eyes around the table cornering her. She started to feel weak and frustrated. She knew her academic records in junior high school almost guaranteed her an admission into any elite senior high school as long as it admitted girls. But with Chairman Mao's class theory as the new admission policy, she now had slim chance because her father was a chief architect. But his education was not hers! She didn't choose to be born in an intellectual's family! The screams inside her were loud and she wanted to let them out. She wanted to put up a fight like a tiger at bay.

With a trembling voice, Hu Nü told the group that her father's family was not rich. Actually, her grandmother had to wash clothes for rich people to support her son through his elementary education. Her father studied very hard; being one of the three top students in his high school and all the way through university, he won scholarships, which covered his tuition and living. She told the group how her father carried his books and bedding on a bamboo shoulder pole. With millions of other Chinese refugees in an exodus during the Japanese invasion, he walked thousands of miles with his school to complete his education. Any time during the war, he could have been killed by Japanese bombs like thousands of other Chinese, and he had many reasons to give up his studies as many students did, but he survived and graduated from the university at the end of the war. Once she started talking about her family, she seemed to remember a lot more stories about her parents. Her classmates listened attentively.

At the end of her talk, Hu Nü swallowed hard and summarized, "It was not easy for my father to receive his higher education. In fact, he was the only one in the entire family to have a university degree. What's more, his education has enabled him to help build the new China after liberation. Father has always been trusted by the Party with important projects." She stopped and let out a sigh of relief.

Her classmates were all surprised at how gutsy Hu Nü had been to tell them about her architect father, who would be considered a bourgeois intellectual according to Chairman Mao's class theory. "Are you saying that your family actually has some Red background?" Wei Dong asked.

"I don't think that was exactly what I have said. What I wanted to say is that the way my father had his higher education was not because his family was rich but because of his determination. And his education has been appreciated by the Party and the people."

"I don't think she likes Chairman Mao's class theory. She doesn't want the new admission policy to be implemented for higher education." Tien Ming tried to pin her down quickly.

Hu Nü was just about to argue with Tien Ming when Mr Soo passed by. He must have overheard Tien Ming's comments. Leaning over the desks that had been brought together for the group discussion, he said softly, "Let's not impose 'big hats' on each other."

"Big hats" was an euphemism widely used in Chinese politics. It referred to political slander, particularly to those who imposed a politically unfavourable label on an innocent person. Mr Soo continued, "We should try to understand the political implications of Chairman Mao's class policies. We should discuss what is going to happen to the school system and future education."

Suddenly Hu Nü realized Mr Soo was protecting her. She could have been easily pushed into a political abyss by Tien Ming if Mr Soo hadn't interfered. She remembered reading about a previous political movement in 1957. Many intellectuals, including university students and senior high school students, were made to wear "big hats" of "Rightist" or "Anti-revolutionary labels." They were sent into exile in remote parts of China. Scared to think about what could happen to her for speaking up, Hu Nü knew that one step further she could easily become the enemy of the people, and then her life would end right here, prematurely, in her teens.

Going to school became a daily trial for Hu Nü. Chairman Mao's class theory was fully implemented with the graduating classes, nothing could save her fate as the daughter of a bourgeois intellectual. For a while she was hoping that her Youth League membership could give her a more progressive profile; after all, only the politically trustworthy young people could join the Communist Youth League. But soon cynicism devoured her naiveté. Wearing the League badge on her chest everyday couldn't change the class status of her family. And this movement was about the class status of every person.

At the end of June 1966 there came a day when the class had to make a collective decision about every student's future. Although Hu Nü held the highest academic record among two hundred junior graduates from No. 2 High School, she was not allowed to apply to senior high schools because of her family background. Instead, she was told to apply only to technical schools. She begged her classmates to allow her to apply to a third-rate senior high school that no students from this class would ever want to go, but she was rejected firmly. Her classmates knew well the ancient Chinese saying, *bu yao fang hu gui shan*, "Do not let the tiger return to the mountain."

"Applying to technical schools, you don't even need to write the citywide senior high school entrance examinations!" Tien Ming said to Hu Nü smilingly. "You just sit at home and wait for your assignment to be mailed to you. How nice and easy."

Hu Nü spat on the floor in front of Tien Ming, then rubbed it off with the sole of her shoe.

Longxiu of Sichuan

After an unusually long rainy season, summer arrived with greater intensity than usual in 1966. The muddy puddles in the big yard where my family lived quickly dried out, and soon residents started to air their sweaters, winter coats, hats, blankets, and cotton bedding in the big yard. By then, my dream of going to a senior high school was completely dead because of Chairman Mao's class policies. I started tasting the bitterness of being an unwanted person, a social scapegoat.

One day, I decided to visit my old girl friend and elementary-school classmate, Longxiu. She lived with her mother, her married brother and sister-in-law, in a ground floor room which had been converted from a garage near the entrance of the big yard. The yard had been built during the Japanese occupation of Wuhan for Japanese officials and their families. There were two rows of garages near the entrance of the gate. During the 1960s, as more people continued to move into the city, the district housing department ran short of apartments, and some families were assigned these garages. Longxiu came from the countryside of Sichuan province with her mother to join her brother and sister-in-law who were already living in one of the garages. I remembered Longxiu's mother, a small, skinny old woman who wore a turban and spoke a dialect that nobody understood. Soon after Longxiu was put in my class at school, we became close friends. We went to school and came home hand in hand everyday. She was quite a few years older than I and physically much stronger. She protected me from street thugs who bothered me on my way home. I helped her with her school work, especially with her arithmetic. However, after I entered Wuhan No. 2 High School and she an alternative school for slow learners, we had rarely seen each other.

I didn't need to knock on the door. The garage door was left open all day long, otherwise it would be a windowless box. "Where is your mother?" I asked, remembering her old mother used to sit outside.

"She went back to Sichuan two years ago," she answered, wiping the surface of a small bamboo chair for me to sit on. "It's too crowded here. Do you know my sister-in-law has two kids?"

"Two already? " I said, feeling embarrassed for not keeping in touch. Looking at my friend, I realized she was a fully developed woman with rounded shoulders and a high bosom. I recalled an incident in the last year of our elementary school.

One late afternoon, Longxiu and I were walking home together as usual. Suddenly she was hit by a stone on the back. She turned around to curse the ruffians behind us. I thought the stone was aimed at me but had hit her instead. I was troubled a lot by the street thugs because they knew I couldn't swear in Wuhan dialect. Before I could pull Longxiu's sleeve and run, the thugs threw a few more stones at her.

"Hey, you dirty boob!" One of the boys shouted.

"You don't know how to tuck in your dirty boobs!" Another boy yelled at us while the rest of them laughed.

"Get out of our school, you country bum!" The first boy shouted and threw another stone at Longxiu. I couldn't believe what I had heard. It was the dirtiest language I had heard, so personal. I looked at Longxiu's chest: her bosom was as flat as mine, except that mine was thin and flat, hers was thick and flat. I looked at her body again from the side, and saw a tight band inside her shirt wrapping her upper body, pressing her breasts down to make her chest look as flat as that of an early teenager.

Longxiu was in tears. I gathered my strength together and shouted back at the top of my lungs, "Go home, ask your mother how you used to suck her milk!" Both Longxiu and I were shocked by what I had just said; so were the thugs. Before they picked up more stones, we started to run. Hand in hand, we ran all the way back to the big yard. We were out of breath. I could see Longxiu's thick chest going up and down.

Since then I became aware of Longxiu's feminine body. She was different from the rest of the girls at school. I started worrying about my own breasts, if they would grow to be so embarrassingly big like hers. However, I could never ask her what kind of bra she wore to press her breasts down flat.

"I've been thinking about you," Longxiu smiled. "I'm so glad you came today." She handed me a small bamboo chair. We sat down in front of the garage in the open air, which was used as her family's sitting room. "You know what, I have joined the People's Liberation Army, Xingjiang Construction Regiment, which came to my school for recruitment. I will be leaving Wuhan in two weeks," she said, her eyes looking into mine.

"What? You joined the farming troop? You mean you're going to plough the virgin land? At the frontiers near the Soviet Union? But you haven't finished your high school yet!" I was shocked by her courage as a grownup woman.

"Yes, I have done just that. I'm over eighteen years old. Back at home in Sichuan, girls were sold at twelve or even younger to marry older men or widowers. My brother and sister are very kind to me, but now this garage room is getting too crowded for the five of us. Besides, I'm not like you, I don't have the brain for school, so I think it better for me to move on and find my own place in the world."

Turning around, I saw a curtain hanging in the middle of the garage. At night Longxiu's brother and sister-in-law slept behind that curtain. Outside it, was a double bed with two pillows and two folded quilts, where Longxiu and her niece slept. In front of their bed, was a short-legged table and a few bamboo chairs. Flies were landing and taking off from the bowls left on the table from breakfast. I didn't know what to say.

"In a week I will get my new uniform. I went to try it on today. I like it very much. I have ordered size medium, a bit loose, so maybe I won't have to tie up my bosom so much."

"So what kind of bra have you been wearing?" All of a sudden, a totally unexpected question jumped out of my mouth.

"You know I can't wear bras for normal girls. I use a home-made thick cotton band to press down my chest . . . Oh, it's so hard to hide my breasts, I would give up ten years of my life, even twenty, for smaller breasts, or even a flat chest." Longxiu looked at me and at my chest. "It's so embarrassing, especially in summer, sweat runs along my armpits and through my shirt, everyone can see what I'm trying to hide. Not to mention that it's terribly uncomfortable to wear a thick and tight cotton band. My skin gets irritated all the time. But I have to wear it, especially when I go to school. You remember that incident, those ruffians throwing stones at me?"

"At us," I said.

She continued, "I will be glad when I can wear a loose uniform, and wear a normal bra underneath. I think I will enjoy working in the open air in Xiangjiang. It will be similar to what I used to do in the countryside of Sichuan before I came to this big city."

"I'll miss you, will you come back for a visit sometimes?" I sounded like a desperate child.

"Every three years, the Regiment will pay for a home trip, if the farming soldier stays single," Longxiu answered. "By the way, when are you going to write the senior high school entrance examinations? You are meant for higher education. And I am meant for physical labour. You should get into the best senior high school and then the best university. I'll be so proud of you in Xingjiang."

"But, Longxiu . . . " I was tongue-tied I decided not to tell her about what had happened to me at school. "But, Longxiu, your parents were poor peasants before liberation, weren't they? So you're an offspring from the Red family. Do you know you don't have to go to a military farm or any farm, senior high schools are going to open their doors to students from the Red families."

Longxiu didn't seem to understand what I was saying. "You must have heard about Chairman Mao's class theory?" I started to wonder whether her school had the same political agenda as mine, since Xingjiang Construction Regiment didn't come to Wuhan No.2 High School for recruitment.

"Yes, yes, I knew the class policies. I couldn't join the People's Liberation Army if I didn't come from a Red family. Your family background is okay, isn't it? With your high marks, you should be able to go to university." She held my hands tightly.

Two weeks later, Longxiu came to say goodbye to my family, wearing a brand new army uniform without badges. The outfit was so loose on her that I could hardly tell whether it was a male or a female figure inside. The following day, I went to Hankou Railway Station to see her off; several thousand young men and women from Wuhan had joined up to become farming soldiers. When the train started to pull out, Longxiu held out her hand to me from the window. "Write to me after you enter the senior high school. Study hard for me, my dear younger sister!" It was too late to tell her what had been decided about my future. I nodded and waved her goodbye.

For the next three years whenever I thought about Longxiu, I regretted not having enough courage to tell her the truth. Three years later in September 1969, Longxiu came back to Wuhan for her first and last home visit from Xingjiang. At that time, I was neither studying nor working, but idling because the Cultural Revolution was still in process. Since idling youth was no news to anybody in China, I didn't have to explain to Longxiu why I didn't go to senior high school. Longxiu brought back a handsome young man, her fiancé. She told me this holiday was also their honeymoon; after they got married, they probably wouldn't be able to afford a home trip on their own for a long time.

Longxiu looked darker and thinner. Her black hair came down from a fitting army hat that partially covered her earlobes. Her well-washed uniform hugged her body now, outlining her high bosom and small waist.

An Overnight Political Storm

In June 1966, with Chairman Mao's class policies fully implemented in the new admission policies for senior high school, I had nothing better to look forward to, as I waited for an assignment to a technical school. Out of the numerous technical schools in the city, though I was interested in none of them, I selected three to put on my application form: Wuhan Plastic Technical School, Wuhan Railway School, and Wuhan Heavy Machinery Technical School. Feeling old at age sixteen and like a person with no future, I started to skip school and stay home to play with my sisters.

On the ground floor below us lived a short old man whose name was Oh Yang. Most Chinese last names have only one character, but his had two. Oh Yang lived alone, yet he occupied a two-bedroom flat; what's more, he even had a housekeeper. He looked strange: on his small skinny face, a pair of small, shiny black eyes reminded us of a cunning old rat. His dry yellow lips resembled a day-old banana peel. He walked with a stick, but he didn't rely on it for support. The stick tapped ahead of him as if he were detecting underground mines. With his stick, he would hit out at the neighbours' chickens whenever he saw them sitting on the entrance steps. The chickens squawked and jumped all over the place, feathers flying in the air. Sometimes he chased kids in the same way. They called him "Old Rat" whenever he waved his stick at them.

Mother told us that Oh Yang was a member of the United Front, a political organization that both the Communist Party and the Kuomingtang had joined during the 1940s to fight against the Japanese invasion. She advised us not to talk to Oh Yang, and in any case to call him bad names. When I had been preoccupied with my school work, I hardly knew of his existence. But since I started skipping school and spending a lot of time at home, I began to notice Oh Yang and his stick.

My sisters and I liked playing hide-and-seek, except we called the game cat-catching-rat in Chinese. We chased each other in and out of the apartment, through the corridor and up and down the stairs, until the person who played the cat caught all who played rats. We were dramatic players, pouncing and scurrying, calling out the cat's "mew-mew-mew" or a rat's "zi-zi-zi." Sometimes we invited the two boys of the Mas to join us. The whole second floor became a wild field of cats chasing rats.

One afternoon, we were in the climax of the game, with most of the rats hiding inside my parents' room. Suddenly from underneath the floor came an unknown sound, a knocking of some sort. The cat and the rats all became still. "How could anybody knock from underneath the floor?" We asked each other.

"It must be the rats living between the floors," Mei said seriously.

We all agreed with her. So we stopped the game, holding our breath and listening attentively at the spot where the knocking came from. Another series of knocks came from under the floor and sent shivers through our spines. We waited for about ten minutes. No more knocks.

Puzzled, we decided to continue our game. The rats hid themselves underneath the table, the bed, behind the curtain, while the cat started to mew, chasing them out of their hiding places one after another; the rats ran out of our apartment into the Mas', the cat ran after them.

Suddenly, all the action stopped and everyone was standing still. Oh Yang, the old man, was walking up the stairs, his stick tapping ahead of him. Without a smile on his face, he asked sternly, "Is your mother home?"

"No." We answered in a chorus.

"In that case, I'll talk to her later about the noise." Turning his back, he tapped his stick all the way down the stairs. We knew now who had been knocking from below our floor. It was Oh Yang, hitting his ceiling.

Later that day Oh Yang and his stick came back up the stairs to our apartment. We were forbidden to play cats-catching-rats at home for good.

In October 1966, some months after the Cultural Revolution broke out, Oh Yang was put under house arrest and his home was searched by Red Guards. Two days later, he committed suicide by taking rat poison.

It was a bright morning in June, 1966. An unusually excited voice came from the radio when millions of people tuned in for morning news: "The University entrance examinations are abolished! The five-thousand year-old feudal educational system in China has been abolished! Celebrate the victory of Chairman Mao's class policies!"

"Abolished? What is abolished?" Hu Nü couldn't believe her ears. How could a five-thousand-year-old cultural system be abolished overnight? Did this mean that from this day on nobody needed to study hard any more, that as long as one was born in a Red family, she could go all the way from elementary school to university? Hu Nü felt darkness shadowing her future. Her generation had been born right after liberation. Since kindergarten, they had been repeating the line "born in new society and growing up under the red flag." There was never any doubt that her generation would be the happiest generation in Chinese history. Now she started questioning if hers could ever be happy at all. She knew innocence sometimes helped produce stupidity, perhaps the innocence of her generation had made it a perfect one to be sacrificed for a great cause.

For the next few days, millions of Chinese turned on their radios in the morning to hear that excited voice of the announcer from the Central People's Broadcasting Station. They were shocked everyday with more and more unexpected news:

"An unprecedented Cultural Revolution has broken out!"

"Sweep away all devils and dregs!"

"Down with the capitalist roaders!"

"Long live the Red Guards!"

Photographs of Chairman Mao wearing the People's Liberation Army uniform with a Red Guard armband filled up the front page of all newspapers. At first the whole nation wondered who these Red Guards were any way, but it didn't take long for people to see that the Red Guards were supported by Chairman Mao himself. In the photographs, the Red Guards looked like university and senior high school students, and the younger ones seemed just around fifteen, Hu Nü's age. Her curiosity was aroused, for whatever happened in Beijing seemed to affect everybody's life elsewhere in China sooner or later. She decided to go to school to have a look.

Wuhan No. 2 High School used to have a beautiful four-season flower garden in front of its U-shaped school building. Hu Nü remembered the garden, which greeted her every morning with its freshness and serenity. During her three junior high school years from 1963-66, she liked to stroll down the narrow dirt paths, reading English or reciting Chinese poetry. Sometimes she sat underneath the tall coconut trees or next to a big green tropical plant called Indian Shot. The plant has a Chinese name too, *mei ron jiao*, meaning beautiful lady palm. Because of its symbolic femininity, *Mei ron jiao* had been depicted a lot in ancient Chinese poetry and traditional brush paintings.

Hu Nü walked cautiously towards the school gate: a huge slogan hanging from a top floor window immediately caught her attention: "Revolution is not a crime; rebellion is justified." Recently she had repeatedly heard this slogan; it was supposed to be a quotation from Karl Marx. She noticed more slogans and big posters on school walls, on the bulletin board, on the daily newspaper board and the Communist League board. Those big posters were made of coarse paper and the words on them were written in black ink. Some were printed with scarlet red acrylic. In the middle of the school entrance hall, many students were gathered behind a permanently installed calligraphy board, on which the Chairman's famous line was embossed: "Study hard and make progress everyday."

As Hu Nü approached the crowd, she could see a piece of off-white cloth hanging behind the huge calligraphy board. She had to push hard to get closer to the board. On the fabric, there was dark-brown handwriting. She read it aloud, together with many other students who were also pushing forward. "Defend Chairman Mao with both my life and death!" A signature and date had been written under the line in the same dark brown colour. Hu Nü started to wonder whether this was a new fashion, since there were so many these days. And overall, why did Chairman Mao need to be defended by a teenager with his life and death.

"He wrote it with his blood, his own blood!" A girl student standing next to Hu Nü was talking. "This is not ordinary writing, it's a blood oath!"

Hu Nü recognized the voice. It was her classmate Tien Ming, who had deprived her of her right to future education. The mention of blood made Hu Nü sick right away. She remembered the live fish she had to kill for her mother's fish soup. Growing up in China, she had heard stories about ancient warriors writing blood oaths to demonstrate their faith. They broke the skin of their index finger with their teeth and then wrote their oath with their fresh blood. Hu Nü didn't understand why this ancient feudal ritual should be copied by a student from this elite high school. Furthermore, writing a blood oath was supposed to be a private event. If someone wanted to prove his or her will, why should it be exhibited in public? Questions started to crowd into her mind, as she tried to push out of the crowd. She wanted to get away from Tien Ming. She was afraid of being confronted by her.

But she couldn't push out; the crowd became more excited as Tien Ming turned around and started to address the crowd: "Fellow students! Fellow students! Chairman has called upon us to start the unprecedented cultural revolution! Let's write our response to our great leader with our own blood! We need to defend Chairman Mao right now!" The crowd was stirred. Tien Ming put her index finger between her front teeth, while other students started to moan or scream. They gave way to her, so she could turn around to face the cloth again.

Hu Nü knew her legs were knocking as soon as she saw blood dripping down Tien Ming's finger. When Tien Ming began daubing on the cloth, Hu Nü could see the drops of blood quickly being absorbed by the fabric. The hysterical crowd started to recede from her sight. In front of her, darkness was moving in. Hu Nü sensed what was happening to her. She squatted down on her knees to avoid falling down like a log.

She had no idea what happened next. When Hu Nü opened her eyes again, she was lying on top of a white sheet in the school clinic. The crowd was gone, there was only one person beside her. It was the school nurse taking her blood pressure. With relief, the nurse said to her, "Your blood pressure was so low ten minutes ago, now, it's back to normal." Hu Nü smiled helplessly at the nurse, who gave her a cup of warm sugar tea.

Twenty minutes later, Hu Nü was discharged from the clinic. On the way out, she had to pass Chairman Mao's calligraphy board at the entrance hall. Even if her reason told her not to look at it, curiosity made her steal a quick glance. The cloth was still hanging on the back of the board. It was covered with irregular stains, smears, twisted writing, signatures, and punctuation marks—all in dark red blood.

Teacher Lo Shen Lin's Resignation

By the end of June 1966, the Cultural Revolution was spreading to the rest of the country from the nation's capital with the speed of wildfire. High schools and universities were first and foremost affected by its unpredictable turmoil. The majority of the population was confused about where the Cultural Revolution was heading. One of those restless mornings, Hu Nü decided to go to school again to have a look.

As soon as she entered the school gate, the first thing Hu Nü noticed was that the front garden was gone. Roses had been trodden down into the dirt and Indian Shot, *Mei-ron-jiao*, shredded. Poppies, chrysanthemums, and many other flowers had been pulled out of the flower beds. The narrow garden path she used to stroll down in the morning was covered with slogans in white paint. One of them read, "Wipe out the bourgeois garden!" This explained why the flowers were outlawed because the word "garden" was associated with bourgeois taste. Hu Nü didn't dare mourn the dead flowers as the famous heroine does in the Chinese novel, Dream of the Red Chamber.

A crowd of students suddenly rushed in the schoolyard from outside. "The General League Secretary committed suicide! Teacher Lo killed himself on the railway tracks!" A tall young man was shouting and waving his arm in the air. Once inside the school gate, he was immediately surrounded by more students "What has happened to Teacher Lo? What has happened to Teacher Lo?"

The tall young man smacked his dry lips with his tongue. Clearing his throat, he raised his voice to make sure the crowd could hear him: "Teacher Lo committed suicide! His head was chopped off by the train this morning! It rolled down the railway tracks! I saw it with my own eyes when a policeman picked it up!"

Hu Nü felt sick in her stomach; her legs were knocking. But she knew she dare not collapse in front of her fellow students again. After she fainted away last time, when Tien Ming was biting her index finger to write her blood oath, her classmates started calling her a bourgeois flower. She leaned on the crowd, trying to gather her strength back. Why did Teacher Lo commit suicide? She was puzzled, so was the crowd. He came from a perfect Red family of poor peasants, he taught political science at school, and as the General League Secretary, he held one of the most prestigious administrative positions at school.

Hu Nü remembered the talk she had with Teacher Lo while she was going through her three-month probation for League membership. He appeared to be very approachable, much more supportive and less judgmental than her own classmates. He was around thirty years old, five feet eight, and quite handsome. On his pale face sat a pair of light-colour plastic-framed glasses. As he saw her off at his office door, he encouraged her with a firm handshake. "Trust the

League and the Party will appreciate your loyalty." Now, why had he killed himself?

Following the crowd, Hu Nü walked upstairs to Teacher Lo's office. It was also the office of the Communist League of the school. A crowd had already gathered in front of the office. From a distance, she could see a big poster on the office door. The title was in huge black characters: "Who is this General League Secretary Teacher Lo Shen Lin of Political Science?" The question mark was twice as big as the letters. Stepping closer to the door, Hu Nü could see what was written on the big poster:

> Teacher Lo is a hidden antirevolutionary, a wolf in sheepskin. He said in the senior political science class that Chairman Mao's Great Leap Forward movement in 1958 was a great setback to Chinese economy. What's more, he didn't carry out Chairman Mao's class policies in our school. Under his leadership, this general League branch has admitted a lot of members from politically untrustworthy families, and at the same time, leaving out students from Red families. We request Lo Shen Lin to resign immediately! We want someone who follows Chairman Mao closely to be the General League Secretary at No. 2 High School! If there is resistance to this request, further revolutionary actions will be imposed!

The big poster was signed by fifty "true Reds" whose parents were revolutionary cadres or higher ranking officers in the People's Liberation Army.

Suddenly the door of the League office opened and let out a group of people. They were dressed in old army uniforms: lemon green cotton jackets and long pants, matching leather belts with big copper buckles, hats of the same colour and style but without the current red-star badge of a soldier. All of them wore a red arm band with Red Guard printed in yellow paint. The head of this group was someone Hu Nü knew right away. It was her classmate Chen Tong, whose father was a commander of the Wuhan Military Region. Behind Chen Tong stood Tien Ming.

Chen Tong took a whistle out of his pocket and blew it. The crowd was instantly silent. Clearing his throat and stepping further from the door frame, he addressed the crowd: "On behalf of the Red Guard Headquarters at Wuhan No. 2 High School, I am here to make the following announcement: After a careful search conducted in Lo Shen Lin's office, we found the following items: his handwritten will, his diary, and some other personal belongings. In his will, he tried to deny his crimes as an anti-Chairman Mao reactionary." Chen Tong flipped the paper in his hands, it looked like Teacher Lo had written a long will. Pulling out a page out of the stack and giving the rest of the loose pages to Tien Ming, Chen Tong started to read from the page:

> I love Chairman Mao more than my own parents who were both starved to death before liberation. To me, Chairman Mao is more than a parent, without him there would not be my life today. I did use the Great Leap Forward as an example to illustrate Marxist economic theory. I was trying to show the students that economic outcomes are important political factors for governing a country. In terms of my service at this school as the General League Secretary, I have always followed Chairman Mao's class policies. That is to rely on the working class, to unite the petty bourgeois and bourgeois class, and to give the children from the class-enemy families an opportunity to choose the side of the Communist Party. I am confident that this is the correct understanding of Chairman Mao's class politics. I declare my innocence. I am not an antirevolutionary. I will not resign from my job. My loyalty to the great leader will never alter. If I can't prove it with my life, I shall prove it with my death.

Chen Tong finished reading the page and said, "He signed and dated his will last night with his blood."

The crowd was disturbed and became restless. "Why should he kill himself?" Several students asked the question. Chen Tong raised his arm above his head, the crowd became quiet again. "Lo Shen Lin killed himself to make a political statement," he said. "Because he was resisting the Cultural Revolution. He didn't trust the revolutionary masses who are the pushing force of this revolution. His suicide was also a protest against Chairman Mao's leadership because our great leader started the Cultural Revolution."

Pointing at his arm band, Chen Tong continued, "This is Chairman Mao's calligraphy. Resistance to the Red Guards means resistance to Chairman Mao himself. Though Lo Shen Lin is dead now, we still need to expose his crime." Chen Tong raised a folded fist in the air, the crowd followed suite. "Down with Lo Shin Lin! Down with antirevolutionary Lo Shen Lin!" Looking around, everyone else raised their arm high. Hu Nü remembered Chairman Mao had said that there was no middle ground for anyone in a revolution; you are either with the revolutionary or against it. Without giving further thoughts, she raised her arm.

After the Red Guards had left the League office, Hu Nü went inside with other students. All the drawers of the desks were pulled out: forms, pencils, a stapler, a few rulers, newspaper clips, books and pamphlets were scattered all over the floor. Hu Nü picked up a League Membership Application Form from the floor and weighed it with both her hands. She remembered some of the most exciting moments in her life: when she was presented this form by the League Secretary of her class; when her application was finally approved after a three-month probation; and especially when she swore under the Communist League flag that she would forever be loyal to the League. The oath was led by Teacher Lo, General League Secretary of the school. He had pinned a brand new League badge on every new member. Those were the most important events in her sixteen years' life. But now with Teacher Lo having become an antirevolutionary, what of the League members who swore with him?

Walking out of Teacher Lo's office, Hu Nü saw another big banner on the door: "Thoroughly Expose Lo Shen Lin—a Hidden Anti-Chairman Mao Reactionary!" She imagined Teacher Lo last walking out of his office, facing this slogan. He must have been deeply saddened, she thought, and hence made his final decision. Hu Nü saw Teacher Lo's head being severed by the wheels of an oncoming train, rolling down the railway tracks marking his final blood oath on the stones in the morning twilight.

A Bourgeois Flower

Students were not allowed to skip school any more. According to a new Party document, all high-school and university students were ordered to go to school and participate in the Cultural Revolution. In the following weeks, big posters swept through schools like a tornado, changing their appearance. At Wuhan No. 2 High School, the entrance hall and the ground floor of the entire building were covered with big posters, exposing the principal, vice-principal, head of each department, and individual teachers, including the deceased Teacher Lo Shen Lin. Most of the big posters were written by senior students and younger teachers who held junior academic positions. Gossip went rampaging through all school corridors like influenza while new victims were targeted everyday.

One afternoon, I saw Teacher Soo's name on a big poster in front of the Chinese Department. It had been put up by my classmates. The title was "Teacher Soo: A Bourgeois Gardener." I was not surprised that my classmates had found out that Teacher Soo's father had been a High School Chinese teacher, as had his grandfather. "What a bore!" the big poster said of him. Then they gave evidence of the accused as a bourgeois gardener:

> Teacher Soo continues his petty bourgeois family trade. Because he is a dyed-in-the-wool petty bourgeois intellectual himself, he has picked students of his own kind and glorified them. In his bourgeois garden are some of his most favourite bourgeois flowers, such as Hu Nü, whose father is also a bourgeois intellectual. She wrote a composition about raising

silkworms. It is full of petty bourgeois sentiments, but her writing was used by Teacher Soo as an example for his composition class. What did he expect us, revolutionary offsprings, to be? We don't want to become bourgeois flowers like Hu Nü.

There was a list of signatures at the bottom of the poster. Standing in a big crowd reading the posters on the wall, I felt my face burning from ear to ear. As far as I could tell this poster didn't really criticize Teacher Soo, but me, his student, instead. I felt like a cornered animal.

I walked into the classroom nervously. Half of the class was present, and to my surprise, Chen Tong was standing behind the podium on the raised teacher's platform. Teacher Soo, our regular home room teacher, was not in the classroom. Chen Tong was wearing an old army uniform and a Red Guard armband. A few other students from families with high-ranking parents were also wearing old military uniforms and fresh Red Guard armbands. They were holding a meeting on the platform when I walked in. I sat down in my seat, waiting for something to happen. Minutes later, the meeting on the platform was over, but the Red Guards didn't all go back to their seats. Chen Tong still occupied the central spot, and four other Red Guards stood with him. They had spaced themselves out on the platform, and they looked like they were going to conduct a trial. I held my breath.

Suddenly, Chen Tong pulled out his leather belt from his waist, raised it up in the air and slashed it all the way down upon the teacher's podium. As the buckle hit hard on the surface, we jumped up in our seats.

"All of you, offsprings from the following five Black categories stand up: landlord, rich peasant, Kuomingtang reactionary, bourgeois capitalist, and Rightist." His eyes swept across every one's face, some students rose from their seats slowly and shamefully lowered their heads. I repeated the five categories inside my head, thank God, my family was not Black.

"Today, I am telling all of you to remember this," Chen Tong turned his back, picked up a piece of chalk and wrote a zigzag line on the blackboard. He reminded me of Teacher Soo, Chen Tong's handwriting was so poor that it mocked the teacher's grand style. He wrote, "A heroic father, a heroic son. A reactionary father, a bastard son." I was shocked by what he wrote. It was profanity! I couldn't believe that Chairman Mao's honoured Red Guards were supposed to swear in public.

"Now all of you who are standing, repeat the line with me three times!" Chen Tong shouted. "A heroic father, a heroic son." He paused, those standing followed him in a chorus. "A heroic father, a heroic son." Chen Tong raised his voice, "A reactionary father, a bastard son." He looked around, "A reactionary father, a bastard son." They were too frightened to argue with him, and repeated after him. He spoke the words once more, and then one more time, and those standing followed him again and again, each time obviously with less pain. Then he ordered them to sit down.

"Now," Cheng Dong said slowly, "you all agreed that you are bastards of your reactionary fathers. I want those of you, who are Communist League members, to think whether you could ever be qualified for the League. But if you have cheated the League and sneaked into the organization, you should withdraw from it now and ask the League to forgive you. Did you hear what I have just said, you bastards?"

There was a general stirring in the seats. I heard somebody sobbing from the front row. It was Wenxin. She came from a capitalist proprietor's family. At fifteen, she joined the League after she had bitterly criticized her father for exploiting the poor before the liberation. I remembered how she had given me a hard time at my League membership evaluation meeting. She suggested I should criticize my father in the same way as she had hers because my father was a bourgeois intellectual. I disagreed with her because my father didn't own any property before liberation. And now she was sobbing in the front seat, but I had no sympathy for her. I also remembered seeing her blood signature among dozens of other names on the white cloth hanging behind Chairman Mao's calligraphy board. She must have been there that day when Tien Ming was biting her finger to write her blood oath. But why should Wenxin do such a thing? In order to look trendy? That sounded just like something she might do! But didn't she know she came from the wrong family, and this revolution was about putting all those from the wrong families under control.

A few minutes passed, the class was sitting in dead silence. Then a rustling sound came from the front seat. Wenxin was standing up. She had stopped sobbing. She walked straight up towards the blackboard. When she stepped on to the platform, Chen Tong and other Red Guards gave her the centre position in the podium. Wenxin bowed to Chairman Mao's portrait in the middle of the wall above the blackboard. "Forgive me, Chairman Mao, forgive me, forgive me," she bowed to the portrait three times and started to cry loudly. She removed her League badge from the left side of her chest, with both hands, she put it down on the podium respectfully. Still crying, she stepped down from the platform; her eyes looked empty, her face was pale. Like a zombie, she walked out of the classroom without a word to anyone or asking permission from the Red Guards. By then, my eyes were filled up with tears. I watched her until I couldn't see her any more. I wanted to be sure she didn't faint. Following Wenxin, four more League members from the five Black families returned their League badges, but they didn't dare leave the classroom.

Chen Tong and other Red Guards resumed their positions on the platform. "You bastards from the five Black families did the right thing today. Only by accepting in public your guilty life, can you start to change. Our next job is to get rid of the bourgeois, feudal, or simply meaningless names in our class." Chen Tong looked around the classroom. "Let's go through the name list and pick out those with bourgeois or feudal meanings."

We looked around at each other as if we had just met for the first time. I saw Shijin's hand go up. I knew someone would be in trouble soon. Shijin's own name didn't seem to have anything to do with the revolution. His parents simply recorded his weight at birth in his name. "Shi" means ten, *jin* is a Chinese weight measurement close to the English pound, so he was a ten-pound baby at birth, a big happiness for his parents. Chen Tong nodded at Shijin; Shijin stood up from his seat, turning around and pointing his finger at Xu Lian sitting behind me. "Xu Lian, do you know the meaning of your name?"

Xu Lian was a shy student who seldom spoke in or out of the classroom. Whenever the teachers asked her a question, her voice would come out so tiny that even I, sitting one row ahead of her, couldn't really hear her. As usual she blushed, and her lips were trembling. Standing up from her seat she said, "it means pure and upright." Surprisingly, she answered Shijin's question with clarity and certainty.

"But what else?" Shijin pursued. "That's what it means to me." Xu Lian said firmly.

Shijin raised his voice. His eyes quickly sweeping over the classroom and back to the platform where Chen Tong was standing, he started to address the whole class: "*Lian* is the word that embodies the complete feudal morals. Do you know, that word was first used by Confucius in his feudal moral doctrine. It was adopted by many emperors in Chinese history. It was also invoked by Jiang Kai Shek in his new morality instructions for Kuomingtang government officials. I think *lian* is a word that is saturated with all feudal and bourgeois meaning. And what's more, it embodies the whole reactionary history!" Shijin sat down satisfied.

"Who gave you this reactionary name?" Chen Tong questioned Xu Lian suspiciously. "How dare your parents name you such? You were born in the new society and growing up under the red flag, and yet your name quotes Confucius and even Jiang Kai Shek everyday! Are your parents nostalgic for feudal old China?" Chen Tong turned around again, picking up a piece of chalk, to write down Xu Lian's name on the blackboard. But for some reason his hand paused in the air as if in slow motion. The class started to wonder why. But I knew why immediately. He had forgotten how to write the character, *Lian* which had thirteen stokes. It was one of the most complicated characters in the Chinese language. During our three years in Junior high school, we were used to various mispronunciations and miswritings of her name. Sometimes even new teachers made these mistakes.

Eventually, Chen Tong wrote another word on the blackboard. I wanted to laugh, but didn't dare. It was not *lian* but *jian*, another character that was often confused up with *lian* by mistake. *Jian* meant "double," or "in addition to," without any negative or positive meaning. He then picked up a piece of red chalk; with all his might, he crossed out *jian* with a big red cross. Now I really wanted to laugh, because it was so comical. I thought Xu Lian must have felt true relief since it was not her name being crossed out. In China only criminals about to be executed would have their names crossed out with red ink, in public bulletins. Therefore nobody wanted to see his or her name being crossed out with red ink. I was pleased for Xu Lian that nobody in the class corrected Chen Tong's miswriting.

Following Xu Lian's name, some other bourgeois names were written on the blackboard. Yu Anna voluntarily put her name on the blackboard to be executed with a red cross. "Anna is a Western name. As a Chinese, I am so ashamed of myself being given a Western name, as if Chinese names are not good enough. But it was my parents who named me. They are both medical doctors, they are both bourgeois intellectuals, that's why they gave me this Western name. Chen Tong, like you, I grew up under the red flag. I want my bourgeois name crossed out!" Anna's revolutionary action was welcomed with a handshake from Chen Tong on the platform. The rest of the Red Guards applauded her.

After Anna sat down, Chen Tong said we should also take a revolutionary action against names that were meaningless. "Are there any names that are trivial in meaning or carry petty bourgeois sentiments?" Chen Tong asked slowly, his eyes shifting across the classroom. Shijin raised his hand again. I wondered whom he was going to attack next. Chen Tong nodded at Shijin.

"What about Hu Nü? Her name 'Nü says merely that she is female. That is meaningless as far as I can see." Shijin dropped his voice, waiting for Chen Tong's response.

"Um, Shijin's analysis seems to make sense with 'Nü' alone." Chen Tong put my name on the blackboard and added a question mark beside it. Talking aloud to himself, he went on, "But 'Hu Nü' together makes better sense. Perhaps we should leave her name alone."

Shijin remained standing. "I want to say, I want to point out my own name as well," he murmured with embarrassment. "My name is not only trivial in meaning, but also embarrassing. It certainly carries my parents' petty bourgeois sentiments at my birth. Ten-pounds, so I was a big fat baby at birth, what does that have anything to do with the communist cause. And our generation is supposed to think about revolution and communism first. I ask myself this question everyday. I really don't want this silly name, I want a revolutionary name." Shijin was so excited that his voice was trembling.

Shijin's name was crossed out on the blackboard, which reminded the class of Yaoqi's name. She had already left school to work in a factory, because she had to help her mother raise two younger brothers. Chen Tong wrote Yaoqi's name on the blackboard and put a question mark beside it. Many students nodded their heads and agreed with Chen Tong. Yaoqi's name told the unusual story of her birth. One could just assume that she was not born in the hospital, because her name stated that her mother had to bite off the umbilical cord with her teeth. This was exactly what her name meant—*Yao* meaning to bite, a transitive verb in Chinese. *Qi* is the umbilical cord. Yaoqi must have been named by her mother who wanted her daughter to remember her eventful birth. Perhaps Yaoqi's mother was smart to bite off the umbilical cord because, she could have contracted puerperal fever if she had used the unsterile house utensils. During the three years at school, the class had noticed that male teachers seldom called Yaoqi to answer their questions. Most male students felt just as embarrassed when calling Yaoqi. They sneered at her through their teeth, as if pronouncing her name was as bad as biting off an umbilical cord. As a result, Yaoqi didn't have to answer half of the questions that I did in a year, simply because my name was one of the easiest to pronounce.

Everyone was looking at Yaoqi's name on the blackboard. Some suppressed their giggles with their hands. Chen Tong picked up the red chalk again and crossed it out with a big red cross. My name was the only one on the blackboard that was not crossed out. It remained beside a question mark.

"Now that we have pulled up the bourgeois flowers and poisonous weeds from our garden, the revolutionary flowers should start to grow. Let's give those students who have rid of their old names a new name and a new revolutionary identity," Chen Tong announced. The whole class moved on to the next stage, of looking for new names.

The names were taken from various revolutionary slogans of the great era. The class recommended *Xiangyang* to me, even though my name was not crossed out. *Xiangyang* describes what a sunflower does everyday by turning its flower face towards the sun. Sunflower had become a favourite symbol since liberation. The Party liked the plant's biological habit of facing the sun, even if it had to turn 360° everyday. The symbol worked this way: Chairman Mao was our red, red sun, we should always be loyal to him, just as sunflowers following the sun. My classmates were pleased to find this new name for me. They believed they now had changed a bourgeois flower into a sunflower.

Shijin, the ten-pound baby at birth, was given the name *Wenge*, meaning the cultural revolution. Yaochi was given the name *Hongwei*, meaning "Red Guard," and Anna *Hongge*, "red revolution." Another girl student whose old name was Huixian, meaning "the fragrance of flower," was given the name *Xiangdong*, meaning "following Chairman Mao Zedong."

By the end of the day, we were all exhausted, having searched for revolutionary names for hours. Chen Tong and the Red Guard committee wanted all of us who were given new personal identities to waste no time to have our new names officially registered. We were allowed a day off to go to the Registrar's Office.

The next morning on my way to the district Registrar's Office, I saw street names being taken down from the telephone poles at street corners. The morning news said that all those names with feudal, bourgeois, or ambiguous meanings had to be replaced by revolutionary names. Soon repetition became a major headache for the city, because there were only a limited number of revolutionary slogans and songs that could be used as a resource for new names. Even

Chinese dictionaries didn't help, because most Chinese words have ambiguous meanings. The better and thicker the dictionaries, the more ambiguous the words seem to become.

"So are we going to abolish our five-thousand year-old language?" People gossiped and laughed on the street. "Just imagine, post offices will be clogged with undelivered mail everyday, if ten streets are all called Hongwei [Red Guards], or Xiangdong [following Mao Zedong], or that kind of stuff."

"The search for new street names continues," the City radio broadcaster announced. "Chairman Mao says that true wisdom comes from the masses. Believing the masses are the true heroes, the municipal government asks the public to contribute its wisdom and to help solve the shortage of new names for our streets." A week later the masses had found a solution. It was suggested that by giving numbers to the street which had identical names, we could overcome the limit imposed by the existing revolutionary vocabulary. Some of the biggest cities in the world, such as New York had adopted the same method in naming their streets. Of course, we didn't really need to copy this from the West. After all, our revolutionary masses had a better solution than just numbering the streets. The street where my family lived used to be called Three Sheep Road, which was parallel to One Cycle Road, Two Jumping Road, Four Season Road, Five Luck Road, Six Peace Road, Seven Colour Road, Eight Happiness Road, Nine Wine Song Road, and Ten Sisters Road. Now all of these complicated names were replaced by Red Guard First Road, Red Guard Second Road and so on to Red Guard Tenth Road.

"The combination of a new name with a sequential number is a true invention of our city. It beats the simple numbering system in many Western cities," City Radio happily announced. "Chairman Mao says 'revolutionary masses are the true heroes,' now we have proved it."

The next morning, when I arrived at the District Registrar's Office, I was shocked to see half of the building was scarlet red in colour. In the bright morning sunshine, I almost mistook it for fire. Then I saw a group of Red Guards walking in and out of the building with ladders, long-handle brushes, and pails of red paint. I understood then, the other half of the building would soon emerge red from their brushes.

There was a long queue in front of the building for individuals to change their names. I had to wait for three hours for my turn. I noticed most people in the line were between their late teens and early twenties. After chatting with some of them, I was embarrassed to admit that I would be one of the three Xiangyang ("facing the sun, or sunflower") in the line. There were five Xiangdong ("following Mao Zedong"), four Hongwei ("Red Guard"), four Weidong ("defending Mao Zedong"). And two newborn babies, a boy and a girl, both were named Wenge ("Cultural Revolution").

Rebellious Blood

Hu Nü was delighted to see two rows of sunflowers in front of the school building. "How nice! They are celebrating my new name!" she said to herself. In the flower beds, the school gardener was transplanting wheat and cotton plants.

"Grandpa Zhang, why are you transplanting wheat and cotton plants in the flower beds?" she asked curiously. "They are not flowers, are they?"

The old gardener raised his head. With a wink at Hu Nü, he said, "I'm not too sure about that, or about what is a flower, what is a weed any more. Chairman Mao himself said that we should plant some wheat and cotton in the city, so the urban population can see where their food and clothes come from. I am following Chairman Mao's instructions. I got the wheat and cotton plants from a hundred kilometres away yesterday, so city youth like you can see them." He smiled under the brim of his big straw hat.

"Is that true?" Hu Nü couldn't believe that the great leader himself had actually spent time on minute subjects like wheat, cotton, flowers or weeds. She asked the gardener, "Did the great leader suggest rice seedlings as well?"

"No, no, no. Not rice, just wheat and cotton. That's why I'm not planting rice."

"You're definitely very loyal to him." She waved him goodbye.

With her new name, Hu Nü felt she was no longer a bourgeois flower. As a sun flower, she actually felt a renewed interest in going to school. After all since the university entrance examinations were abolished, nobody talked about the senior high school admission examinations any more, assuming they were also abolished. Therefore the applications they had filed for senior high schools or for technical schools had all become invalid. Hu Nü felt a secret joy that nobody was going to university or senior high school in fall. She was not really worried about where she or everyone else would be going next school term.

After one-third of her class had their names changed, it became totally chaotic and confusing. "Wenge" was Shijin, "Hongge" was Anna, "Xiangyang" was Hu Nü, and "Xiangdong" was Huixian. The new names sounded so close to each other, it was as if suddenly they had all became brothers and sisters. Hu Nü noticed she had problems responding to her new name, unless her old name was added as well. This was really ridiculous, she thought, because one couldn't possibly be on the revolutionary side and the feudal side at the same time. One day, her new name did get her involved in the heat of the Cultural Revolution, together with many other young people.

In was an afternoon in early July, a telephone call from a city cemetery asked No. 2 High School to send a truck load of Red Guards to carry out a mission in its territory. Most Red Guards of the school happened to be somewhere else in the city, carrying out similar missions to clean out feudal or bourgeois remains. Hu Nü's class was summoned immediately by the Red Guard headquarters. There was a truck waiting for them outside the school gate. It wasn't until the truck started towards the cemetery that Hu Nü and many on board realized they should not be there because they were not even Red Guards. The few Red Guards on the truck said it didn't matter because a revolutionary mission like this would need the joint efforts of ordinary folks.

"Actually," said one of the Red Guards, "this is a great opportunity for those who want to join the Red Guards, you can demonstrate your revolutionary spirit and prove your loyalty to Chairman Mao." With this encouragement, standing hand in hand, they all swore they would do whatever Chairman Mao called on them to do. Hu Nü said she wanted to join the Red Guard because the great leader himself wore a Red Guard arm band.

As soon as the truck stopped, Hu Nü realized they were at the cemetery nicknamed the Big Garden, where foreigners were buried in Wuhan during the wars. The cemetery was situated right behind the District Registrar's Office. Two days before when Hu Nü had come here to change her name, she looked through the locked European-style wrought iron gates. She could see tombstones scattered inside a few acres of land. Growing up in Wuhan, she had heard many ghost stories about the Big Garden. Her friend Longxiu told her that on July 7, the day when ghosts were allowed to return to earth, she was passing by the Big Garden, when she saw two ghosts with long noses and blue eyes waving at her. She also heard children crying. Other friends living nearby had also encountered ghosts on various occasions. Hu Nü had never met any ghosts, not did she want to see them, but she believed in the stories. Every time Hu Nü passed by the Big Garden, she prayed for the lost souls to rest in peace. Though Wuhan was not their native land, they had happened to die here, they should rest in peace in her city.

The truck stopped and they all jumped down. The gates of the cemetery were wide open. The leading Red Guard from the school told everyone to line up in two rows, facing him, so that he could give them their assignments. With his hands at his waist on both sides, he started to address the group about the significant task they were about to conduct: "Our task today is to destroy these foreigners' tombstones and reclaim our territory. Those foreign invaders, missionaries, and blood suckers came to China before liberation, using various excuses, such as trade, religion, education, medicine, and whatsever, and they undermined our independence, divided up our land, exploited our people, weakened our economy, and colonized our nation and culture. Now so many years after their deaths, and sixteen years after the liberation, they are still occupying our land. Today, we Red Guards will reclaim the land from these foreign devils. Here are some spades, iron bars, hammers, and chisels. Pick up your tools, let's fulfil the historic task that only the Red Guards can undertake." He finished, they clapped hands and followed him. They marched into the Big Garden with their tools in their hands, singing the latest revolutionary song, composed from Chairman Mao's words, "Revolution is not a crime, rebellion is justified."

Hu Nü felt blood running hot in her veins. She couldn't recall the last time she had felt this way, perhaps it was when she joined the Communist League. She recognized the excitement of belonging, being part of her generation again. She wished she were a Red Guard and wore an arm band.

This was the first time for Hu Nü to be actually inside the Big Garden. She was fascinated by a totally different world in front of her, not because it was the world of the dead, but because it was part of European culture, which was totally alien to her generation. Spreading out in front of her eyes were high and low tombstones with all sorts of designs. Weeds and climbers went all over them. Without their intrusion, she imagined this would be an extremely tranquil and peaceful place all year round. The only sound of summer would be the constant long chirping of cicadas and crickets. At least half of the tombstones were carved in English, the others Japanese, Russian, French, and languages that she couldn't identify. The tombstones were mostly marble or granite, with carved motifs of a cross, Christ on a cross, a wreath, or a cherub with wings. It was the first time for Hu Nü to see the actual image of Jesus Christ on a cross and angels with feathered wings. Born in New China and growing up under the red flag, her generation was raised in a religious vacuum.

Hu Nü moved gingerly in front of the tombstones, secretly enjoying the European masonry, trying to comprehend the messages on them. Suddenly, a voice from behind startled her, "What are you waiting for?"

Jumping around, she saw Shijin, now renamed, Wenge (Cultural Revolution). He was holding up his iron bar over a small angel's statue behind her. She wanted to stop him, so that she could have a look at the statue first. But it was too late, his iron bar came down, chipping off the angel's wings. Hu Nü heard herself murmuring, "Oh, my God." The iron bar came down again and again until the statute was completely defaced, before Shijin finally stopped.

"How many have you destroyed?" he asked Hu Nü. She looked at the iron bar in her hand, clean and dustless. Then looking at the disfigured angel, she wanted to say to Shijin that he now had truly lived up to his new name. Suddenly she saw underneath their feet a horizontal tombstone partially revealed from the trodden weeds.

"Let's see what's here," Hu Nü suggested. They went down on their knees to read the epitaph together. With his fingers, Shijin scratched and rubbed off the soil covering the words, so that they could read the whole epitaph clearly:

Herc lies in peace Tom Jackson, born June 30, 1940 in Montreal, Canada, died May 20, 1945 in Wuhan, survived by his loving parents, missionaries from Canada to Sichuan, Northwestern University. Forever remembered with love by his parents and his Chinese nanny Qin.

Shijin unconsciously made a God-bless-me sign with his hand. Hu Nü let out a deep sigh of sadness. They looked at each other without saying a word. Then Shijin pulled back some dead grass to disguise the flat tombstone, and Hu Nü scattered a few handfuls of loose soil on top of it, and they quickly left the spot. Later the two of them worked in a team. Most of the time, they disfigured Japanese army officers' tombs. Whenever they had to hit something else, they said their prayers and apologies first, telling the ghosts that it was not their decision to disturb them but the great leader's.

It took the students the whole afternoon to disfigure the stately appearance of the Big Garden. Most of them had bloody blisters on both palms. The next morning, the Red Guards' headquarters at No. 2 High School received a thank-you telephone message from the

District Registrar's Office. The revolutionary cadres and staff in that office thanked the Red Guards for cleaning up the foreign dregs in local history. The municipal government had planned to build a seven-floor apartment building at the site of the Big Garden. It was only because the construction workers were scared to touch the foreigners' tombs that the plan couldn't proceed. Thanks to the Red Guards' fearless spirit, the Big Garden had been finally reclaimed by the people. A construction team would march in next week with digging machines to pull out the rest of the tombs.

By then the Party committee of the school and the regular administration had completely collapsed; daily school events were arranged by the Red Guard headquarters. Two days after Hu Nü and her schoolmates went to the Big Garden, the Red Guards at No. 2 High School were given another such task to cleanse a Buddhist temple of its feudal and superstitious practices. Hu Nü and her classmates went there in the school truck. It was much harder for Hu Nü to go to a Buddhist temple than a Christian cemetery, because her maternal grandmother was a dedicated Buddhist. Grandma, who lived in a small village in the Zhejiang Province, meditated everyday, ate simple vegetarian meals, and wore home-made clothes. From time to time her mother invited Grandma to come and live with them in the city, but Grandma declined, saying, "A Buddhist lives in peace."

The truck stopped in front of a small temple that didn't look like a temple at all. Its front gate was modest, unlike the gates of most temples. There were four red wooden pillars in front at the street, but the paint had already cracked and started to peel. Hu Nü thought it wouldn't be a bad idea if the Red Guards, who were painting the district Registrar's Office, could do the job on these pillars.

There were three monks and five nuns living in the temple. The master was an old man whose eyes were half closed, as were his lips. He wore a dark brown robe down to his ankles. He didn't seem to notice that a truckload of Red Guards had entered his temple. Maybe he didn't even know there was such a thing called the Red Guards. The nuns had shaved their heads entirely. Hu Nü had to look for the delicate feminine features in their faces before she could tell they were women. But the nuns were more alert than the monks since they quickly gathered in the kitchen area as soon as they saw the truck arrive, while the two monks continued to sweep the yard.

There was a room in the back of the temple. Hu Nü went there to have a look. A nun quickly ran over and put a lock on the door. "These are the mops we make for the market, we sell them to cover our living costs. We are self-sufficient."

"Is that so? That's admirable." Hu Nü replied. "So what is our mission here?" It seemed to her that the monks and the nuns were very well organized. Labour was shared among them. Their lifestyle seemed simple and self-sufficient, as recommended by Chairman Mao to the Chinese people.

Then Hu Nü remembered the Five Hundred Buddha Hall. She decided to sneak down there to check out her fate. Many years ago she had gone to a large Buddhist temple with Grandma in Hangzhou. Grandma told her how to find out about her fate. If you entered the Five Hundred Buddha Hall with your left foot first, you began counting the Buddhas on the left side until you reached the same number as your age. If you entered with the right foot first, you began counting from the right side. At age seven Hu Nü counted up to a smiling Buddha, which Grandma said she surely meant a happy childhood. Since then she had never been to a temple, and now she was anxious to find out her fate before the Red Guards destroyed the statues.

There was nobody in the Five Hundred Buddha Hall. Brass candle holders were scattered around on dusty altars. Hu Nü felt the cold metal of the candle holders and the hard congealed wax drippings. She realized she had forgotten to note with which foot she had stepped into the hall. Now she had to go out and reenter, but the result would not be the same since she had already messed up her fate. She was quite annoyed at herself, when she heard a woman screaming in the yard. Quickly she came out of the Five Hundred Buddha Hall. There was a Red Guard throwing out mops from the room locked earlier by the nun.

"What are you doing with these mops?" The Red Guard was questioning the nun. "Why did you lock them up if you are not using them for superstitious practice? We're going to burn these witch-craft tools."

The nun was crying, begging the Red Guard for mercy.

Hu Nü sneaked back into the Five-Hundred Buddha Hall, and waited for the noise to disappear. But the noise didn't abate at all, it had just begun to rise, as a bonfire was being made outside in the yard. More screams came from all directions in the temple. Hu Nü came out of the Five Hundred Buddha Hall again. This time she saw the old master chasing a Red Guard who was carrying a pile of hard-cover scriptures from the main hall. The old master's eyes were wide open now, charged with anger and contempt.

His hands held together in front of him, "Merciful Buddha for-give . . . forgive me . . . ," he cried and went down on his knees as the scriptures were thrown into the bonfire. The books were instantly swallowed by hot red flames of the bonfire, and it made a loud, cracking noise.

A Red Guard shouted at Hu Nü, who was still standing in front of the Five-Hundred Buddha Hall. "What are you waiting for? There are a lot of feudal sciptures in the main hall. Come with me!" Hu Nü ran after him like a ghost, they went into the main hall, where the monks and the nuns did their daily meditation and chant-ing. Behind the tall Buddha in the central hall, there were several tall bookcases, where the scriptures were kept. They must be very pre-cious and valuable to the temple, Hu Nü thought. But remembering Chairman Mao's teaching, she knew there was no middle ground for her to choose here, she was either with the revolutionaries or with the feudal superstitious priests. She quickly assessed the situation, knowing her choice would make no difference to the fate of the temple. The Red Guard ahead of her had already gathered all the scriptures from the two tall bookcases. He asked Hu Nü to check the last bookcase, if there were any scriptures left there. Hu Nü opened the bookcase doors, and saw more books inside, together with sitting mats and folded brown robes on the shelves. She decided the sitting mats and the robes were probably less valuable than the scriptures. She grabbed the mats and the robes with both her hands. Kicking the bookcase doors closed, she ran out as fast as she could.

"They're all here, you don't need to go back in any more!" Hu Nü told two Red Guards coming towards her. They helped her throw the sitting mats and the robes into the bonfire. The fire made a whooping sound, licking the silk robe and sitting mats with its red tongue. Instantly ashes were flying up and dropping down all over the ground. The clean and tranquil yard of before had been transformed into a cremation site.

The Red Guard movement was spreading from the schools to the larger society. Suddenly various sorts of Red Guards came into existence in factories and government offices. The monopoly and dominance of the original Red Guards organized by children from the higher ranking cadres' families were challenged. All kinds of big-character-posters and manifestos of different revolutionary organizations were posted everywhere on the streets. Certain neighbourhoods were targeted. Hu Nü heard that the homes of her classmates whose families belonged to the five Black categories had been searched by Red Guards. Most of the home searches were unwarranted; requested by neighbourhood committees, they were conducted by various revolutionary mass organizations. At the beginning, the targets were simply the five Black categories, and shortly after that, a new target was added to the list, the "capitalist roaders", who were Party leaders themselves before the Cultural Revolution.

In the big yard where Hu Nü's family lived, half of the high ranking municipal cadres saw their homes searched. Their chauffeurs and housekeepers, some of whom had worked for their families for twenty years, were given a ticket to go. Chauffeurs were government-paid, so they went back to the personnel department to be reassigned, but housekeepers lost their jobs for good. One day on her way to school, Hu Nü saw neighbours gathered at the entrance of the big yard. It turned out to be a gathering for neighbours living in the garage-converted rooming homes. They had met to express their resentment at those living in large buildings in the big yard.

Before the Cultural Revolution broke out, those living in the garage-converted rooms were not totally unhappy about their condition. Most of them came from the countryside, like Longxiu's family; any kind of house in the city was better than what they had in the countryside. That was why they had tolerated the windowless garage with no drinking water or indoor lavatory. Now the Cultural Revolution gave them an opportunity to express their anger at these living too comfortably in the same big yard. They wanted to speak out, to challenge the unfair system, and they needed a target.

Who would be an appropriate target? They didn't want to attack the deputy minister, whose four-member family plus a housekeeper occupied the entire Building No. 1. No one knew if he would come back to power next year. What about the chief editor of the city's daily newspaper? His family had four members and a housekeeper, they occupied half of Building No. 5. Although the chief editor was under scrutiny, his wife still held a significant position in the Department of Women's Affairs in the provincial government. The other families living in Building Nos. 2, 3 and 4 were still in power. Every morning their chauffeurs arrived in shiny black cars, waiting patiently downstairs for the bosses. Their housekeepers still kept their special appointments with the local markets twice a week, and had boxes and baskets of food delivered at the door. For years the neighbours in the garage-converted rooms had kept a watchful eye on the families of the seven inner buildings. They knew who was who as clearly as what kind of food each family ate daily.

They went through the list of families in the big yard. They stopped at Oh Yang's name. Who was that short old man anyway? Neighbours knew he had been a United Front member, but that was a long time ago when the Communist Party had to unite Kuomingtang to fight the Japanese. Kuomingtang was defeated in 1949, Jiang Kai Shek and his troops had withdrawn to Taiwan, and the United Front had become only a name in history. The people of the garages cared as little about the historical name as they did about Oh Yang himself. All these years, the weird old man seldom exchanged a greeting with anybody in the big yard. He wore the same grey suit all year round, and he walked in and out of the big yard daily in the same manner with a stick knocking ahead of him. Neighbours remembered him beating their chickens with his stick, or running after their children with it. Nobody liked him for sure, and, everybody resented him for occupying a two-bedroom apartment and keeping a housekeeper busy. He certainly belonged to the remains of the feudal dregs that this Cultural Revolution meant to wipe out.

The neighbours living in the garages decided that Oh Yang was their best target. When Hu Nü was on her way to school, she saw neighbours writing a big poster. A huge slogan had already been finished and left on the ground to dry: "Down with an old Kuomingtang—Oh Yang!" As she was reading the slogan, a man in his fifties came up: "What is your attitude towards the Cultural Revolution in our big yard, pro or con?"

"Ah, you must be Longxiu's brother," Hu Nü said warmly.

"Yes, I am." he answered briefly. Looking at her seriously, he rephrased the earlier question, "Are ya with the Cultural Revolution in the big yard?

"Of course," she answered without thinking about the question.

"OK, ya Red Guard?" He looked at her arm suspiciously. Hu Nü knew he was disappointed that she didn't have an arm band on.

"Well, I'm not a Red Guard yet, but I have been with the Red Guards on various missions. We have wiped out a few feudal and bourgeois dregs from our district." She didn't want her neighbours to think she was an idle youth. It was important for them to know that she was involved in the movement that was currently changing the fate and face of China.

"Good, glad to hear it. Now, we need help. Can ya get us a truckload of Red Guards today?"

"What? What for?" Hu Nü was surprised at his request. She wished she wasn't having this conversation at all; she didn't really want to get involved in neighbourhood affairs. For years Father had taught her an old Chinese adage, that a clever hare does not eat the grass around its nest. "We, the revolutionary masses in the big yard, have decided to launch a revolutionary campaign against Oh Yang. He lives below your family in Building No. 7. We hope families in your building will be on our side." Longxiu's brother gestured towards the people working on the big poster.

"But why, Oh Yang? " Hu Nü asked. "He is not a capitalist roader."

Longxiu's brother looked at her suspiciously, "But ya probably don't know that he was with the United Front. Before liberation, he represented Jiang Kai Shek and the Kuomingtang, your mother would know all about this. Anyway, can you get us some Red Guards this afternoon? We want to conduct a house search."

Looking around, Hu Nü saw Longxiu's sister-in-law and other middle-aged housewives who lived in the garage rooms. She knew what they would think of her if she said no. She remembered the time when Oh Yang came upstairs with his stick when they were playing cat-catching-rats. Since then her mother had forbidden them to play the game. She herself had been saying "Oh Yang is coming to get you" to scare off her younger sisters when they refused to go to bed at night. And now she sensed the Cultural Revolution was about to catch Oh Yang.

"I'll do my best." She promised the neighbours.

Schedules at school were irregular these days, many students started skipping school again as heat became more intense in June. And those who did come in the morning went home for lunch. After lunch it was time for siesta or heading down to the swimming pool or the Yangtze River for a swim. Fewer students returned to school in the afternoon. And the Red Guards at No.2 High School had been busy everyday, carrying out missions in the district. Hu Nü waited and waited until it was almost too late to present her neighbours's request.

"Why didn't you tell us earlier?" the chief Red Guard in the headquarters said. "Now that most people are gone, there is little I can do." There were only two female Red Guards in the office cracking roasted watermelon seeds. They frowned as Hu Nü walked into the office. The look on their face told her they had no interest in going out at this time of the day to do a home search. Finally the chief Red Guard made it clear to Hu Nü that his last two Red Guards on duty could go with her, but the masses in the big yard would have to be completely responsible for the home search.

At two-thirty in the afternoon, the three young women were walking towards the big yard. Under the fierce late June sun, Hu Nü could see the two Red Guards sweating through their uniforms.

"They are here! They are here!" Kids, playing cat-catching-rats at the entrance of the big yard, yelled at the top of their lungs. Adults sitting under the big willow tree stood up immediately, stretching their backs, rubbing their sleepy eyes. They couldn't believe there were only two Red Guards with Hu Nü. "Where is the truckload of Red Guards with red flags?" Longxiu's brother asked.

"There is no vehicle, and there are no more Red Guards. They went out to other missions," Hu Nü said. She knew they had been waiting for hours and now they were badly disappointed. Some of the neighbours sat down again on the benches, shaking their heads. Hu Nü felt like washing her hands of this neighbourhood cultural revolution. She wanted to go home and make sure her younger sisters were alright. But Longxiu's brother said their revolutionary action shouldn't falter. He said a big poster and a banner had already been put up on the wall of the building, the political atmosphere was ripe for a major action. Since Oh Yang was not at home right now and his housekeeper wouldn't dare to stop them, they couldn't afford to miss this opportunity!

The neighbours gathered under the big willow started to march toward Building No. 7 with the two Red Guards in the lead. Immediately a search was carried out in the two rooms of Oh Yang's apartment. Seeing the garage neighbours fully in charge, Hu Nü sneaked out and went upstairs to check on her sisters.

Later that evening, Mother came home with more news. She said nobody seemed to know where the two Red Guards came from, but she heard that the revolutionary masses and the Red Guards had arrested Oh Yang when he came home in the evening. A criticizing meeting had been scheduled for three o'clock the next afternoon under the huge willow in the big yard. Hu Nü asked Mother who was watching Oh Yang and where they had kept him for the night. She said he would be in his own apartment and some voluntary guards from the garages would be with him on shifts throughout the night.

The next afternoon, residents from the big yard met under the willow to criticize Oh Yang. Red flags on poles were flying high along with graceful long willow branches, colourful slogans were pasted on the garage walls here and there. Neighbours came with their short-legged wooden chairs or bamboo stools. The crowd was even bigger than the day before.

It was three-thirty, half an hour past the scheduled time, when two voluntary guards emerged from Oh Yang's apartment, but without Oh Yang.

"Bad news!" a guard reported to the neighbourhood committee. "Oh Yang committed suicide at noon by swallowing a package of rat poison and drinking a lot of water. He has gone beyond the stage for anyone to criticize him."

"What a pity!" The masses were disappointed that they were unable to show the old fool the power of the people. Nevertheless, it was good news that the old fool was dead and wouldn't be able to occupy the two-bedroom apartment any more. A family of five from the garages would be assigned Oh Yang's unit. While the neighbours were gossiping about who was likely to get the apartment, another voluntary guard brought over Oh Yang's stick. On behalf of the revolutionary masses of the big yard, Longxiu's brother stepped on the stick, broke it into two pieces, and threw them into the garbage cart parked under the willow tree.

The meeting was cheerfully dismissed.

Hunger Strike

The Cultural Revolution had become an uncontrollable machine. Not only schools collapsed, but also society as a whole fell into unprecedented chaos.

One bright June morning, the Red Guards at No. 2 High School were surprised to see that a so-called Cultural Revolution Working Team had entered the school the night before. The team was made up of public servants and soldiers. It had been sent in by the municipal government to curb the speed of the Cultural Revolution. Its task was to reinforce an overall social order and to keep students on campus. The chief school administrators, principal and vice-principal, deans of all departments, and deputy secretary of the League had put out a big red banner in front of the school: "We Warmly Welcome the Cultural Revolution Working Team!"

The Red Guards were upset. Why were they not informed? Did Chairman Mao know about this? This was a counter-revolutionary action against the Cultural Revolution launched by the great leader. It didn't take them long to find out Cultural Revolution Working Teams had entered more than twenty universities and high schools citywide. So who had made such a decision overnight? Why didn't the Central China Broadcast Station say anything about the Cultural Revolution Working Team? The Red Guards concluded that the decision must have been made by a few resistant municipal leaders who stood obviously against the Cultural Revolution. No sooner had the Red Guards realized the complicated situation they were caught in, than another big banner, written in black ink appeared on the opposite wall of the welcome banner. It said: "Cultural Revolution Working Team Get Out of No. 2 High School!"

The Cultural Revolution Working Team put up an official announcement on the school bulletin board at the entrance hall. It declared that in the following week all students should go back to their classrooms; graduating classes should discuss their assignments, while the rest of the school would start its summer vacation in early July. The bulletin infuriated the Red Guards. As if a spark had fallen on dry hay, instantly the whole school was on fire. A new layer of big posters covered the entire school, calling the Cultural Revolution Working Team "Dictator," "Cultural Revolution's Fire-Extinguisher," "Anti-Mao Zedong Thought Team," etc.

The next morning, the Red Guards were even more upset to find that their headquarters had been boarded up and locked. Anger surged among the students, and the whole school was ready to explode. Red Guards were gathered in the auditorium to discuss emergency strategies. A collective decision was made: they would go to the municipal government to protest against its control. They would request the Mayor to officially withdraw the Cultural Revolution Working Team from universities and high schools across the city. But if their request was rejected, or if the Mayor refused to meet with the delegates, they would start a hunger strike. The Red Guards decided to march on the municipal government office. Carrying big banners requesting the Cultural Revolution Working Team to withdraw, several hundred Red Guards and students left the school on foot around noon. Meanwhile, some Red Guards from the school biked to other schools to organize a citywide campaign against the municipal government's intention to abort the Cultural Revolution.

Hu Nü was in the crowd. She had been to school almost everyday and had watched the developments of the events carefully. She was as much upset as the Red Guards about the city government's handling of the Cultural Revolution at its grassroots. She decided to join the march, although she knew she couldn't stay long because she had to pick up her youngest sister from the kindergarten in the afternoon.

It took them an hour and half to get to the municipal government offices on foot. The receptionist on the ground floor called the Mayor's office on behalf of the students. As expected, the Mayor said he was too busy to see the students today, but he asked them all to go back to school and discuss their issues directly with the Cultural Revolution Working Team. The students were enraged by the Mayor's treatment of their request. A second emergency decision was made on the spot by the Red Guards: they were here to stay until the Mayor met with them and agreed to withdraw all the Cultural Revolution Working Teams. The Red Guards would start their hunger strike.

They gathered on the ground floor of the municipal government building. Chen Tong, the leading Red Guard from Hu Nü's class, addressed them: "We, Chairman Mao's Red Guards and revolutionary youth, are facing a serious political challenge! This municipal government is not supporting the Cultural Revolution. It has rejected our reasonable request to meet with the Mayor and to discuss various urgent issues concerning the future of our city in this unprecedented Cultural Revolution. This is because this government wants to maintain the old social order under the old government machine. We will start our hunger strike at 2:00 p.m. sharp today and continue until the Mayor receives us and accepts our request. Students who are not Red Guards are free to leave, but if you feel as strongly as we do about this cause, please stay with us because we need your support." Chen Tong finished his speech and raised his arm: "Defend Chairman Mao with our life and death!" The whole crowd shouted after him, raising their fists in the air. It was 1:45 p.m. In fifteen minutes, they were supposed to be ready for a hunger strike.

I had fifteen minutes to make up my mind. I went to the washroom. I needed time to think about the whole issue. Squatting in the washroom cubicle, I started debating with myself: "How long will this hunger strike last? I'm not even a Red Guard, why should I sacrifice my health? If the Red Guards control our school system, I still won't be allowed to go to senior high school or university. Since my family is not Red, why should I join the Red to further deprive myself?" After asking myself these questions, I concluded that I didn't want to join the hunger strike.

Five minutes before two o'clock, just as I was about to leave the washroom I heard a whistle outside. I already felt hungry, since I hadn't had lunch. But how could I sneak out of the building without being noticed by my classmates? I went down to squat in the cubicle again. Another ten minutes passed, I still didn't know what to do. My feet went numb.

Perhaps another half hour had passed; the noise outside quieted down, a loudspeaker was set up in the hall. Against the background of music, Chairman Mao's sayings were being read. "There are always sacrifices in a revolution, death often happens. But if we have to die for the people, it is a cause worth dying for . . ."

My mind was disturbed; I started to feel the guilt of a coward. I went down to the squatting position again to reconsider my decision. I thought about my parents, who wouldn't know where I was.

I started worrying about my youngest sister, who would be waiting for me to pick her up later in the afternoon. She would be leaning against the doorway of the kindergarten, crying, until my mother finally came to get her in the evening. "Oh, I'm not just sacrificing myself for the revolutionary cause, I'm sacrificing my whole family to the cause. But if I could get away without being seen by anybody, I wouldn't have to make these sacrifices."

I decided to waste no more time. I made sure there was no familiar voices in the washroom before I came out from my cubicle. But my heart sank as soon as I saw Anna, whose new name escaped me at that moment. Before I could feel my feet again, she asked me, "So what are you doing here?"

"I was in the washroom," I answered spontaneously.

"I came in to drink some water. The hunger strike has just started, the only thing we can take is water." She looked at me, "Are you with the hunger strike?"

"Oh, yes." I hated my tongue whenever it was faster than my brain. I regretted immediately for not telling her my true decision. I drank some cold water from the tap, standing there without knowing what to do. "Do I have to change my decision because of her? What would they say about me if I walk out from here?" I asked myself. "Now that I voluntarily jumped into the pit, the only thing I can do is to take my chance."

I went back to the entrance hall, dragging my feet, as if the power of hunger had already devoured my strength. I sat down with the crowd on the floor; it was hot and humid outside, but the cement floor inside the hall was cool on the backside. We leaned on each other for support and the last row of students leaned on the wall. Through the loudspeaker, Chairman Mao's saying on human sacrifice were repeatedly read, and slowly I began to understand why I was there. I repeated the quotation in my mind. The leading Red Guard asked us all to repeat the quotation with the loudspeaker: "There are always sacrifices in a revolution, death often happens. But if we have to die for the people, it is a cause worth dying for . . ." I suspected everybody else was asking the same question as I had asked in the washroom, because this was a voluntary sacrifice. That was why we all needed the reassurance from the great leader to consolidate our faith.

One hour passed. Two hours went by. Three hours, and then four hours passed. Time seemed to have slowed down. Every minute became a painful duration. I was still worried about my youngest sister at the kindergarten and about how and when my parents would find out where I was. Four hours after we started the hunger strike, we were told that the local radio had already broadcast the news, so parents of No.2 High School should know their children might be at the hunger strike if they had not arrived home in the evening.

Golden twilight came in through the revolving glass door. I could see the dark shadows of the trees outside getting longer and longer. Employees of the municipal government had all left for home, lights in the offices were turned off but not in the entrance hall. The whole building seemed much bigger, impenetrable, and even mysterious. Then the moon rose, casting its cool silver light through the glass revolving door into the building. I looked around me, on the cement floor of about two hundred square feet, where one hundred and twenty young men and women were leaning against each other, hungry and tired. Some were dozing off, others were chattering, but nobody seemed to be as restless as I was.

Some parents came to look for their children. Names were called through the loudspeaker, the crowd started to stir when some students stood up and went outside to meet their parents. A general excitement began affecting us all because we realized we were not alone. The loudspeaker started to play the most popular revolutionary song "Looking up for the Northern Star," which described the emotional attachment of the Red Army to Chairman Mao during the Long March from 1935 to 1938. The music was slowly weaving its sentimental words into a meaningful cause for us. Suddenly someone patted my shoulder, I turned around "Did you hear your name being called through the loudspeaker? Your parents are here." Anna was standing beside me.

"Oh, really?" I couldn't believe this. I listened to the loudspeaker again.

"Hu Xiangyang, please come out to meet your parents. Hu Nü please come out to meet your parents."

"Oh, I'm sorry. I didn't realize it was my name. " I apologized for not responding to my new name. Since I had my name changed, I seemed to have lost my personal identity. Sometimes I thought I was nameless just like everyone else. I knew I could get into a lot of trouble for saying this aloud, if I was not with the hunger strike for a great cause.

Getting up from the floor, I felt dizzy, the whole world was spinning under my feet in darkness. Panic seized me that hunger had exerted its full power over my body and soul. "Did my parents both come? What am I going to tell them? What is my reason for joining the hunger strike?" I remembered Father's lifetime philosophy of noncommittment. He would think I must be really stupid to get into something like a hunger strike.

My parents were standing under a willow tree, waiting for me. The soft long branches were moving back and forth, gently brushing their shoulders as I descended from the stairs. I couldn't remember any other time when my parents were so intimate with each other and even romantic. I felt like a stranger, an intruder approaching them to disrupt their moment of peace. Seeing me coming down the stairs, they both rushed forward.

"Mao Mi, Mao Mi!" they called my nickname, forgetting that I would feel ashamed if fellow students knew that I had more than one bourgeois names. My parents had nicknamed me after our family cat, when I was one year old. "Mao" with a first tone, meant "cat" in Chinese, but it was also close to Chairman Mao's last name, which however had a second tone. "Mi" was a homonym of a cat's mew in Chinese. I had told them never to call me by the nickname in front of my schoolmates.

I quickly brushed away my annoyance at their sentimentality. As soon as I came closer, my mother stuck something in my hand. It was a piece of chocolate. "Put it in your mouth." She ordered.

"Mother, I can't. Nobody is eating, just drinking water. I can't betray them." To my own surprise, I sounded like a believer.

"How do you know?" My mother said. "We saw two students wearing worn-out army uniforms at the little store, they were buying cookies, though I'm not sure they are with the hunger strike. Perhaps you shouldn't be so naive."

I was surprised my parents didn't even ask me about the reason for the hunger strike and how long we planned to go on. It disturbed me a great deal that they seemed to think I had been brainwashed by the Red Guards. Why didn't they ask me to go home with them? The music through the loudspeaker was turned down, and Chairman Mao's saying was read again, "There are always sacrifices in a revolution . . ." My parents seemed to have a lot more to say, but they swallowed it.

"Don't worry. I'm fine. I won't die if I don't eat for a day or two." I tried to comfort them, and at the same time, I rejected their judgement. I felt sorry for the gap between us. They didn't know that I was not a believer and every minute since the hunger strike started, I had been restless and uneasy about my own involvement. I wished they would give me a hug. Maybe through body contact I would be able to be myself again. I might be able to tell them that I didn't really believe in the sacrifice, and I would rather go home with them now. But I knew Father would never think about giving his daughters a hug. As a Chinese man, he was not supposed to show his emotions. Mother couldn't do that in public either, she didn't want my classmates to call me a bourgeois flower.

I went back to join the crowd inside the entrance hall. It was around midnight, the lights were turned dim, and the music was switched off. On the cement floor students stretched out all over the place. We had had a long frustrating day without food, we should at least get some rest. I was looking for a spot where I could lie down or lean on a pillar, if not a girl friend. Around the pillars there were already people leaning or lying around. I was still looking for a spot when I caught sight of Anna being caressed by Shijin in a corner. My heart suddenly started to jump faster. I had heard rumours about the two of them falling in love, but since it was against school regulations for students to become lovers, I never thought anything like that could actually happen in my class. But there in front of me Anna and Shijin were in each other's arms. I felt so ashamed of what I saw that my innocence was betrayed in the same way it would have been had I taken my mother's chocolate. Without giving them a second look, I went to lie down in a far corner all by myself.

Morning music woke me up. My body was weak and my limbs were aching. There was a nurse from the Red Cross going around checking everybody's blood pressure. I heard her reporting to the Mayor's office that generally all students suffered from the low blood pressure syndrome. She suggested that the students be given some hot sugar tea. Soon, two buckets of hot sugar tea were put in front of us with mugs on a tray. But Chen Tong rejected the offer on behalf of all of us. The buckets were left on the floor for two hours before they were removed.

Although the students' delegation was received at noon by the Mayor with journalists from city newspapers and broadcasting stations, its request to have the Cultural Revolution Working Team withdrawn from all universities and high schools was rejected. On the other hand, the Mayor requested the Red Guards to end the hunger strike immediately and go back to school the following day. The Red Guard headquarters decided that the hunger strike had to continue. A telephone hot line was set up, so that with every passing hour, the whole city was informed of our struggle. We also sent a telegram to Beijing to inform the great leader Chairman Mao himself that we were not afraid to die for his Cultural Revolution.

Twenty-four hours passed, then thirty-six hours, and finally two days.

We passed the stage of hunger pangs. I remembered my mother saying if you didn't eat on time, your liver would use its storage to support the body, but if you still didn't eat, eventually you could exhaust your liver, and collapse and die. After two days' of the hunger strike, we were all lying down on the cement floor without bothering to get up. A few students fainted. The nurse from the Red Cross gave them an injection. Shortly after they came to consciousness, they came down from the emergency table and went back to the strike site.

I decided to close my eyes and shut off my hearing as much as I could. I wanted to hang on, so I wouldn't faint. Since the time I fainted in front of so many students watching Tien Ming bite into her index finger to write her blood oath, my classmates thought I was a coward or a spoiled bourgeois brat. Looking around me, I felt secretly proud of myself that after three days of hunger strike, I hadn't given up physically or mentally. I was determined to continue until we won the battle.

The clock struck the sixtieth hour of our hunger strike, time had become meaningless. I had stopped looking at the big electric clock on the wall. To make the passing more tolerable, I managed to open a new space inside my mind, in which I saw my sixteen years' life unrolling like an unedited documentary movie. I saw Mother aging from a young woman more beautiful than me into a withered old lady with a bent back, suffering from osteoporosis. I saw Father hitting my sister with his belt behind the curtain. I could also see Ma Nai-Nai walking between her apartment and the kitchen, baring her two dry sagging breasts in summer days. I saw Mr Lo Shen Lin's head being cut off by the fast-moving wheels of the train. There were also Oh Yang's little rat's eyes glittering and then getting dim before they closed for good after the rat-poison effectively took over his body. He could never catch us playing cats-catching-rats again. Then I saw Longxiu's fully developed feminine body, I couldn't help feeling my cold breasts under my bra. I wished Longxiu were here, she would cuddle me like an elder sister. I had always wished that I had an elder sister or an elder brother, whom I could talk to or seek advice from. What had happened to my younger sisters? How could they function without me? How had they got to school or kindergarten the last three days? Had I died from the hunger strike, would people remember me as a revolutionary martyr as they did the heroes and heroines who died in the wars? Would there be a monument on which our names would be carved?

More and more students fainted. The voice from the loudspeakers couldn't penetrate my mind any more, I was too tired to care about what was going on around me. Suddenly I felt someone patting my shoulder and whispering in my ear, "Hu Xiangyang, are you okay? Are you conscious?"

"Hu Xiangyang? Who is it? Oh, that's my name. I'm sorry I must try to respond to my new name faster next time." A voice was talking inside me, but it was so difficult to open my eyes. I saw Chen Tong's shiny red face bending over mine. From his mouth came the strong smell of tahini sauce, which was used in the hot-'n'-dry noodles, a popular breakfast in Wuhan. After three days' hunger strike, even if I didn't feel hungry any more, I could still remember exactly the smell and taste of my favourite breakfast. "Did you eat hot-'n'-dry noodles? Did you eat? You traitor!" I looked into his eyes and shouted angrily.

He withdrew from me; resentfully he squeezed the following words out from between his white teeth as if he were eating the hot-'n'-dry noodles at the very moment: "Yes, to tell you the truth, I did. I have to eat for the revolutionary cause, because I am a member of the negotiating team. I cannot lie down like you, there is a lot of work to be done. I hope you understand the different tasks we have been assigned to are all for the same cause of Chairman Mao's Cultural Revolution." With a contemptuous look at me stretched out on the floor, Chen Tong jumped over a couple students and went back to the table where the city hot line was set up.

Eighty-four hours had passed since we started the hunger strike.

An agreement was reached between the Red Guards and the municipal government that all the Cultural Revolution Working Teams were to be withdrawn immediately. Rumours said the Wuhan municipal government had received a telephone call from Premier Zhou Enlai in Beijing. When our final victory was broadcast through the loud speaker, hot tears were surging inside my eyes and gushed down my cheeks. A final understanding of myself dawned on me— I was a member of the young generation born in a new society and growing up under the red flag. I had done what I was brought up to believe. I had lived up to Chairman Mao's expectations.

The crowd quickly dispersed itself. Cars and military jeeps were arriving to pick up the Red Guards by parents with high ranks.

Anna's parents, who were both medical doctors, were also waiting outside in their hospital's ambulance. So Anna and Shijin were taken directly to the hospital for a check-up. Twenty minutes after the news of the final victory was announced, I found myself with a few other non-Red Guard students remaining at the site gathering our energy. The Red Cross nurse was nowhere to be seen, nor were the journalists, as I edged slowly out of the revolving glass door trying not to collapse.

It was a bright summer day. I couldn't open my eyes in the sun, but I could see the big willow under which I had talked to my parents on the first night of the hunger strike. My legs were soft as if made of cotton. I started moving slowly towards the bus stop outside the municipal government building before I realized I had no money at all. Squinting, I saw the hopelessly long dusty road ahead of me. I made up my mind that I was not going to walk home this time. I would get on the bus and tell the driver that I was a participant in the hunger strike. I hadn't take one mouthful of food for three and a half days. I was a hero of the city, I deserved a free ride home on the city's public transportation.

Standing at the bus stop, daydreaming, I felt a pair of arms supporting me from behind. "Mao Mi, were you at the hunger strike?" I leaned back toward the voice. It was my childhood sweetheart, Hua, from the elementary school.

Hua and I had not seen each other for more than three years since we parted after the junior high school entrance examination. Hua's family came back to China in 1952 from America. His father was an aeronautical engineer and his mother, a concert pianist. Hua was born in the United States, his younger brother and sister were both born in Wuhan. Upon graduation from elementary school at age twelve, we were already attracted to each other, so we both applied for No. 2 High School. But he did poorly in the entrance examinations and ended up being assigned to a third-rate high school. Since then we had lost contact.

"How did you come along, at this time, after all these years?" I was overjoyed to see him. He used to be my height in elementary

91

school, but now he was over six feet, almost a head taller than I; his western nose which was so different from Chinese noses still caught my attention first. Besides his nose, I recognized his soft hazelnut eyes and his naturally curly hair. Suddenly I became aware of my own haggard appearance. I wished we could have met some other time in a different place instead.

"Let me call a three-wheel rickshaw and take you home." He waved at a passing vehicle. He nearly lifted me up to the seat, then climbed in beside me. We were sitting in the two-seat rickshaw with a canvas back partially covering our heads. The rickshaw man probably thought we were out seeking a few juvenile kisses, taking a romantic half an hour's ride in his rickshaw. It would be too bold a thing to do in the Cultural Revolution. For our convenience and for his safety, he pulled down the canvas door flap. In the cradle of the seat, I felt Hua's broad shoulders behind me, his warm arms around my waist. I let my exhausted body lean on his, which felt like a solid wall. By the time the rickshaw stopped at Building No. 7 in the big yard, I was too tired to say goodbye to him.

Two days later, Hua came to visit me at home. I had almost recovered from the hunger strike. There was colour in my face and my short hair was washed and combed straight down to my ears. I wanted to ask him a lot of questions, about what had happened to him and his family since we parted three years before.

"I have officially disowned my parents," he said, shocking me.

"No, you didn't do that!" I felt as if I had been hit on my head. I lost control, I heard myself shouting at him: "Why did you do that? You're so stupid!"

"In order to join the Red Guards." He looked at me with the kind of stubborn naiveté I believed my parents saw in me on the first night of the hunger strike.

"You stupid young man! I am so sorry for your parents." I started to cry without knowing exactly why. I didn't cry at the hunger strike, why would I cry for his family?

I wished I could tell him about the bitter taste in my mouth. Having gone through eighty-four hours of the hunger strike, minute by minute, I had grown out of my blind loyalty. I had made up my mind that this was the last time I would sacrifice myself or my family.

I wished I could tell him all this, but the tone in my voice had already given him the signal that I had lost interest in him.

Part Three

Go to the Countryside

Between 1966 and 1969 China witnessed the most turbulent era in its recent history. While the Cultural Revolution was sweeping over the nation, high schools and universities were shut down. Factories were occupied by different groups of revolutionary organizations. Street fights ravaged most cities. Numerous deaths of ordinary people occurred on the streets, in the name of the revolutionary cause of defending Chairman Mao, the great leader, the great teacher, the great herdsman, and the great commander. Afraid of flying bullets, residents in Wuhan gave up their ancient habit of sleeping in the open air on hot summer nights. Everyone stayed indoors instead.

Daily newspapers highlighted Chairman Mao's sayings with red ink, and his photographs were sometimes enlarged to occupy the entire page. All radio stations used the same music, "The East Is Red," to start the day and to end the night. In between the daily news programs, Chairman Mao's sayings were read repeatedly. Public interest in the Cultural Revolution had diminished after destruction and chaos. People secretly wished this revolution would somehow come to an end soon.

The majority of students had stopped going to school entirely. There was virtually nothing to do there, especially if one didn't want to be involved in street fights. Hu Nü stayed home, taking care of her younger sisters and cooking for her family. While idling time away, occasionally she took out her mathematics books: the numbers, diagrams, equations, and problems were still there, but not her interest. She heard that her classmates from higher ranking families had joined the Liberation Army and gone to military academies. But the rest of them were so bored that they were ready to take any opportunity just to be useful again.

On a grimy early winter morning in 1968, Chairman Mao decided to disperse the idle city youth to the countryside. He instructed a group of Red Guards to go to the countryside and carry on the revolution there, and to receive re-education from the peasants. He pointed out that under the vast sky and in the open spaces, city youth could be more useful. Millions of idle youth, who had been in high school and university before the Cultural Revolution, were stirred by the call of the great leader.

"Why does Chairman Mao want to get rid of us? What does it mean to receive a reeducation from the peasants?" Hu Nü asked Mother. Father had a long time before been transferred to a different city. Mother had no answer, nor did anybody else. Nobody was allowed to question Chairman Mao's strategic decisions. She decided to go to school to have a look.

Her heart sank as soon as she saw what had happened to her beloved No. 2 High School, which she had attended everyday with pride for three years before the Cultural Revolution. All the windows were broken, most of them were covered with dirty black ink and strips of big posters. The front garden had been taken over by weeds, for the gardener had been dismissed a long time ago. The huge three-floor, U-shaped school building wore the sad look of a trauma survivor, layers of big posters peeling off it from everywhere. Most of the classrooms and offices were locked and some were blocked from inside by desks and chairs. Standing in the entrance hall, Hu Nü recalled how, at the beginning of the Cultural Revolution, her classmate Tian Ming had stood up to sign her blood oath, her action being followed by more than one hundred other students. Now Chairman Mao's calligraphy board, with the message, "Study Hard and Make Progress Every Day," looked as weathered as the rest of the school.

However, there was a fresh red banner hung across the wall of the ground floor at the entrance hall: "Respond to Chairman Mao's Call and Go to the Countryside." Under the red banner, there was an arrow pointing to the door of an office: "Sign Up Here." Hu Nü quickly turned her head away from the direction; she didn't want to sign up for anything. From the hunger strike three years ago, she remembered her lesson. There were a few people wandering about in the building. A few male students from the senior classes were coming in and out of the office. Hu Nü was glad that she didn't run into anyone she knew.

In the following month there was more talk in the newspapers about Chairman Mao's strategic decision to send the idle city youth to the countryside. It was not only a solution for one of the many problems caused by the Cultural Revolution, but also an opportunity for young people to gain valuable experience from real life. Overnight, all young people in the city, including the Red Guards, who had followed Chairman Mao closely during the Cultural Revolution, became the targets of the new doctrine.

One morning, there was a knock on the door. Opening it, Hu Nü saw four young men staring at her.

"Are you Hu Xiangyang?" one of them asked politely.

"I suppose," she smiled back, recalling her new name, which was actually three years old, though, she was still not used to it yet.

"We have an important proposal for you, though you might think it odd that we don't know each other, right?" Another young man said with a mischievous smile. Hu Nü opened the door wide to let them all into the apartment. Her three younger sisters, who had never seen so many young men visit them before, flocked over.

With four young men sitting down around the table, the outside half of the one-bedroom apartment looked crowded. The young men were two or three years older than Hu Nü and they were from the senior division of the school. They took turns to introduce themselves. "I have known you for a long time through your writing," one of them said. Hu Nü noticed his large brown eyes were shining at her, and she was quite embarrassed by the mention of her writing. She hoped he didn't remember what she had written, especially those sentiments that had earned her the nickname Bourgeois Flower at the beginning of the Cultural Revolution.

"Oh, those writings, they are a load of petty-bourgeois sentimentality, they are not worth mentioning," she apologized.

"You know what, I liked that petty-bourgeois sentimentality," the young man with large brown eyes said seriously.

Hu Nü looked at the pair of large brown eyes beneath dark thick eyebrows. "Really?" She was surprised that someone still remembered her name after school had been shut down for three years. That someone still remembered her writing was too flattering to be true.

"It was your true feelings, and it was personal," the young man continued, as if he knew her as a person through her writings. Hu Nü was not so sure what "personal" meant in this context; after three years of Cultural Revolution, everybody in China knew that "personal" interest was a dangerous thing.

"The four of us came to make a proposal to you," the first young man interrupted. "We'd like to form a family with you and your girl friend Ke, so what do you say to that? We hope you are not going to say no to us." Hu Nü looked at him, then at the big brown-eyed youth who was gazing at her, and at the other two young men who were both smiling.

"What? To form what?" She said, was shocked.

While she was struggling to understand him, the first young man raised his arms in front of him to form a circle. "You see, we want to form a group to go to the countryside together. The group ideally should include both men and women, and we'll live in the same house, share housework, and help each other in every possible way."

"Oh, I see," she murmured, trying to picture the situation.

"So, here we are, four strong young men. And we need four women. Two of us have sisters who want to join us, but we need two more women. Since we knew your writing, we thought we knew you too. We came to invite you to join our group." This time the big-eyed young man was talking, the other three stood up and bowed to Hu Nü with an arm-sweeping gesture of sincerity. She and her sisters burst out laughing.

On a winter morning, right after the New Year of 1970, Hu Nü said goodbye to her mother and sisters. With her sleeping bag tied up and carried in military style on her back, she took a northwest-bound train together with thousands of youth from the city. There had been an official farewell ceremony at Wuchang Railway Station for the city's four million people to see their children off to the countryside. The railway platform was decorated with red banners; a temporary stage was set up with a microphone and several loud speakers. The mayor gave a speech. A student representative swore to the public that they would work hard in the fields and they would not disappoint their parents and folks of their city. Finally amidst the noises of drum, music, and fire crackers, the train slowly puffed out of the station. Thousands of hands were reaching out from the train windows and thousands more hands stretching out from the platform, waving goodbye. Hu Nü's parents couldn't come to the railway station to see her off. Mother had to take care of her younger children all by herself now with Hu Nü's departure, while Father worked in another city.

As soon as the train picked up speed, the regular rhythm of the wheels brought a chill into the cars. There was no heat except for the warmth of their youthful bodies leaning on each other. Hu Nü was sitting with seven young people in their early twenties, among whom four were the young men who had came to visit her at home, two were their sisters, and the fourth young woman was her classmate, Ke. They were going to establish a student home somewhere three hundred kilometres away from Wuhan. This was the first that they had ever sat so closely to each other. At first she felt somewhat strange. But, by the time they reached their destination, a county named Tang, they were already calling each other by nicknames.

Daughter of An Ex-landlord

The village awaiting us was called Three Tile Roofs situated on a hilly landscape thirty kilometres from County Tang, where the railway station was. There were only three families living in the village. Two middle-aged brothers, married with children, occupied two houses with tile roofs. We were given the third one, attached to theirs. It had a one-bedroom design with a sitting room at the entrance and an interior bedroom through a door frame. The four young men were to share the two beds in the sitting-room area, and we four women would use the two beds inside.

There was neither electricity nor running water. Water had to be fetched from a pond half a kilometre away and carried back in two big wooden buckets hanging by ropes on the tips of a bamboo shoulder pole. We were told by the brigade leader that it was the men's duty to carry water home and to attend the vegetable garden, and women's duty to cook, make shoes and clothes, and raise children. So the eight of us were divided up into four housework teams as "man and woman" in order to share daily household chores. I was paired with Xin, the big-eyed young man who had said he liked my writing.

The peasants were extremely hospitable. There were about thirty families in our brigade spreading out in three villages, of which our Three Tile Roofs was the smallest one. Since it was winter, there was little work in the field, and the peasants took turns to invite us to dine with their families. For each meal we paid *15* fen per person. (100 *fen* = 1 *yuan*; today 15 *fen* would be worth less than a Canadian penny.) We were happy that we didn't have to cook our own meals, and we had an opportunity to get to know the peasants one by one.

Having been invited by most of the families in the brigade, I was surprised that we had not been invited by the family next door. We didn't even know their name. So one quiet afternoon, my curiosity led me to knock on the door partially hidden under the heavy hay roof. A young woman in her early twenties opened the door; she was wearing a floral padded cotton top and black padded cotton pants. In her hand she had an unfinished cotton shoe sole that she had been sewing.

"Hello, how are you?" I said, smiling at her and stretching my hand out.

Before I could introduce myself or explain why I had come, a startled look came upon her face. Her mouth flew open, her eyes filled more with fear than surprise. The muscles on her face twitched visibly before a helpless smile formed. "Are you sure you want to come inside my house?", she asked me suspiciously, stepping back.

"If it's not convenient, I'll come back some other time." I apologized for my intrusion. Maybe our next-door neighbour was a hermit.

"No, no, it's convenient, it's just . . . , nobody ever came to visit us. That's why I'm surprised to see you. Come in, please. My name is Chun." She had recovered from her earlier shock. Now she talked like a young woman to her peer.

I sat down with her at a square table in the middle of the room. She went to the kitchen to make tea. Looking around, I saw the clay walls were much smoother under the hay roof than our bumpy walls under the tile roof. Also the hay roof gave a much warmer feeling inside compared to the tile roofed houses we had visited lately. Chun set three tea cups and a pot of tea on the table. She sat down facing me across the table. While she was pouring tea into the cups, I wondered who the third person was. Perhaps she was married and her husband was inside.

"Have some hot tea, please." Chun put down a cup in front of me, "I'm bringing a cup to my grandpa. He rests inside." she said softly.

I was slowly sipping the hot tea, gently blowing away the tea leaves from the brim of the cup, when Chun came to join me. We smiled at each other. I could tell she was in her early twenties, like me. Her pink complexion was a result of working outdoors, especially in the cold winters; she had round eyes and a round face. I asked about her family. She said there were three of them: her elder brother, herself, and their grandfather. I thought that a strange combination. "What about your parents?" I asked. Looking at me for a while, then swallowing a big mouthful of tea, she said: "They have been dead for years." I felt sorry for an inappropriate question on my first visit. But before I could say something more appropriate, Chun continued, "They were executed by the government during the land reform movement in the early 1950s."

My heart sank. Suddenly I understood why Chun said nobody

ever came to visit them and also why we were not invited to dine with her family. Her family belonged to the class enemy. Was this why her family was the only household that didn't have a tile roof?

"My brother and I grew up with our maternal grandfather, so we don't really remember our parents," Chun explained with a helpless smile.

I nodded silently.

The next morning I woke up with two inches of snow on my bed; my clothes, which covered my duvet as an extra layer of bedding at night, were completely white. I thought a hay roof probably wouldn't leak like this tile roof. Outside, the village was covered up with snow. The tile roofs and the hay roof were all as white as the trees and bushes and everything else. It was extremely beautiful. The eight of us came out to put the first set of footprints on the snow. We were yelling and shouting with pleasure, making a snowman, padding its barrel body, when the party secretary of the brigade walked into the yard, puffing a long pipe.

"Morning, university students!" he greeted us formally.

"Morning, Party Secretary Chen!" We were glad to see him.

"What's new besides the snow?" We were dying for news about the outside world. Since coming to the village a month ago, we had not received a newspaper.

"That's why I'm here to have a quick meeting with all of you," he said, sucking on his pipe.

Immediately we all went inside and sat down around the table, men on one side and women on the other. Party Secretary Chen in the middle. He started the meeting with the trendy routine of wishing Chairman Mao a long, long life and Mao's best friend, the military commander Lin Biao a permanent good health. It turned out the meeting was about me visiting the ex-landlord's home the day before. I couldn't believe gossip could travel as fast in the countryside as it did in the city.

"Do you know they are the ex-landlord's relatives?" Party Secretary Chen asked me with his pipe pointing at the eastern side of wall we shared with Chun's family.

"No. Nobody ever told me anything about their class. I only thought they were like everybody else and we could pay a friendly visit."

"A friendly visit? They belong to the enemy class. Why didn't you ask your neighbours on this side? The Chen brothers, they are poor peasants." He now puffed his smoke towards the western side of the wall we share with the Chen brothers.

"I won't visit them again," I promised. I felt bad about doing such a stupid thing, bringing embarrassment and shame to our group. I probably had given Party Secretary Chen some ideas about why we city youth needed re-education from the peasants.

"I suggest you study Chairman Mao's class struggle theory together and develop some necessary political skills. So in the future you will be able to recognize who your friend is and who your enemy." Party Secretary Chen closed the meeting.

I wanted to say that Chun was not a class enemy because she herself was not a landlord. Like all of us she was born in new China and grew up under the red flag. Her parents, who were our class enemies, had already been executed. Regarding the children of class enemies, Chairman Mao said they should be allowed to choose politically. They were not necessarily enemies of the people. If they chose the side of the people, they should be given their opportunities. I wanted to explain Chairman Mao's class struggle theory to Party Secretary Chen, when I remembered Father's warning, "Disaster comes from your own mouth." I decided to bite my tongue and swallow my argument.

Spring came. Before the land had thawed completely, we followed the peasants to the fields. We learned to plant rice seedlings and to move quietly in the paddies to avoid leeches. Then we sowed cotton seeds in the fields and peanuts on hilly terraces. To prevent peasants from eating raw peanuts during sowing, the brigade leader mixed peanuts with fresh cow and chicken manure. In May, we cut wheat for two weeks and this was followed by nightly threshing and processing, during which the brigade rented machines from the commune. Then came the long hot summer of weeding. We weeded the rice paddies four times and cotton fields nine times until fall arrived with its harvest season. Rice had to be cut and dried and threshed. Cotton needed to be picked from the plants and dried and seeded. After the harvest was over, all brigades carried their best products to the commune's grain station on hand-pulled carts or shoulder poles and sold them to the state. In November, the accountant of each brigade would publicize the annual income of every household. For 1969, an adult male labourer in our brigade made about five hundred *yuan* annually; an adult female labourer made about four hundred *yuan*; half of these amounts were made by the male and female youth labourers under sixteen years of age.

We were anxious to know how much each of us had earned after working for a whole year side by side with peasants in the fields. Near the end of the first year, our hands were covered with calluses; we had shed our pale city skins for a dark brown country tan. We were still living together, although the subsidies for our settlement had long run short of our needs. We had borrowed money from the brigade to buy our daily food. The borrowed amount would be shared evenly and deducted from individual incomes at harvest time. Like everyone else in the brigade, we were bonded to the brigade economy, which was in turn bonded to the productivity of the land.

At the end of November the brigade held its annual meeting. Men and women, old and young, were dressed up for the occasion as if it were a national holiday. Everybody was excited and anxious. The brigade leader started the meeting by wishing Chairman Mao a long, long life and Lin Biao, good health. Then it was the accountant's turn to publicize each household account. First he read the income of each person and then the household total. Then he subtracted the amount of money borrowed by the family during the year, and finally, the account balance. The brigade listened quietly. People looked around for the family whose income was read. They cheered the successful families and showed sympathy towards families with meagre sums.

The eight of us, "university students," as referred to by the peasants, were listed at the end of the brigade ledger as a new household. The names of the four men were read first. Three of them earned about five hundred *yuan*; Xin made four hundred *yuan*, the amount earned by an adult female labourer. Everyone looked at Xin; the brigade leader gave a half-hearted explanation of why Xin earned less. Being physically thinner, as everyone could see, Xin was not as strong as the other three young men. Xin's face turned red. He stood up and asked angrily, "But I didn't do less work, did I? I was always given the exact same assignments as other men, students or peasants, why should I be paid less?"

"Silence! Silence!" The brigade leader shouted. "If you have any problem with the assessment, you can go to the commune office. After all, you are here to be re-educated by us, the assessment of your contribution also includes your attitude towards the brigade." Xin sat down heavily on his chair, his hands cupping his head. Taking out his cigarette package, he stuck one between his lips and lit it with a lighter. I watched him with sympathy, wondering whether he was going to accept this judgment.

Suddenly I heard my name being called. In fact I was the very last person listed in the brigade ledger. I had earned two hundred *yuan* after a whole year's toil, which was not even enough to cover my share of what the group had borrowed during the year to buy our rice and vegetables.

"What? I don't believe this. I am not a youth under sixteen, am I? I worked as an adult female labourer, why am I paid as a child?" I stood up, speaking fast, staring at the Brigade Leader.

"Wait a minute, wait a minute," the brigade leader raised his voice. "Do you remember on the first day you went to dig the mud on the frozen river bank, your leg went through thin ice and you almost fell into the river? You were so scared you even cried at the spot. There is no doubt that you were a city brat when you came here, not to mention you have visited the ex-landlord's relatives. You should think about your behaviour." He knocked the head of his pipe on the back of a chair. "Every household in this village has a combination of labourers, full male labourer, full female labourer, and then half labourers. The distribution of labour in the household of the university students should follow the same pattern, am I right?" The brigade leader laughed, his white spittle flew.

By now the crowd was tired. Mothers were ready to put their sleepy children to bed. Men were yawning and asking each other for a cigarette. The meeting was dismissed.

Two days after the brigade end-of-year meeting, Xin asked me whether I wanted to move with him to Peach Blossom Village. A good friend of his wanted to join him in a new settlement. Since Three Tile Roofs was too small to take another student, not to mention its bias against anyone who was physically smaller, he was thinking about moving to the neighbouring brigade. He said it would be nice if I could move with him. I was surprised by the idea at first, but after giving it a second thought, I knew it might work for me as well. Mother had asked whether my sister Mei could join me. So the four of us could settle down in a new students' home.

New Year's Eve of 1970, the day before Xin and I moved to Peach Blossom Village, we said goodbye to most of the families in our brigade. I paid the negative balance of my account with the fifty *yuan* I had brought from home. That night eight of us drank to our departure. At nine o'clock someone knocked at the door. Chun, our next-door neighbour under the hay roof, came to say goodbye.

Chun and I went inside the bedroom to talk. She said that she had waited until it was dark and made sure that no one saw her. She didn't want to get me into more trouble. However, she said she had to say goodbye to me, because I was the only person, as far as she could remember, who had ever visited her home and invited her to visit in return. She sat down on the edge of my bed. I held her hands in mine. I wanted to give her a token of friendship, so I took out my collection of Chairman Mao's badges. I had about one hundred pieces, among which the biggest one had a diameter of five inches, and the smallest one was only the size of a small finger nail. I asked her to choose whatever she liked. She picked up the one that had the Yangtze River Bridge underneath Mao's head. "I like this one, because you said your home is close to the river."

"Yes," I was surprised that she remembered. Chun's hand was searching inside her pocket. Pulling it out, she put something in my palm and immediately wrapped up my hand with hers before I could see what it was. She held our hands together for a long minute or two before she slowly let go. Opening my hand, I saw a small gold pin inside my palm. It was a tiger pin! It was so delicate that I could see the rings on the tiger's tail. "Where did you get this treasure?" I was surprised. I had never seen anything so beautiful in my life. Since the Cultural Revolution, jewellery had been considered an illegal bourgeois possession, nobody dared to wear a ring, a brooch, or a necklace. My parents didn't have any jewellery, so I had never touched any jewellery before.

"My mother gave it to me," Chun said. "I guess she wanted me to remember the year I was born." "So you were born in the year of the Tiger!" I couldn't believe it. "You are also a tiger girl!" I jumped up. "We were born in the same year, do you know?" I held her shoulders tightly with my arms.

"I wanted you to have this pin and remember me," Chun said softly.

"Of course I'll always remember you. I'm not moving far away. Come and visit me whenever you have time." I had totally forgotten the class struggle theory.

"I heard you and Xin are getting married, is that true?" Chun's eyes gazed at mine, glowing mischievously.

"What? What are you talking about? Who is getting married?"

"You and Xin. The gossip is all over the brigade, even the brigade leader said so."

"What did they say?" I was shocked by the rumour.

"They say since it's illegal to have an affair before marriage, you and Xin decided to move to another village and get married," Chun said.

"Oh. . . I see, that's why we decided to move to another village." I repeated sarcastically. "Why do some people always tell lies about other people?"

Outside, under the cloudy grey sky, the howling wind was sweeping through the bleak wintery landscape. From underneath our single-layered tile roof, a chill was descending with bits and pieces of dead leaves and occasional gushes of powdered dirt. A heavy snow was about to cover up the entire landscape with its mysterious white coat of innocence. I let out a deep sigh from my chest to calm the anger rising in my veins.

Peach Blossom Village

Following the week of the Chinese New Year, Xin's friend Huang and my sister Mei both arrived at Peach Blossom Village. The four of us started living like a family. The guys always made sure there was enough water in the huge terra cotta container in the kitchen, and the firewood was cut and piled up neatly behind the stove. We were next door to Brigade Leader Wang, his wife Xiuzhen, and their two-year-old son. Perhaps because they were young themselves, we found it easy to talk to them. We could even have fun together as neighbours. We learned to grow vegetables from the brigade leader, so like every other family in the village, we had seasonal fresh vegetables from our own garden. By then Xin and I were more or less used to physical labour in the fields and had adopted the peasants' life pattern as well. After working in the fields, the women of the house would start cooking right away, while men would carry water from the drinking pond, work in the garden, or prepare firewood. When all outdoor chores were done, the men would come into the kitchen to help feed the fire.

I became the chief cook in the kitchen. In both summer and fall, we used dry wheat or rice stalks for fuel; we only bought firewood for winter after the grain stalks were used up. Wheat and rice stalks were twisted into bundles to make them last longer inside the big stove. Someone had to sit in front of the stove to keep adding new bundles into the flames while another person cooked in the big wok above the fire. Whenever I was cooking, Xin always came in to help me feed the fire. As he sat in front of the stove, his face would be lit up by the flames. Sometimes we talked about various things while the flames licked at the bottom of the wok. Other times he gazed at the flames, completely lost in his own thoughts. I would leave him there to ponder over whatever was occupying his mind.

One day Xin came to help me as usual after we returned from the fields. Sitting in front of the stove and waiting for me to tell him when to light the fire, he seemed completely preoccupied. He didn't even look up.

"Xin, please ignite," I said.

"Sure." He struck a match and threw it into a bundle of dry hay inside the stove. Immediately there was a roar of fire under the wok. "Ah, I wish I could do that with my life," Xin sighed, mumbling to himself.

"Of course," I responded accordingly. I thought he must be thinking about his future. How much we wished to be somewhere else, doing something more interesting than physical labour, the so-called re-education from the peasants! The fire made a humming sound under the stove. Xin's face was lit up red. Looking up at me, his big brown eyes glowing, he said, "Don't you know, you silly girl, what I mean?"

"What? What?" I thought I heard the fire roaring.

"Don't you know I am in love with you?" Xin was staring at me.

My heart was pounding fast against my chest, when I realized I hadn't heard him wrong. Of course, I had sensed his affection for me, but as a girl from a good family, I was not supposed to reveal my feelings towards a young man before he did.

"I'll die if I don't tell you this today. Ever since we first met, I have been in love with you. In fact, even before we met, I was in love with your writing." Xin was looking at the flames.

"Oh, oh, my writing, that pretty bourgeois sentimental stuff," I murmured, without knowing what to say exactly. My ear was drumming with the roaring flames and my face burning hot. I recalled the gossip in Three Tile Roofs before our transfer. I wondered if he had anything to do with the rumour. Xin kept adding more fuel into the flames without looking at me. Bright red shadows from the fire danced up and down on the kitchen walls.

"Xin, I smell burnt food!" I lifted up the wooden lid of the large iron stove. The pungent smell of burnt rice met my nose. I looked around, there was no one outside the kitchen, both Huang and Mei were in the house, I said to Xin softly, "Let me think about this." I didn't know what else to say. It was both exciting and embarrassing to know a young man had had a secret desire for me.

Xin and I started to spend more time together. We shared reminiscences about our high school, about childhood dreams, about the Cultural Revolution, but mostly we talked about our future. We didn't know if we had to spend the rest of our lives in the countryside with the peasants, married, with a family. After our lengthy discussions, we always reached a negative conclusion about this. We believed our condition was temporary, part of Chairman Mao's strategic planning of ending and repairing the damage from the Cultural Revolution. By sending all of us city youth to the countryside for a real-life experience, Chairman Mao had easily completed the task of dissolving the Red Guards. Once again he had moved and handled millions of us with a single instruction. Now that we had settled down in the countryside, our future depended on future urban and industrial development. Without knowing how long this re-education would last, Xin and I decided to curb our desire for each other until we returned to the city. The worst scenario was that if I became pregnant, and then we would have to get married in the countryside, we could end up staying here for the rest of our lives.

At Peach Blossom Village, we each had a single bed. My sister and I slept inside the bedroom. Xin and Huang slept in the sitting room. At night I listened to the two men reciting poetry from the Tang Dynasty before one of them fell asleep. Mei and I talked about how we used to fight and play with our two younger sisters, and we worried about Mother working full time and taking care of two children by herself. Every morning at six o'clock, Brigade Leader Wang got up. Before he blew his whistle to wake up the whole brigade, he would come over to our side and knock on our door. "Get up, Xin," he would call. I could tell that the brigade leader regarded Xin as the head of our household.

One day, Huang got a telegram from home. His sick old father was dying in the hospital. Huang asked the brigade leader for two to three weeks' leave of absence. He left immediately for the railway station to catch the evening train. With the three of us remaining in the household, and my sister not interested in cooking after working in the fields, Xin and I were left with each other most of time in the kitchen or in the sitting room after dinner. One night after I said good night to him, and blew off his oil lamp for him, he grabbed my shoulders silently. In the darkness, he kissed me on my lips and all over my face. I was afraid that Mei could hear us from inside. I pulled myself away from him, but lying down in my bed, I wished there was no wall between us.

During the last week that Huang was away, Mei's high school teacher Miss Liang came to visit. In order to make it more comfortable for the visitor, I gave my bed to her, so she could sleep in the inner bedroom with Mei. After dinner when I told Xin that I would be sleeping in Huang's bed that night, he was delighted. At night after Mei and her teacher went to bed, I asked Xin to go to bed first. I didn't want to undress in front of him. I blew out the oil lamp and then quickly got into Huang's bed. In the darkness, I could see Xin's bright eyes shining at me, his dark hair on the pillow on his bed, and his duvet well wrapped around his body. The distance between the two beds was less than two feet. I was embarrassed by such closeness. Xin stretched his arm out, his hand touched my ears, my eyes, my nose, until it found my lips. Then it started to go down my neck and to my breasts. I didn't know what to say except to let him feel me.

Early next morning, I woke up as soon as the brigade leader knocked on the door with "Get up, Xin." Xin mumbled an answer as he sat up in bed, half sleepy. Suddenly he realized that I was in Huang's bed. He turned to me and said gently, "I love you." My heart was pounding. "I love you too." I vaguely remembered how he felt my breasts the night before.

At breakfast, Mei said she needed to take three days off to accompany her teacher to visit some other students in a neighbouring county. They would set off for the railway station to catch the morning train. Looking at each other, Xin and I knew we would be alone for two days before Huang's scheduled return. We couldn't wait for the sun to go down and for the day's labour to end.

After dinner brigade leader Wang, his wife, Xiuzhen, and their son came over to play cards as they did from time to time. Xin treated Wang to cigarettes and I gave the kid and his mother some candies. While playing poker, Xiuzhen told me that Chun in Three Tile Roofs had set a wedding date.

"Where is her future husband's home?" In the countryside a bride moved to the household of her husband upon marriage.

"Two hundred kilometres north of here," Xiuzhen said.

"Why does she want to marry someone that far away from home?" I asked. Most marriages were between neighbouring villages.

"You know Chun's parents were executed in the Land Reform Movement because they were landlords before liberation. No woman wants to marry a man from a landlord's background. Chun's brother is thirty-nine years old this year, but still he couldn't find a bride. What they are doing now is called 'exchanging brides' in the countryside, meaning Chun is going to marry another landlord's son, and this man's sister will marry Chun's brother."

"Just like that, the girls are exchanged as brides, so their brothers can each have a wife. You see, otherwise, the two men would probably stay single for the rest of their lives." Xiuzhen looked at me and Xin to make sure we understood the custom.

"It's convenient to have a sister around the house," Xin said sarcastically.

"But if Chun is married to someone else who belongs to a better class, she and especially her children wouldn't be called landlord's descendants any more, is that right?" I asked.

"Yes, that's true. The class status of a family is decided by that of the man." The brigade leader nodded at me.

"If Chun does that for herself, her brother will probably never be able to find a wife, women from better classes don't want to marry a landlord's son," Xiuzhen explained.

"But that is so unfair to Chun," I said. "And of course, it's unfair to anyone."

"You're right. If you think it's unfair to Chun, what about the other girl? What about any woman who marries a landlord's son?" Xiuzhen said with sympathy. I felt a bitter taste in my mouth.

After the Wangs left us, I was still preoccupied with Chun's arranged marriage. Xin asked if I wanted to wash and go to bed. I had forgotten he and I were alone in the house, and earlier we had been looking forward to a quiet evening by ourselves.

"Where do you want to sleep?" he asked me, his big brown eyes shining with expectation.

"In my own bed," I said absentmindedly.

After I had changed and lain down, Xin came over and sat on the edge of my bed. He was fully dressed. He bent down and gave me a full kiss on the lips, and then he put kisses all over my face and my neck. His hands started to feel my breasts. Suddenly I felt a longing for his touch from inside my body. Xin's right hand kept moving underneath my robe, until it reached my crotch. I was afraid, I didn't know what he would want to do next. His hand stopped when he looked at me with embarrassment. "Could I?" He asked timidly.

I nodded, though I knew I was supposed to discourage him. A good girl was expected to say "no" when her boy friend was sexually aroused. But I couldn't stop myself from wanting him as well. I was surprised he didn't ask to see me undressed, perhaps his imagination could satisfy that desire. For a while both of us were so concentrated on the movement of his hand that we even stopped talking. My body seemed to rise along with the touches of his hand. Shortly, his index finger started to penetrate my vagina. I knew it was too late to stop him.

We spent the following night enjoying the same kind of intimacy. Xin was sitting on the edge of my bed, kissing and feeling my body before his index finger finally penetrated me. Then he said goodnight to me and went back to his own bed in the sittingroom.

Two days later Huang and Mei both came back; Huang looked exhausted because of his father's funeral, and Mei disturbed. She went straight to bed and didn't go to work in the fields the next day.

A Yin Yang Person

Mei started to receive mail regularly following her teacher Miss Liang's visit. It was the handwriting on the envelope that first caught Hu Nü's attention. It had what was generally considered a masculine style because of its strong downward strokes and the bony structures of its characters. Xin and Huang were impressed by the strength and energy in the handwriting, and they thought therefore that Mei must have a boyfriend.

Shortly after, Mei began to ask for leaves of two to three days regularly at the end of each month, so she could go to the county Tong where the railway station was. When asked why she went there, she said, simply to see a friend. Who had so much attraction for Mei that she didn't mind walking thirty kilometres each way? Hu Nü was puzzled, but she didn't want to tell her parents. She blamed herself for not looking after her sister; when Mei wanted to go away with her teacher she didn't even try to keep her. It seemed to her that it was after Miss Liang's visit that Mei had started to behave differently.

It was not until the Chinese New Year in 1970, when they all went back to Wuhan for a month-long holiday, that Hu Nü finally found out about Mei's secret friend. During the holiday season, her family was busy everyday. At first, their parents didn't notice that Mei was out everyday with Miss Liang. She simply said she went shopping or to a movie with a friend. Suspicions were aroused only when she started to stay out at night for several days in a row. Her parents got very upset. When questioned, Hu Nü told them that Mei received letters regularly from someone who might be Miss Liang. Her parents immediately concluded that Miss Liang probably had a brother whom she was trying to set up with Mei.

That Chinese New Year's Eve was the first family reunion since Father was sent to a state farm in 1967. But Mei didn't come home, her absence ruined the New Year atmosphere. Father drank silently while Mother put dishes on the table without naming them. Hu Nü and her two younger sisters, eleven and nine, walked around the apartment on tiptoes. Around eight o'clock in the evening, they heard every other family in Building No.7 start their New Year's Eve dinner, talking, drinking, and laughing. The Hus ate in silence, because of their second daughter's absence. At about nine o'clock, heavy footsteps came on the staircase, it was Mei finally coming home.

She sat down at the table heavily as if exhausted, but didn't pick up her chopsticks. There was a lot of food on the table. Mother said she could warm the dishes up. But Father insisted that Mei tell what had happened, and why she was out at night, and with whom she spent time. Mei stood up. It looked like she was ready to leave home again. Father yelled at her to sit down and to tell the truth. Mei didn't say a word. Instead, grinning, she turned the whole dinner table upside down. All the dishes fell on the floor: meat balls were rolling out of the bowl; the stand-by fish jumped out of its thick sauce; deep-fried lotus root pieces wheeled themselves to the corner of the room; tofu plopped on the floor along with roasted peanuts, spoons, chopsticks and bowls.

"Are you insane?" Mother rushed over and slapped Mei on the face. "Where did you go? Who were you with? Where did you sleep at night? shameless slut!"

Hu Nü waved at her two younger sisters, and quickly they went to the inside part of the bedroom. Mei didn't say a word. They heard her slamming the door. Mother was crying while Father was kicking the dishes on the floor and cursing his bad luck for having four daughters.

It was a Chinese custom to sit through the New Year's Eve and wait for the dawn of the New Year. That year, long before the fire crackers were lit to celebrate the arrival of the New Year, the Hu family had put out their light and gone to bed in silence.

They didn't talk about the New Year's Eve during the holiday season. Five days after the New Year, Father went back to the state farm in Henan Province. Mei came home from time to time, and sometimes she ate with the family but usually without talking to anyone. She had lost weight, her slim figure became even smaller and her face grew paler.

On a late afternoon during the last week of their holidays back in the city. Xin urgently knocked on Hu Nü's door. His big brown eyes were shining with emotion. "What's wrong?" Hu Nü asked, letting him in.

Xin looked around the apartment. Only Hu Nü and her two younger sisters were at home. Sitting down in a chair to catch his breath, Xin whispered to Hu Nü, "Do you know who this Miss Liang is Xiao Mei spends so much time with?"

Hu Nü shook her head. She remembered Miss Liang was a tall woman, at least five feet seven, taller than most Chinese women, definitely much taller than Mei, who was only five feet two. Miss Liang had short hair, a pale face, full lips, and she wore spectacles. She was ordinary except for her height.

"So what did you find out about her?" Hu Nü asked anxiously.

"There are quite a few big posters about her on the wall outside of their school. Apparently, she is a *yin yang* person." Xin said hesitantly.

"What? What is she?".

"A *yin yang* person." Xin repeated. Hu Nü tried to think of the meaning of the two words. *Yin* meant cloudy or shady, or of the moon, or of the female, while *yang* meant bright, sunny, of the sun, of the male.

"It means she is a woman during the day, and a man at night," Xin explained, "that's what the posters have said. I'm not sure how the transformation can actually happen. The posters said that, Liang is sexually attracted to women, especially younger women, because she herself becomes a man at night."

An eerie feeling started to descend through her spine, chilling her blood. It was the first time in her life that she had heard about such a thing as a *yin yang* person. Hu Nü asked Xin anxiously, "What do they do, do you know, I mean a person like that, what does a *yin yang* person do to someone like Mei?" She was thinking about her relationship with Xin and what they liked to do together. During the holidays, they spent a lot of time with each other. Hu Nü's parents didn't know Xin was their daughter's boyfriend, but his parents knew about their relationship. The old couple had started treating Hu Nü as a future daughter-in-law.

"I guess they do exactly the same thing as we do, kissing and playing with each other." Two years older and having grown up in a working-class area, Xin knew many things that Hu Nü had never heard of.

"I don't believe this . . . " She didn't want to hear this any more. It was too disturbing and it challenged her imagination. "Don't tell Huang about this, please, I definitely don't want my parents to know this. They have already been hurt by Mei's strange recent behaviour."

Hu Nü's parents had been very strict with their eldest daughter when it came to boys. Though she had been attending a boys' school, no male classmates had ever come to visit her at home before the Cultural Revolution. Her childhood sweetheart Hua was the only boy ever invited home. After he left, her parents would question her about what they did, what exactly they had talked about. After she went to the countryside, this strict parental control over her life seemed to have loosened up a little. During the holidays, Xin dropped by often, though he pretended to be a schoolmate only, a fellow youth who happened to be in the same village as Hu Nü. Before her parents, he didn't dare to show any intimacy, nor did she ask him personal questions that could cause her parents to be suspicious.

Hu Nü didn't know why she always wanted to prove to her parents that she hadn't changed from the straight A student she had been at Wuhan No.2 High School before the Cultural Revolution. Somehow she seemed to want them to believe that she was not attracted to boys, and was not interested in fashion. She was their eldest daughter, occupying the place of the eldest son who was never born. She wanted them to be proud of her. For the same reason, Hu Nü felt it was her responsibility to help her parents raise their younger daughters. But if she had failed, in the case of Mei, she wanted to protect her parents from knowing the worst details.

New Opportunities

On a cold winter night at Peach Blossom Village, the brigade leader came over for a visit. Hu Nü made hot tea, and Xin took out the cigarette package he had bought from the commune store. Sitting down at the table, the brigade leader seemed to have something important to say.

"Good news!" He couldn't control his excitement. Sipping his tea and looking at the four city youth gathered around him, he said with a big smile, "Your opportunity has finally arrived."

"What opportunity?" they asked simultaneously like little school children in a classroom.

"Today I attended a meeting at the commune office. We were told that factories and companies from the city are coming to our county to hire students. Those who have been in the countryside for two years and worked hard are going to be given opportunities first."

"Really?" They looked at each other, they wanted to jump up and shout "Hooray" to this new opportunity. But they didn't want the brigade leader to think that they disliked the countryside. At least it was not true about Peach Blossom Village. Their brigade leader understood that the city youth didn't want to spend their entire lives in his village.

After the brigade leader left, the four of them were so excited that they sat there talking away after midnight. Xin and Hu Nü had been in the countryside for over two years, Huang and Mei for about a year. So it seemed that the latter two would have to continue for another year before they could have their opportunities.

The next morning, when the sun rose, Hu Nü felt for the first time since the Cultural Revolution started in 1966 that there was a new hope on the horizon.

In a week, Xin got a notice from the commune office that he was one of the first fifty students who could fill in a form. He asked why Hu Nü was not chosen, since they had come together to settle in this countryside. The answer was that it would take a little bit of time. Hu Nü started to imagine her life without Xin. She felt unbearably sad.

Xin came back from the commune with more news. The company that had come to hire students was a military supply factory in the deep northwestern mountains of Hubei Province. The enrollment qualification specified that trainees must be from a Red family, working class, poor peasant, revolutionary cadre, or revolutionary soldier. Suddenly, class politics, which had not been so important in the last two years in the countryside, returned to dictate their fate again. The Brigade Leader asked Xin whether Hu Nü came from a Red family. He answered vaguely that her family was not Black. As family background was designated solely by the male lineage, Hu Nü finally understood why no women wanted to marry Chun's brother in Three Tile Roofs. Which woman wanted to have her future children's blood tainted by the descendant of a landlord?

Xin came from a working-class family. He was adopted at age three by an old couple who became his parents. He told Hu Nü that he didn't want to look for his biological parents. He had no interest in knowing their kinship to him, since they had given him up for adoption when he was only three. His new parents loved him dearly, and they were both Party secretaries of local businesses.

"I wish you could come to the factory with me," Xin said, holding Hu Nü's hands tightly after they had finished all the housework in the kitchen. "Maybe I could request that, after I am hired. There are always nonmilitary jobs that family members can do, for example teaching kids at school, you won't mind doing that, will you? I think that can be arranged definitely after we get married in the not-too-faraway future."

Hu Nü thanked Xin for thinking about her and especially about their relationship, but she didn't want to go to a place where she was categorized as politically untrustworthy while everyone else was a true Red. It seemed to her that she and Xin would have to part.

Two weeks after his medical check-up, Xin was officially hired by the military factory. By then the whole village knew he came from a Red family and both his parents were Party members. Women in the brigade, especially Xiuzhen, the brigade's leader's wife, thought it was strictly unfair that Hu Nü was not given the same opportunity. "It really shouldn't matter what kind of family the woman belongs to, as long as her man came from a good one. That's how it works here, why doesn't it work with his factory? Now what about your relationship?" she asked.

"I don't know. Maybe I have to say goodbye to Xin," Hu Nü told Xiuzhen honestly.

Hu Nü went to the railway station to see Xin off. The thirty kilometres between the village and the county took them a good three hour's walk. On the way Xin told her that his factory actually made machine guns, the kind used in Vietnam by the militia to shoot down American military helicopters. He said he wouldn't be able to give her any more details about the factory once he got there, it was against the security regulations. She should remember never to ask him questions about the products of his factory. She could only talk about personal things in her mail. "You think I can come and visit you one day? Will the factory allow that?" she asked him.

After giving this some thought, Xin said that could probably be arranged. "That's why I want to marry you. Once we are married," Xin stopped walking, his big brown eyes looked sincerely into hers and his hands held hers in front of his chest, "I'm pretty sure I can ask the personnel department to hire you at the factory."

Xin boarded the train along with a happy crowd. It reminded Hu Nü of three years before, when they had boarded the train together at Wuchang Railway Station to come here. At that time, they were almost strangers to each other. How similar the situation was right now, except that she was not wanted in this new journey ahead of him.

Two weeks later, a letter came from Xin. He was very happy about the new job. He had started his three-year apprenticeship to become a machine operator. His monthly pay during this period was 25 *yuan* (today about $5 Canadian). In three years, he would be paid 36 *yuan* a month. He said an apprentice was not allowed to get married, so they had to wait until he completed his training. He budgeted his money thus: if he could save 10 *yuan* per month, he would have 360 *yuan* by the end of his three-year apprenticeship. Then he would be paid 36 *yuan* per month, and if he could save 16 *yuan* a month for a year, he could have an extra 192 *yuan* in a year, and a total of 552 *yuan*, enough for their wedding. "By then," he said in his letter, "you'll be twenty-four and I will be twenty-six, we'll be more mature to start a family than we are now."

Xin called Hu Nü his "sweetheart" in his second letter, using an English word she had never heard before. After she looked it up in her little pocket English-Chinese dictionary, she blushed. She warned him of his petty bourgeois sentiments, which could invite political criticism if discovered, and yet she also told him how much she liked the English word, because of its direct expressiveness. In their situation, it said more than any Chinese word could ever have said about their feelings for each other. Xin said in his following letter that he learned the word, "sweetheart," from a female technician, who had been separated from her husband, a professor of mathematics teaching at Wuhan University.

Shortly after Xin left the village, Huang was called by the commune office to fill in a form. Hu Nü started to panic. Huang had been in the countryside for only a year and two months, and yet he had been called. What was wrong with her? Was there really something bad in her family? She knew her family were not Red, but far from being Black—-landlords, rich peasants, capitalists, Kuomingtang officers, rightist, or capitalist roaders.

Hu Nü remembered that Huang's deceased father was an old school teacher, which meant his family belonged to the same class as hers—-intellectuals, or petty bourgeoisie. He told her that after his father's death, he had changed his family status to working class, which was his mother's family background. Hu Nü was confused. One could not change the family one was born in, because one parent had died, or Chun's brother in Three Tile Roofs would not have to trade off his sister for a wife. But Huang said this could be done only when the living parent was the financial provider of the family, and that was his mother.

"My mother's family were poor peasants; she herself was a worker, and she also helps support the family. Does that mean I could change my family background to 'poor peasant' or 'working class'?" Hu Nü asked Huang hopefully.

"Not when your father is the major provider."

"I hate to say this, but, in a very selfish way, your father's recent death actually was a good thing, because it helps advance your future. Am I right?" Hu Nü was almost immediately ashamed of her own cynicism.

"Yes, you're quite right. I wouldn't have this job opportunity at a military plant had my father been alive today."

Huang was hired by another military plant. It manufactured parachutes. The factory was also situated in the deep northwestern mountains in the province, close to Xin's factory. Hu Nü was glad for them both. At least they would be able to see each other during weekends and holidays.

The two sisters were left in the village by themselves now in a household without men. The brigade leader and the Party secretary didn't like the situation at all. To them it would have been more appropriate to let the female students go back to the city or factories first. Now that the men were gone, the brigade heads wished the sisters could soon be on their way out.

Hu Nü started carrying two half buckets of water on the shoulder pole. From time to time, she also carried grain and hay from the brigade office to their home. Every other day she had to carry water from a ditch to their vegetable garden. She learned to walk like a man with a gentle swing and a good rhythm. She also learned to change the bamboo pole from the right side of the shoulder to the left while walking. This helped her ease off the pain from the blisters on her shoulders.

Overseas Relationship?

When the third winter came in 1971, there was a severe shortage of firewood in the village. The brigade leader and the peasants had no objection to Mei's request to take an earlier holiday in the city. Hu Nü decided to stay behind in case of job opportunities. The day after she saw Mei off at the railway station, she stopped at the county office. By then there was an Educated Youth Office set up to provide hiring companies with candidates' files. She went in to ask why her sister and herself had not been called to fill in a form.

A middle-aged local county cadre received her. He introduced himself as "Lao Chen," Old Chen. Lao Chen listened to Hu Nü with sympathy. According to him, most of the students who came with Hu Nü or even a year later had filled in some kind of forms except those from the Black families. Hu Nü could hear her heart beating against her chest. Apparently more than a dozen companies were here to select students. Lao Chen said most students from the Red families had already departed for their new jobs in industry, now many from petty-bourgeois family background were being selected and were scheduled to leave soon. He asked Hu Nü whether she knew Anna, whose parents were both medical doctors.

"Anna, of course, I know Anna. How can I forget her?" Hu Nü exclaimed. "Her name should be Hongge? She was my classmate in high school." She was excited that she could even recall Anna's Cultural Revolutionary name. By then, people had realized that the revolutionary names caused too much confusion to be practical, so a lot of people went back to using their original names. Talking about Anna made Hu Nü feel the gap between now and then, here and there. It was almost three years since she came to the countryside.

She sensed that something was seriously wrong in her family, something of great importance that she was not aware of. "Could you look up and see whether there was anything negative wirtten about my family?" she begged Lao Chen. After looking at her for a moment, Lao Chen stood up and went to his office to pull out a file from the locked cabinet.

"Are you sure your parents have told you everything about their families?" Lao Chen asked her suspiciously. "I also mean their extended families, including their brothers and sisters?" He took another look at the file folder in his hands.

"I think so, anything you think that I don't know?" Hu Nü asked timidly.

"I am not supposed to tell you what is in your file. But I am very sympathetic with you, I will let you have a quick peek at this part."

Lao Chen walked towards his desk, Hu Nü following him. She thought that any second he could change his mind and tell her to simply go back to the brigade and wait for her call. But Lao Chen didn't change his mind, he put down the open file on the desk, and waved at her to come closer. She couldn't believe that he would risk his job to let her see her secret.

There were a couple of pages stapled together in the middle of a white folder. Lao Chen pointed at the column titled "Relatives." In the space below were four Chinese characters with a question mark: *hai-wai-guan-xi*? The handwriting looked hastily done and the ink smudged.

"Overseas relationship? My family? What does that mean?" she asked in surprise.

"It means that there is some suspicion that one of your parents has some relatives living overseas. Do you know anything about it?" Lao Chen asked.

"Oh, no. No. No. We don't know anyone from abroad. My parents both came from relatively poor families in the countryside, I have never heard that we have any relatives in other countries." Hu Nü spoke as firmly as she could, because she knew that with overseas relatives, her future would be doomed for good. During the Cultural Revolution, having relatives overseas was considered as the worst family trait, ten times worse than Black-ness. In some cases, families with overseas relatives were suspected as foreign intelligence agents and saw their homes searched by the Red Guards.

"Let me give you a hint. This file came back from your father's institute. He is a chief architect. The suspicion is about his side of the family. You might want to check that out." Lao Chen closed the file, put it back inside the cabinet, and locked it with a key.

Walking out of Lao Chen's office, Hu Nü's mind was filled with questions. She started to go through the list of her father's relatives in her mind: her only aunt was a housewife married to a railway worker who had died two years ago of tuberculosis. Of the two uncles, one was a medical doctor, the other a locomotive driver. She heard from her mother that her father originally had two more brothers, but they had both died. One was drowned in a flood, the other one was drafted by the Kuomingtang and died in the war of liberation. So who would be the overseas relationship that made her unemployable?

She left the county office with a heavy heart. Absentmindedly, she started walking towards Peach Blossom Village. Evening was descending earlier in the winter, she knew she had to get home before darkness blotted out the road.

But after walking for an hour on the bleak wintry road, she changed her mind. Turning around, she started walking back towards the county and the railway station. She decided to go back to Wuhan to ask Father about his brothers. Perhaps he could clarify the situation.

Twilight disappeared in the horizon. Darkness came like a thick winter coat. Hu Nü was the only person walking along the frozen country path. When she arrived at the railway station, the door of the waiting room was still open, but there were no passengers inside. A naked light bulb hung there casting despair over four bare wooden benches. The ticket window was closed. She knocked, there was no response. The wind was blowing the door back and forth, making a long creaking noise. She started to panic. Then she went to read the schedule on the wall, the last train for Wuhan had left two hours ago.

"Am I going to sleep here tonight?" she asked herself because it was too late to walk back to the village.

Stepping out of the waiting room, she was the only one on the empty street. She couldn't help shivering in the cold. Walking a little, she saw a small noodle restaurant still open. She pushed the door and went in. There were a few peasants sitting at the table in the middle of the room, each with a bowl of noodles in his hands. The smell of sesame oil mixed with fresh green onion in the cold air made her mouth water. She ordered a big bowl of hot and dry noodles her favourite.

The peasants at the table, all men, started shifting. They gave her the nicer and cleaner side of the table to sit. Then they all went back to enjoy their noodles, slurping almost in unison. By the time her bowl of noodles came, they had already finished theirs. Some wiped their mouths with their sleeves, a normal practice in the countryside, others started asking her questions, brown soy sauce still stuck around their mouth.

"So, what are you up to at this time of the day, university student?".

"I wanted to take the train to Wuhan tonight, but it was too late. I don't know what I'm going to do now, my village is thirty kilometres away from here." She told them the truth, seeking advice.

"Why didn't you set off earlier? Didn't you know the last train leaves here at four o'clock in the afternoon?" an older man said, looking at the rest of them sitting at the table. They nodded in agreement.

"I should know the schedule better, but I have an emergency. So I didn't think." Hu Nü didn't know how to explain her situation to them.

The older man was smoking a pipe, puffing out grey smoke circles over the table. "Emergency?" He repeated. "I'll tell you what you can do. But first of all, let me ask you, are you brave?"

"What? Brave, why?" She didn't understand him.

"Brave, so you are not afraid of riding a freight train with us to Wuhan tonight, because it's illegal." Some of the peasants got up from the table. They looked at the older man suspiciously, as if he had betrayed them. "We have to help this young woman, she has an emergency. Did you hear that?" he said firmly. Those who had stood up, sat down again.

"So, are you brave?" a young man from the opposite side of the table asked Hu Nü.

"I think I am, depends on how risky it is. Will we be caught by the railway police?" She knew that only vagabonds and criminals rode freight trains. Many of them were involved in stealing and smuggling goods. The railway policemen were tough with the illegal riders once they were caught.

The peasants at the table were waiting for her answer. "Or you could check in at one of the two inns in town and take the passenger train at noon tomorrow," the older man suggested softly. "But if you decide to go with us, you'll get to Wuhan early tomorrow morning. You will have to make up your mind by the time you finish your noodles, because we'll be leaving here soon."

Hu Nü nodded yes with her mouth full of noodles.

Outside, it was now pitch-dark. A thin layer of ice had formed on the pebbled street. From a nearby village came occasional dog barks. Hu Nü stumbled along with the group of six peasants towards the freight yard. They pulled tight their almost identical home-made, black, cotton padded coats. Walking swiftly in more or less the same manner, they hunched their backs, stuck their heads forward, and pushed their bare hands into the opposite sleeves to keep them warm. They wore the same kind of knitted black hats, and home-made black shoes with cotton soles. Some of them occasionally coughed and spat. Hu Nü had to run to keep up with them.

When they turned at the end of the main street, she could see the shiny dark rails ahead. There were several freight cars parked separated from one another. Since her father worked for the Railway Bureau all his life, Hu Nü knew a bit about the railways. One of the men walking at the front turned around, as if suddenly, he had remembered that she was with them. The older man stopped at the same time, and whispered to Hu Nü, "Keep up. Don't make any noise, we are getting closer now." She nodded without raising her

eyes from the ground, fearing she might slip on the ice.

The group stopped at a single freight car parked on a pair of side tracks. The man at the front checked the number on the side. He made a gesture to the rest of group. "Get on," he said quietly. Two of the men started to pull the heavy metal sliding door in opposite directions. Inside, it was dark and empty. The men all jumped up into it. Two of them put out their hands for her. Holding on to their hands, she let them pull her up from the ground. The two guys then pushed the sliding door back, and she heard a click as the door closed.

Inside the car, there was absolutely no light. Hu Nü remembered an old Chinese saying describing real darkness as being so dark you cannot see your five fingers. She stretched out her hand; indeed, she couldn't see her own five fingers. She put both her hands against the wall, feeling her way forward and away from the breathing sounds of the men. She knew a freight car was quite big inside; she wanted to find a corner to sit down by herself. She reached the other end and found a corner.

After about half an hour, footsteps came along the tracks, and she heard the sound of metal hitting metal, made by a hammer on the wheels. Hu Nü knew it was the mechanic checking the wheels. Shortly after that came a sharp, long whistle. From a small crack in the wall of the car, she could now see a thin strip of green light blinking. The men were so quiet that she couldn't even hear their breathing any more. Suddenly, they were shaken up by the shock of the locomotive hitting their car. They began to move. The wheels made a scratching noise on the rails as they went from the side tracks onto the main tracks. She could see some blue lights now from the small crack in the wall. She knew they were coming to a freight yard to join other cars going to the same destination.

After more jerking backwards and forwards, there came the long blowing of a whistle three times, followed by the loud puff of the locomotive. They were off! It didn't take long for the wheels to pick up a galloping rhythm. Listening to the regular sound of the motion, Hu Nü almost forgot that she was sitting on the cold, bare floor of a freight car. The men started chattering; they began to smoke. The tension they had all felt earlier was released in the rhythm of the wheels. She closed her eyes, to get some sleep.

She was sleeping when she felt a cold wind brushing her face. Struggling to open her eyes, she saw a man standing at the door. It was open about a foot wide, and he was leaning to one side. She wondered what he was up to, then realized he was urinating. "That feels better," he said with deep relief. Another guy came over to the door and did the same. Hu Nü closed her eyes and tried to get back to sleep.

Outside, tree branches were moving swiftly past them. A branch scratched the man standing at the door. He yelled and jumped back. Orange twilight appeared on the horizon, signalling a new day. The men stood up, stamped their numb feet and stretched their sore backs. Hu Nü got up on her feet too, walked over to the open door.

"Did you have a good sleep in this moving cradle?" the older man asked her with a big smile.

"A very nice sleep," she smiled back, even if she couldn't help shivering.

"Tell us what is your emergency?" He asked.

"About my future," she answered vaguely.

"Is it about a job in industry?"

"How did you know?" she was surprised.

The older man scratched his head, pretending he was thinking hard. "Because the university students in our brigade left one by one. All of them have been hired to work in some sort of industry or in the office in the city. So are you hired?"

"I wish," Hu Nü said slowly. "That's my emergency."

"Maybe you should use some of your family's *guan xi*," the older man said seriously. *Guan xi* referred to relations or acquaintances whose influence one could use. "What are your parents? Are they revolutionary cadres?" He seemed to know how to laugh at her and her family.

"My father is an architect, one of the types that have no power at all, my mother works for the neighbourhood shoe factory organized by women, who otherwise would be unemployed. They have neither power nor *guan xi*." Hu Nü gave the peasants an honest account of her family background.

The men had stopped talking. She knew they were all listening to her. "I don't know how long my sister and I will have to stay in the countryside. I hope to find out more about my family background from my father when I see him this morning."

The peasants expressed their sympathy, by clicking with their tongues as they listened to her. After she finished, the old man said: "Now I remember you said your village is thirty some kilometres away from the county. I tell you what, if there's some real bad luck, no company or factory ever wants to hire you or your sister, and you have to spend the rest of your lives in the countryside, why don't you think about marrying someone in our village? Our village is the closest to the county and the railway station, and our village is the richest in the whole county." He spoke sincerely.

"Yes, we can promise you. We'll look after you and your sister really well. Married women have an easy life in our village," a young man added.

"Just keep that in mind, if you have to stay in the countryside for good."

Hu Nü wanted to thank the peasants for their consideration, but her heart began sinking into an unfathomable black hole. She didn't hear the peasants' talk about her. "Overseas relations?" If she could just tear up her file and burn the pieces.

Portraits of My Uncles

The freight train stopped in the yard in the suburbs of Wuhan at about five o'clock in the morning. Emerging from the car, Hu Nü saw the whole yard cloaked in the grey winter twilight. The city was waking up from sleep, there was nobody around yet.

She got home at breakfast time. Mei, who had come home the previous evening on the passenger train, was surprised to see her sister back. Mother was still working in the neighbourhood women's shoe factory. Father was back in the city as a chief architect for the new railway project that would connect Hubei province with Sichuan, Guizhou, and Yunnan provinces through the mountains. Her two youngest sisters, Ping and Ning, were both in elementary school. Hu Nü thought it was good to be home if only to enjoy electricity and running water.

Father was extremely busy. This new railway between the central and southwestern provinces was part of Chairman Mao's strategic plan against the West. If there was a war with the West, the northern Chinese heavy industrial base and the eastern Chinese light industrial base would be targets. Mao's plan was to shift industrial distribution from the coastal provinces to the inland central-western and southwestern provinces. A railway was essential for this. Mao ordered the Railway Ministry to "get on the horse" with the construction. The Railway Ministry summoned its chief engineers and architects from various state farms, where most of them were receiving their re-education from peasants. Upon being called back, Father was immediately assigned a job in the new project.

Hu Nü was lucky to catch Father before he set off to the project site in Xiangfang, three hundred and fifty kilometres northwest of Wuhan. As soon as she stepped into the apartment and saw Father was home, she asked him the question that had occupied her mind all the way from County Tang to Wuhan: "So what is this 'overseas relations' with a question mark? It was put down in my file by the personnel department of your institute."

"Overseas relations with a question mark?" Father repeated. He was in the middle of his breakfast, while Hu Nü sat down on the other side of the table. "This must be the new information they have inserted into my file, it's about your Second Uncle, the one who disappeared in the war."

"Do you mean he is still alive?"

"That is the new information," said Father.

"But where did he go? Why did they put a question mark instead of a period?" She asked.

"That is because they are not sure. This trouble was caused by your Third Uncle many years ago." Father swallowed a mouthful of rice. "In the fall of 1948, around the time of the liberation of Hangzhou, Second Uncle sent two letters home from Taiwan. He had a fiancée at home, a child-bride growing up in our family. He wanted to apologize to her for not being able to marry her." Father reminisced slowly. "Your grandparents made Third Uncle marry Second Uncle's bride, who is your Third Aunt today. At that time, Third Uncle was very progressive, he wanted to join the Communist League. So he handed over the two letters to the local League branch without even showing them to me. I'm pretty sure these two letters were kept in his file ever since." Father put down his chopsticks.

Hu Nü remembered how difficult it was for her to be accepted by the Communist League. "So did he join the League?" she asked.

"No. That is the sad part. He was rejected."

"I cannot believe how stupid he was," she said, though she was not supposed to despise an elder. "But then why didn't I have any problem being accepted by the League in 1966?" With a suspected 'overseas relations' in her file, her League application would have been easily rejected. Having an uncle in Taiwan would destroy anyone's future, because Taiwan was categorized as a political and national enemy.

Father was silent. He couldn't explain to his daughter why Third Uncle did what he did. But he tried: "The reason you didn't have any trouble before was because I never admitted to such a suspicion. Since Second Uncle didn't send more mail back after 1949, I assumed he had died shortly after the troops had withdrawn from the mainland to Taiwan. At the beginning of the Cultural Revolution, my colleagues went to your grandparents' village and to my two brothers' employers. This 'overseas relations' was what they probably had dug up from Third Uncle's file. These people want to bring me down, so they can be given important tasks. I have refused to sign their paper, but it didn't stop them from inserting it into my file, and then being copied into yours." Father had never said that much about his family before.

His breakfast had gone cold. Hu Nü looked at Father from the opposite side of the table, and she felt a surge of sympathy. He had fought for his own integrity and dignity. He tried to protect his children, but he hadn't been able to protect himself.

Later that evening, Mother gave more details about Father's siblings. Father had one elder sister and four younger brothers. His sister was illiterate. No family in the village would send a first-born girl to school. She grew up helping her mother in the house, before she was engaged to marry her cousin at age fifteen. Being the eldest son in the family, Father was sent to school at the age of six. His interest in learning and his hard work made him the best student in his class. From elementary school through university, his academic excellence won him scholarships every year.

Two years younger than Father was Second Uncle, who also went to school, but he knew that he would be the one among his brothers to join the army, so that the rest of them could live civilian lives. Since childhood, Second Uncle had a child-bride, a cousin growing up in the family. This was arranged by the parents. Second Uncle was not happy with the arrangement. At age eighteen, he was drafted into the Kuomingtang troops. Two years later the troops were defeated and forced to withdraw to Taiwan. Second Uncle went with them. He managed to send two letters home. According to the customs of the village, his parents made Third Uncle marry Second Uncle's child-bride.

Third Uncle was the most handsome man in the village. Hu Nü remembered the first time she went to Hangzhou. At the railway station, Third Uncle came with a large bouquet of fresh flowers in his hands. Hu Nü had never seen her parents buy cut flowers for anyone, and she was most impressed by Third Uncle's style. He had a square jaw, and big dark brown eyes with thick eyebrows. His high forehead was covered with shiny thick black hair. He brought her an English-Chinese dictionary for her eighth birthday, as if he knew at that time that his niece would become an English teacher later in her life.

Mother said Third Uncle wanted to become a locomotive driver since childhood. But he didn't want to marry his elder brother's child-bride, who had grown up as a sister to him in the household. She was small, timid and old-fashioned, definitely not his type of woman. His parents made him swear that he would marry her, or they would not be able to close their eyes at their death beds.

Fourth Uncle, on the other hand, was the child disliked by both his parents. He would wet his bed at night. His parents had tried different doctors and therapies. From dog meat stew to donkey's kidney soup, they spent the little money they had hoping to find a cure for him. They failed. He would still occasionally wet his bed, even at age eighteen. They gave up on him, chased him away from the dinner table, gave him leftovers to eat and rags to wear. Catching him wet in bed, his father beat him, his mother cursed him. They called him a punishment from Buddha for all the sins and wrongs of their previous lives. Even Second Uncle's child-bride looked down upon him. She prayed secretly to Buddha that she would not have to marry him.

Fifth Uncle, who was only twelve years older than was Hu Nü, was also born in the year of the Tiger. As the youngest son in the family, he was spoiled by his mother. At age five, he would still unbutton his mother's top and suck her breasts in front of the whole neighbourhood. One day he took a bowl of rice and sat on top of a ladder. The ladder fell, and he broke his jaw and lost his front teeth. Mother said that since then he changed completely. Fifth Uncle became a meek lad, just like a tiger who had lost its teeth. Later, after Grandmother died of breast cancer, he decided to become a medical doctor.

"Why did Third Uncle hand in his brother's letters to the Party secretary?" Hu Nü asked Mother. "Why didn't he show them to his elder brother?" She couldn't understand why Third Uncle chose to wash the family dirty linen in public and betray his whole family.

Letting out a deep sigh, mother said, "Third Uncle was only sixteen years old at the time of Liberation. I remember he was a cheerful and energetic young man. He went to his dream Locomotive Drivers' School. And in two years, he graduated and got a job as a locomotive operator in the Hangzhou Railway Bureau. He started to drive freight trains between Hangzhou and Shanghai. Everyone in the family, including Grandparents, knew he had a girl friend in

Shanghai. But later, after Grandmother had breast cancer, she wanted to see Third Uncle marry the child-bride before she died.

"Grandmother was a true feudal matriarch," Hu Nü concluded. She recalled that Grandmother had wanted to give her away as a child-bride.

"Third Uncle ran away from home for two months," Mother continued. "But as his mother's health deteriorated, Father found him and he came back home. Third Uncle married the bride that was never his, hoping by following his mother's will, he could bring about a miracle cure to her health. Two weeks after his wedding, Grandmother died peacefully in her bed at home. Maybe his filial devotion did work a miracle on his sick mother, who didn't suffer much pain. However, the pain has been endured ever since by Third Uncle and Third Aunt."

"But Mama, why did he hand in his brother's letters to the Party?" Hu Nü didn't see any connection between the two events.

"He wanted to join the Communist League, so he could belong to the group of progressive youth. At his evaluation meeting, he was asked to clarify his marriage to his brother's child-bride. He was criticised for helping prolong the feudal tradition of arranged marriage."

Hu Nü remembered her own experience of such a meeting, in the spring of 1966, when her application for the League was evaluated. She was asked to criticize Father. To most of the League members in her class, Father was a bourgeois intellectual who deserved to be criticized rather than respected. Hu Nü also remembered how her classmate Wenxin bitterly criticized her parents who had owned a small corner store before Liberation. Anna did the same with her parents, who were medical doctors. There was also her childhood sweetheart, Hua, whom she met after the hunger strike at the beginning of the Cultural Revolution and had never seen again. She remembered their last meeting when he told her he had publicly denounced his parents, because they were overseas Chinese returned from America.

"In order to prove to the League that he didn't make the decision, and that in fact he was a victim and so was his wife, Third Uncle gave his brother's letters to the League secretary, who then gave them to the Party secretary," Mother recalled. "What he didn't expect was that his application to the League would be rejected because of the new information he had provided. Since then he has never been trusted at work. His route was changed from Hangzhou-Shanghai to a small county route, and from driving freight trains that carried industrial and military products to those with agricultural products. He was pressed for more letters from his brother in Taiwan. Since there were no more letters from Second Uncle or even news about whether he was still alive, the case stayed open."

Now Hu Nü could see how Second Uncle's two letters of 1948 became the evidence of 'overseas relations' in her file and an obstacle to her opportunities.

"This is really unfair, Mama, because I have never met Second Uncle in my life, how can someone assume that he would cast any influence on my political view?"

"I never met him either. He had left China before Father and I even met," Mother said. "It is unfair."

"But I thought politics is about fairness," Hu Nü responded, "otherwise, why should there be so many political movements?" Indeed, if it were not for justice and fairness, what were the goals of the endless political movements in China?

She started to forgive Third Uncle.

A Virginity Test

Mother worked ten to twelve hours daily in the neighbourhood shoe factory with her fellow women workers. My two younger sisters went to school every morning. Mei went out with Miss Liang every afternoon. She stayed late and sometimes overnight at Miss Liang's place. I resumed my cooking duty for my family.

During the holiday season, Father was extremely busy. We seldom saw him. Most of the time he was at the headquarters, three hundred and fifty kilometres away from home. His new position at the strategic new railway project raised our status in the neighbourhood. Whenever I bumped into a neighbour, I had something new and exciting to say. "By the way, my father is back from the farm. He is working in the headquarters of the new railway project, the one, you know, strategically planned by Chairman Mao himself."

"That's great . . . ." The neighbours didn't always believe me, knowing that Father was not even a Party member. But they would say, "We're glad for your family." Sometimes someone would ask, "Are you hired to work in the city? A lot of students have been hired by factories and companies."

"I guess soon . . . I should also have some good news soon." I would lie and almost believe it.

"But where is my opportunity? How likely will a company select someone with overseas relations?" I asked myself everyday. Though I didn't have an answer, I had found an argument.

There was something illogical here. If Father was trusted by the Party to work on Chairman Mao's strategic new task, why couldn't his daughter be given an ordinary job? After all it was his brother, not hers, who was the problem. If "overseas relations" didn't affect Father's career as a chief architect, why should it affect his daughter's life and future?

I decided to speak directly to the Personnel Department of the new railway project headquarters. I rehearsed my first few sentences several times: "I would like to see the comrade in charge of the Personnel Department." Then when I was let in, "I would like to talk to you about my future job opportunities."

On a bright winter morning, I walked into the new railway project headquarters on the eighth floor of the Wuhan Railway Bureau Building, designed by my father in the late 1960s. I was let in by a tall male receptionist.

"What is the purpose of your visit?" he asked me, his eyes sweeping over me from head to toe.

"I want to talk about my job opportunities," I said honestly.

"What job opportunities? Are you an engineer?" he asked, his cigarette resting on the edge of an ashtray was smoking.

"No, I am not. But my father is one of the chief engineers in this headquarters."

"Who is your father?" He quickly picked up a pen and a notepad. After he had written down Father's name, I told him about the difficulty I had had with previous hiring companies. I said, "I don't understand if my father can be trusted with an important national task, why can't his daughter be hired as a worker?" Standing up, the secretary tore the front page from the notepad. He gestured to me to sit down on the sofa, he crushed his cigarette and went to knock at the door of an inner office.

I sat down on the sofa, waiting anxiously. Five minutes later, the door of the Head Office opened. The secretary came out, closed the door behind him gently. His face was beaming. "I have good news for you. Comrade Chou said he will speak to our Railway Bureau's hiring committee about your situation. He believes a special case can be made. You will be hired by our Bureau."

I stood up, remembering it was always polite to stand up while talking to an elder or an important person. "You mean our Railway Bureau is hiring as well? What kind of jobs, do you know?" I asked earnestly.

"Yes, yes, we are hiring just like any other industry. In order to help the children of the railway employees, the Railway Bureau Party Committee has decided to hire two hundred students in the near future, from the countryside. The job, as far as I know, is exclusively for the new railway line between Wuchang and Yichang. Most of you will be stewards on the express train." He spoke rapidly as if reciting from a written script.

"Oh, stewards . . . " I sounded disappointed. Stewards on a passenger train were perhaps at the bottom on the social ladder of the railway system. The job didn't need any education, developed no skills, and was extremely tiring. A steward's job consisted of checking tickets, serving hot water, selling snacks, opening and closing the door, and sweeping and washing the floor when the train reached its destination. There was also another problem—stewards had a notorious reputation for being morally loose. Growing up as a Railway employee's child, I had heard enough rumours about female stewards sleeping around with fellow male stewards, locomotive engineers, drivers, and conductors. I had never thought about becoming a steward when I grew up.

"You don't want to be a steward? Do you look down upon service jobs?" The secretary's smiling face turned stony, his voice became harsh and unforgiving.

"That's not what I am thinking. Please don't misunderstand me. Since I like travelling, a steward's job is probably all right for seeing the world."

"All right, then. I guess now you can go home, and in fact you should return to your village, and wait for the good news." The receptionist opened the door for me. I left the office with an awkward smile.

I laughed at myself, once outside the Personnel Department. How could I have linked a steward's job with travelling in the world? Instead of taking the elevator down from the eighth floor, I decided to walk down. I recalled the peasants I had ridden with a month before. What would they say if they found out that I had beome a steward on the railway line they travelled on? Maybe they would come to my car for a free ride.

I returned to Peach Blossom Village, knowing that in the near future I would be hired to work as a steward on a train. So when the call came for me to fill in the form, the whole brigade was excited, except me. Everybody thought working on the train was the best job they had ever heard of, much better than working in the deep mountains to make weapons and military supplies. Because the Railway Bureau was one of the largest national industries, it offered its employees an iron rice bowl. I forced myself to look happy, though from time to time, I lapsed into depression. The brigade was only too glad to see us leave one by one. The brigade leader said to me that after I left, Mei could stay in the city until her opportunity came. I thanked him for being so considerate. It would be very hard for my sister to live alone in the village by herself.

Two weeks later, I went to the county hospital for a medical check-up with fifty other students listed with various companies. We gathered at the county office to pick up our medical forms. From the items listed in the forms, this looked like a serious medical examination. The results would determine whether one would actually be hired. The candidates were summoned in front of the county office, then we walked towards the county hospital in two lines.

Walking next to me was a young man with thick glasses. "How are you?" I said to him. His face was tanned and his hair bushy. Had it not been for the thick glasses, I would easily have mistaken him for a local peasant. I asked him what company was interested in him and what kind of job he expected to do in the future.

"Education Bureau, to be an elementary school teacher." The young man answered unemotionally.

"Oh, I see. Do you want to be a teacher?"

Knowing that teaching was one of the least desirable jobs since the beginning of the Cultural Revolution, I regretted asking him about his feelings for the job.

"You see, I have very poor eyesight, so factories would never hire me. You probably don't believe that this is my third medical check-up. I have been rejected twice already because of my eyesight."

I was surprised that someone could be rejected twice. "So, you think you will be able to pass the test this time?" I asked him, and then to brighten his day, I said lightheartedly, "After all, who cares if a teacher wears a pair of glasses or not?"

"I think it still matters, because as an elementary school teacher, you are expected to teach several subjects, including physical education." Looking at me through the windows of his lenses, the young man continued, "But this time, I'm not going to let them turn me down."

"But how?" I was curious. "Have you got better glasses?"

"No, but the chart is in my mind, as long as I can tell which line, I know the signs on every line, including the bottom line," He whispered to me.

"What are the last two lines?" I asked him in a whisper,

remembering that I sometimes had problems seeing the last two lines.

"The second last is, left, right, left, up, left, right," He recited without giving a second thought. "Do you want to know the bottom line? It is left, up, left, right, down, left."

The eyesight examination chart used a capitalized "E" scaled down in many rows. Each "E" was positioned to face a different direction, so the person under the examination was expected to point out the directions of each "E." I asked him to repeat the last two lines, so I could memorize them. By the time we got to the hospital, we both were ready to show our perfect 1.5 eyesight.

"Boys step to this side, and girls to that side."
As soon as we entered the hall of the hospital, we saw a nurse of about fifty years old. Facing us, her arms stretched out, she repeated, "Boys this side, girls that side." It had been years since I had heard this kind of greeting.

"Why are male and female students separated?" someone raised the interesting question.

"Because, because," the nurse was searching for an explanation, "your reproductive system is also going to be examined. Do you know what that means? You will be requested to take off your clothes." The nurse had lowered her voice to a whisper. She smiled.

"Woo, is that true?" We made a noise of surprise.

"What is the reproductive system any way?" asked a small young woman standing at the front.

We who stood at the back tried to stand on our tiptoes to get a quick look at whoever had asked the stupid question. Someone in the crowd responded, "Are you so stupid that you don't even know where you came from?" The rest of us burst out laughing.

"No more questions, separate now! Boys this side, girls that side!" We got up, a gender line was drawn down the middle. "Boys to the Optician first to check your eyesight, then to the Ear, Nose and Throat next door. Girls come with me to the physician and gynecologist first. Then boys switch with girls."

There were twenty female students. Looking around, I tried to see if I knew anyone in the crowd. But I didn't find any familiar faces, so I followed the nurse quietly. When we arrived at our destination, she counted the ten people at the front and waved us in. A middle-aged man checked me. He asked me what kind of jobs I would be hired to do.

"Steward in a passenger train from Wuchang to Yichang," I told him precisely.

"Have you had any problem with your heart?" He asked, his stethoscope was placed on the left side of my chest.

"No, never." I answered firmly. "Is everything all right?" I asked anxiously.

"You have a murmur in your heart. I don't think you want to work on the train, it would be too stressful for your heart." He gestured to me to turn around so he could listen to my back.

Watching him pull the stethoscope from his ears, I begged him, "I have never had any heart problems, and I was very athletic in high school. This must be caused by the stress I have had recently, please, don't write it down in my chart. I want to get out of the countryside, I don't care what kind of job I will be doing, please."

The doctor's hand stopped halfway in the air. He didn't say a word for a long minute, then he put down his pen and picked up a rubber stamp. Pressing the rubber-stamp into the ink pad first then brought it down on my chart. "Take care of yourself. Remember, don't ever get too tired. Change your job as soon as you can." He handed the piece of paper back to me. I was so grateful to him that tears filled up my eyes.

"Thank you." I turned around to look at him one more time before walking out of his office. His stethoscope hanging around him like a necklace, his thick pepper-grey hair covering his forehead, perhaps he had his own daughter in the countryside waiting to be hired.

After the heart check-up, X-ray, blood and urine tests, I came to the department of gynecology. I had never been checked by a gynecologist before, there had been no need. To me and to many young women of my age, only married and pregnant women saw an obstetrician and gynecologist. We felt uneasy mentioning the words of

144

these specialists, let alone going to them. There was a small crowd outside the doctor's office in the corridor. As I came close, I saw a slim, pale-looking young woman crying in the centre of the crowd. She was wearing a flowery shirt, her thick black hair fell on her shoulders. Tears streaming down her face, she was shaking a piece of paper in her hand: "What am I going to do? What am I going to do?"

I asked a tall woman standing at the back of the crowd why the young woman was crying. "The doctor wrote in her chart that she is not a virgin. She is afraid the Railway Bureau will reject her."

"The Railway Bureau? I am also with the Railway Bureau," I said. Pushing myself through the crowd, I asked the pale-looking woman, "What's your name? Are you a descendant of a railway employee?" She looked at me. "Yu Qing. And yours?"

I told her my name and that I was also a railway employee's child. "Don't worry. We can go and talk to the hiring team. I believe they are responsible for taking us back."

"But they might think I am a bad person, because of this line," her finger was pointing at the words in her chart. "I'm not a loose person, I did that only with my boy friend. He promised me as soon as we both get out of the countryside, we'll get married."

"What did you say you just did with your boy friend?" A few students were confused.

"How can the doctor tell who is not a virgin?" Another student asked.

In Peach Blossom Village, I had heard gossip about a villager who found out his bride was not a virgin on their wedding night. According to the custom, three days after the wedding the newly weds were expected to return to the bride's home village with a lot of food. The groom refused to go with her, and her village found out that she was not a virgin. As both her family and her village had lost face, she was permanently kicked out from her home.

I remembered asking Xiuzhen, our brigade leader's wife, what virginity exactly was. She giggled with her hand covering up her mouth, and then whispered to me, "It's a piece of skin called hymen growing inside your vagina. When it's broken it bleeds. That's how your husband will know whether you are a virgin or not on your wedding night."

"How thick is this hymen? How easily can it break?" I was quite worried upon hearing about this virginity test for the first time in my life. "Does a woman know when it breaks?"

"Well, it's hard to say." Xiuzhen was thinking loud. "I heard it could also break from physical labour or sports."

From that time on, I was worried about my own virginity. Since I had done track and field for three years in high school, perhaps my hymen was broken a long time ago. I also believed that if my hymen was not broken during sports, my boyfriend Xin's finger must have broken it later.

"What did your boy friend do to break your hymen?" I asked Yu Qing quietly. She looked at me with surprise. I knew I shouldn't have asked such an embarrassing question. I was only too worried about my own virginity. A nurse appeared at the door of the examination room, and called out a few names, mine included.

Following the nurse, I stepped into a gynecologist's examination-room for the first time. The gynaecologist was a white-haired woman, with reading glasses on her nose. "Are you the last group?" she asked, yawning.

"Yes, we are." We answered like a chorus of elementary school kids.

"OK, girls. Undress from waist down, and come one by one to this examination table." She went behind a curtain, the nurse picked up our charts. Standing there, we were too embarrassed to do what we were told. Looking at each other, we started to loosen our belts, but nobody volunteered to take off her pants. After a few quiet minutes, the nurse stuck her head out from behind the curtain impatiently "What is the problem with this group? Do you want to be checked or not? The doctor is tired. Hurry up!"

A tall girl went ahead with her pants on. In less than five minutes, she emerged from behind the curtain with her pants down her ankles. While she was pulling them up, the nurse waved at me. I hurried forward in the same manner. Behind the curtain, there were two examination tables; one with stirrups and foot holders on both sides, the other one was just a bed. The doctor was sitting in front of a desk. As I had no idea about what to do next, the expression on my face must have been ridiculous, because the doctor burst out laughing. "I am not a tiger, am I? I'm not going to eat you up, am I?" Her joke made me laugh.

I thought maybe she was born in the year of the Tiger as well. "I am a Tiger Girl," the words were on the tip of my tongue, but I knew it was irrelevant.

She gestured to me to come forward. "I know you're a good girl, now drop your pants." I wasn't sure if "a good girl" was not just one of the routine encouragements doctors and nurses gave to their female patients. As she was tapping my shoulder, I loosened my belt completely and let my pants drop down to my ankles. She pulled down my underwear and looked at my genital area, as I stood before her with a red face. She then pressed on both sides of my naval and downwards a little bit. "Does it hurt?" She asked.

"Never," I gave her a firm answer.

"Is your menstruation regular?" she asked.

"Yes, very regular." I said without hesitation.

Gesturing to me to turn around, she pushed my back down somewhat to examine my anus. "OK, You're done." I pulled up my pants and stepped outside the curtain.

Ten minutes later the nurse came out the door again, and gave us back our charts. My chart was empty except for a red mark made by a rubber stamp.

"How could the doctor tell Yu Qing is not a virgin? I talked to myself while walking down the hall. Does that mean I'm still a virgin? Do boys have a hymen? How can the doctor examine their virginity?"

A New Journey

Two weeks after the medical examination, I received an official notice from my new employer, the Railway Bureau. I would be expected at the New Workers' Orientation Camp in two weeks. Peach Blossom Village was so happy for me that my peasant friends invited me to dine with their families every evening. I started to feel sorry about leaving these simple and sincere folks who treated me with respect and gave me love and support. I had been working side by side with them in the fields for three years. How could I not realize that I had become part of them as they had been part of my life? But the peasants seemed to know in their hearts that the educated youth would not live in the countryside permanently.

I took a north bound train to the city of Xiang Fan, another hundred kilometres north of County Tang. The Orientation Camp was set up there to give the two hundred new workers a two-week training. There were more females than males among the new workers. We were divided into ten smaller groups for the activities. The workers in my group elected me as their group leader, so I was in charge of physical training, political studies, cleaning up the camp site, and other duties. The ten group leaders met the trainers everyday before and after daily activities. The trainers were middle-aged male cadres from the Personnel Department of the Passenger Transportation Division of the Railway Bureau.

The first three days of our training were spent studying Chairman Mao's famous three articles: *Serve the People*, *In Memory of Norman Bethune*, and *The Foolish Old Man Who Moved the Mountains*. Most of us knew the three articles by heart, since we had studied them hundreds of times during the Cultural Revolution. Some new workers said they'd rather go back to the countryside to work in the fields than sit here studying Chairman Mao's three old articles. Near the end of the three-day political studies, we were requested to post our written oaths on the wall. Everyone had to swear his or her complete obedience to the Party. The oaths were first read at the new workers' assembly before they were pasted on the walls for others to read.

Even though the two hundred oaths all sounded the same, the trainers said it was necessary for every new worker to realize that he or she must not make any personal demand at the job assignment. We must obey the Party's decisions unconditionally. Finally the serious moment came when we were to be assigned our positions. Among the two hundred new workers, ten women were selected to be trainees for broadcasting. Their job would be to announce the names of the up-coming railway stations and services, tune into the news and play music tapes from time to time. Ten men were picked to be trainees as cargo officers in the luggage cars. Twenty men were selected to be professional chefs for the dining cars, while twenty men and women would be trained to be waiters and waitresses. After these specific jobs were assigned, the rest of the new workers were considered trainees as future stewards.

I didn't hear my name called at all. Sitting there in the crowd, my face was burning hot. Why was I not selected to be an announcer? Didn't the leaders know that I spoke a standard Beijing accent? The other group leaders were all given special jobs. Why was I rejected? Suddenly I felt I wanted to go back to Peach Blossom Village where the peasants had always treated me as an equal.

I decided to see the trainers about my interest in becoming an announcer. After dinner, most of the new workers went downtown to see a new movie. I decided to see whether there was an opportunity to catch the trainers in their office. I strolled down the camp and saw a light in the office. I knocked on the door gently. Mr Fu, who had lots of smallpox scars on his face, opened the door with a surprise: "Don't you like movies? Why don't you join the rest of the new workers?"

"I would like to take a few minutes of your precious time, if that's all right," I said politely.

"Come in then," he opened the door wide to let me in. On his desk were lots of papers, it looked like he was still working.

"Comrade Fu, I want to be an announcer if it can be reconsidered. I speak Beijing dialect well. I love writing and broadcasting. Of course, having said that, I still submit my personal wish unconditionally to the Party's will." I didn't dare to bore him with details of how to make broadcasting more interesting.

"Sit down, young comrade, and calm down." Mr Fu pointed at a chair on the opposite side of his desk. I sat down. From the opposite angle, I could see how smallpox had mapped its territory into this man's flesh. Perhaps a little excited because of my visit, Mr Fu's face was covered with uneven red patches here and there. His eyes, expressing disapproval, were blood shot. I could see disgust and contempt in his eyes. Right away I knew I was wrong to come and talk about my job.

"Do you know how much trouble I have gone through in order to get you out of the countryside?" Mr Fu's voice forced me to look at him again. "Had it not been for the note from the head office of the new railway project, I wouldn't have done so, and I don't think anyone else would have gone a hundred kilometres to your commune to hire you!"

"I am very grateful to you." I had no idea that I owed Mr Fu personally a big favour. Now I knew it was he who had given me this new opportunity.

"Now, in terms of your job assignment, there is nothing else I can do for you except for what you've been given, a steward's position. You know your family background better than I do. Your father is a chief architect, a bourgeois intellectual. Before liberation, he went to university to study and so he became educated, while workers like myself were deprived of such an opportunity. So his daughter must do physical labour instead, and we must give working class children better opportunities, such as an announcer's position." Mr Fu's sharp voice and angry eyes forced me to lower my head. I felt like a criminal.

Suddenly, the door of his office was pushed open from outside. The other trainer, Mr Gao, came in. "Hello, Comrade Gao." I stood up. Waving with a cigarette between his fingers, he gestured me to sit down and to continue my conversation with Mr Fu. Smiling at

Mr Gao, Mr Fu said: "This young woman wishes to be an announcer. What do you think?"

Mr Gao looked at me and answered, "Personally, I think it's good that you came forward to talk about your wish with us. Whether it can be realized or not is another issue, isn't it?"

I nodded. At least Mr Gao didn't read me as an ungrateful brat as Mr Fu had done. Soon enough Mr Fu changed the topic back to what he and I were earlier talking about before Mr Gao came in. "The reason that you cannot be selected to be an announcer is your family background. In addition to your bourgeois intellectual father, do you know your family has 'overseas relations'? Do you know what that means? It means you cannot be trusted with any important job, definitely not with broadcasting, which is the brain and voice of the train. With all the electronics and radio devices, you may even be able to get in touch with your uncle in Taiwan. Then, the whole train could be subverted by your sabotage."

Mr Fu's words brought back the worst nightmare I had had since the beginning of the Cultural Revolution. I was reminded again that I could never be trusted because of my unwanted family background. I was devastated. Like a tiger at bay, a voice roared from inside, bursting out from my throat. "I was born in new China and grew up under the red flag. I love Chairman Mao and the Communist Party as much as my peers from the working-class families. I have never met this uncle who disappeared in the war. I think it is strictly unfair to say that I would get in touch with him using the radio system in the train." I stopped. The office was so quiet that I could hear my own breathing. A feeling of relief was creeping in and soothing my inner pain.

"You are too emotional tonight to talk rationally, go back to your camp and get some rest. Tomorrow, you'll see better why the Party has made such decisions." Mr Fu stood up and opened the door for me. Realizing there was no point in continuing this conversation, I stood up. Mr Gao came up to the door and patted me on the shoulder, "Of course you know, this is not the only opportunity for new workers to be selected for more desirable jobs. There will be many other opportunities in the future." I nodded, though I wasn't sure if

152

I would be interested in hearing about new opportunities in the future.

Walking towards the camp, I could see myself growing old in the train running between two destinations. Stewards generally retired earlier to ground jobs, such as in a laundry room or bakery in the railway station. But before my retirement, my life would consist of endless repetition of certain activities: opening the doors, locking up the doors, serving hot water, washing the floor, and cleaning the toilets. While the wheels went clanking on the rails, and the locomotive roared through dark tunnels and across wide fields, I would see thousands of arrivals and departures in the next twenty years.

The last day of our orientation, before we were scattered to different places for further training, we had a gathering to commemorate the beginning of our new journey in the work force. Each group was supposed to give a performance at such an occasion. We could see two groups were practising a group dance as their presentations; several groups were rehearsing singing. Our group wanted to be more creative. We decided to write a poem: "A Long Journey to Begin." A young man and I took the lead male and female solo roles, other parts were assigned either to male or female assemblies or the mixed chorus. We practised our poem until everyone could recite the parts. One stanza read:

A seed is about to push through the soil
A baby bird will take off in the blue sky
A young poplar branch will grow into a leafy tree
A fish dreams of the deep sea
We are new railway workers
with broad shoulders
We are young men and young women
with dreams
We are a new generation
to be trusted
in a long journey
on a new railway line
for a new life, yet to begin

Our poetry performance was the last presentation of the day. After group singing and dancing were over, our emotional recital lifted the gathering to a spiritual height. The audience gave us a standing ovation.

After the celebration was over, I was still absorbed in the excitement of the poetry recitation when a young man came up to me. It was Ho Ping, another group leader. We knew each other from daily report meetings with the trainers. Ho Ping was tall and masculine with a dark skin; often he looked as if deeply engaged in thought. Stretching his right hand out at me, he said: "Congratulations! That was a great presentation!"

"Thank you," I said politely. "The success belongs to the whole group."

"But it must be your idea originally," he smiled mischievously. "The mass needs a leader."

"I don't see myself as a leader. I don't think I could ever become a leader either," I said honestly.

"But you are, don't you see? You have the natural talent to be one." He surprised me with this compliment. I didn't know what to say.

"I have two movie tickets for tonight. Would you like to join me?" he asked anxiously. "And we can talk more about poetry, I like poetry too," he added.

"I haven't made any plan for tonight yet. I guess, I could join you to see the movie that I missed the other night." Ever since Xin left Peach Blossom Village, I hadn't been out with anyone.

It was early spring. The air was chilly, but sprouts had started to push through the soil, spring showers were turning the grass green. After the movie, Ho Ping suggested we take a stroll. Xiang Fan was an ancient city. We decided to stroll along the old city walls. There were other young couples there, walking, leaning against the zigzaging ancient walls, holding hands. I could feel the pressure of the moment, this was a romantic spot. I asked Ho Ping what high school he had graduated from. "Wuhan No. 2 High School," he answered automatically.

I couldn't believe this! "You are kidding, we are schoolmates! What year were you?"

"1966 Junior High, and you?" This was almost too coincidental to be true. I stopped walking, "Which class did you attend?"

He knew immediately that we belonged to the same year. "Class One," he said, waiting for my answer.

"Class Three," I said, he grasped my hands. "I knew there was something in you I seemed to recognize from the very beginning. It's your writing, of course, it's your writing. The teachers used your writing as samples in their teaching, am I right?"

Leaning against the old city remains, we were completely lost in our reminiscences of the school days. We talked about Teacher Lo, who jumped in front of a train and killed himself. I found that Ho Ping had also gone on hunger strike in the hall of the municipal government office building. Ever since, his stomach ulcer had got worse.

It was beginning to get late. "Should we go back to the camp?" I suggested.

"Yes, I'm thinking about the last line of your poem. 'We, a new generation to be trusted,' and then 'a new life yet to begin.' I wish I could . . . I wish I could begin my life's journey from here and now." He seemed troubled by his thoughts.

"Why not?" I asked innocently.

"I wish I could start my life like the rest of you on a fresh new journey. But you know, I started it some time ago without knowing what kind of trap I was getting myself into. Now I am trapped by what I've done in the countryside." He spoke as if he were confessing.

"Can't you solve the problem and free yourself from it?" I was trying to help him without knowing what his problem was. Ho Ping was silent. "Let's walk back to the camp, shall we?" he suggested.

We walked down a quiet street. By then there were few pedestrians or vehicles about. Ho Ping was silent all the way, I didn't want to disturb him. As we got closer to the camp, he stopped. "Tomorrow we'll part. As you know I will be trained for cargo. I won't be able to see you often. But I want to tell you what's bothering me, if you trust me."

"Of course I do," I responded. The temperature had dropped, I could see our breath.

"You know, I had a girlfriend in the countryside, we did some stupid thing together. I got her pregnant, then she had an abortion in the commune clinic. She contracted some kind of infection, so ever since she has been sick. The worst thing is what happened recently. Her name was also listed with the Railway Bureau, even though she is not a railway employee's descendant. My father got her name on the list, so we could be hired together by the Bureau." Ho Ping's eyes were a dark cold night, I couldn't see a light in them.

He paused a while, then resumed. He said: "But guess what has happened, rotten luck! The gynecologist in the county hospital wrote in her chart that she is not a virgin. So the Railway Bureau judged that she is a loose woman and didn't hire her. Now she is all alone in the village, and here I'm blaming myself for doing such a stupid thing with her when I was immature." He spoke angrily, his fists beating his chest.

Suddenly, I shuddered. The face of a small, pale-looking young woman in the hospital appeared in front of my eyes. I asked Ho Ping, "What's her name?"

"Yu Qing. She is my ex-girl friend now, it's impossible to keep a relationship over long distance. But I still think a lot about her and about my past in the countryside. Here I'm starting a new job and a fresh journey; I don't want to be forever burdened by the guilt. I hope you can understand me and help me cut off this lingering pain."

I didn't know what to say. I had nothing to say to him. Yu Qing's tear-streaked face was still floating in front of me. When I first arrived at the New Workers' Orientation Camp two weeks ago, I was actually looking for her, hoping the Railway Bureau had made an exception of her case as it did mine.

Ho Ping's words also reminded me of a recent letter I had received from my own boyfriend Xin. He had stopped using the word "sweetheart." A distance, both physical and emotional, had developed between us.

It was quiet on the streets. The world around us was dreaming of tomorrow. A fresh dampness from underneath my feet had already penetrated my shoes. Before I quickened my footsteps, I turned around to give Ho Ping a final look: in this once schoolmate and now colleague, I saw only a stranger.

Part Four

An English Teacher Who Forgot the Alphabet

She sat in a man-driven rickshaw. The driver, who spoke only the local dialect and couldn't really have a conversation with her, was humming to himself. Soon they left Xian Fan Railway Station behind and came down a treeless boulevard. Gray cement buildings lined upon both sides of the new boulevard with construction sites here and there. This was her second time in Xian Fan, the ancient and new industrial city in the northwestern part of Hubei Province. Two years ago, when she was first hired from the countryside by the Railway Bureau to be a steward, she had come here for the new workers' orientation. This time she had come for another job and to live here, perhaps for a long time.

In the past two years, when she was a steward, her train had passed the city twice a week, each time making a twenty-minute stop. During the twenty minutes, the stewards were expected to stand by the doors of their cars like guards. Not too long ago her boy friend Xin had come all the way from the northwestern mountains to see her for just the twenty minutes she was standing at her post. She knew it was his formal way of saying goodbye; since then she had not seen or heard from him. As the train was pulling out of the station that night, and their joined hands separated, they both knew it was not possible to keep up a relationship over a long distance. Her family background, with an uncle possibly still alive in Taiwan, disqualified her for any job in his military company.

The rickshaw man looked like a happy fellow. But when his wheels turned from the wide new boulevard into a narrow street and then into a web of lanes, he started ringing his bell madly. She noticed the lanes were lined with rows of identical bungalows, their doors all facing south. Some of the doors were open, revealing crudely finished interiors: with cold gray cement floors below the street level, thin white walls, and naked light bulbs hanging from low ceilings. Outside, on many of the door frames, New Year red couplets, though weathered, were still legible. She sensed these were the railway residences, where her school was located.

Before the rickshaw stopped, she had already heard children's voices, reading at the top of their lungs in unison: "We are Chairman's Mao's good children. We study hard. We love the Party. We love the people." The driver stopped at the foot of a new three-story building. She realized the school didn't have an entrance gate yet. He put her luggage down on the ground: a small suitcase, a traveller's canvas bag, and a tied-up square package of bedding. She was left there to explore her new world.

Looking around, she saw no teachers outside, nor children in the playground. She had time to straighten up her jacket and take a deep breath. "Hello, how do you do? My name is Hu Nü," she greeted the school building, with one of the few English sentences she could still remember. It sounded odd to her own ear. This was 1972, six years after the Cultural Revolution had shut down all high schools. She had not spoken English for that long. She knew she was not going to introduce herself in English today, though she needed to practice her English badly.

Suddenly, the school bell rang. From every classroom, students came pouring out. Little boys and girls from the ground-floor classrooms, early teenagers from the second floor, and much taller pupils from the third floor. Immediately, Hu Nü was surrounded by a crowd. Students brought her and her luggage to the door of the Education Director's office on the second floor.

After meeting the Director, the School Principal and the Party Secretary, by the time Hu Nü was introduced to the high-school division, the whole school was excited about her arrival. "Teacher Hu!" "Her name is Hu Nü!" She heard her names chanted outside the office. "She is our English teacher!" The students were as excited as she was. Some stuck their heads inside the office door, giving her a sly smile, then quickly ran away.

The high-school division office gave Hu Nü a warm welcome. She was quite impressed by the number of well-educated intellectuals in this office. Ms Li and Ms Liu, both teaching mathematics, were originally engineering students at Beijing University. Selected by the government, they were sent to the Soviet Union to complete their education and training in the late 1950s. Also from Beijing University were Mr Ma, a professor of astronomy, and Mr Zhang, a professor of economics. Now Mr Ma taught high school physics, and Mr Zhang politics. Since all of them came from politically untrustworthy Black families, they had been sent here from Beijing to be re-educated by the working class during the Cultural Revolution. When the school system needed more teachers, they gave up their engineers' jobs to become school teachers.

There were four single female teachers of her age at the school. They shared two of the standard row-house bungalows next to each other just outside of the campus. Again students took her and her luggage there. The layout of the bungalow homes was simple: a rectangular room of about four hundered square feet and a tiny attachment that looked like a kitchen, with two doors, one opening outside, the other inside.

"Welcome to the female teachers' residence!" A smiling young woman with big eyes stretched out her arms. "My name is Tao. You must be Hu Nü, our new English teacher."

"Yes, I am," Hu Nü smiled back, a little overwhelmed.

Another young woman walked out from inside the attached area of the house. "I'm Fang, welcome home."

"Thank you very much." Looking around the "home," Hu Nü saw two beds in the rectangular room. One was taken, the other one was obviously waiting for her. By the side of each bed, there was a school desk and a chair. She noticed that the kitchen was used as another bedroom.

"We are just about to go to the canteen. Would you like to join us?" Tao picked up a couple of bowls from inside her desk. "Dinner is served between five and six, if you are late, there will be nothing left. And there are no restaurants nearby." Fang picked up her set of utensils while handing a bowl and a spoon to Hu Nü. "Come with us, you can borrow mine and unpack later."

It was a five-minute walk to the railway workers' canteen, a big brick house with at least six double doors widely open. It was simply a big hall without tables or chairs. Upon entering, people swiftly lined up in front of the eight serving windows, stretching their necks out to read the menu written on the two small blackboards hanging between the windows. Hu Nü lined up behind Tao and Fang. Soon enough she noticed Ms Li and Ms Liu also in line. Men and women smiled at her.

"Hu Nü," she heard someone calling her from behind. Turning around, she saw a little girl, who was hardly school-age yet. Hu Nü smiled at the girl and at the child's mother. "Are you the new English teacher?" she asked. Hu Nü blushed, everyone seemed to know who she was before she had even introduced herself. She felt warmth all around her. Maybe finally she was arriving home. Maybe she belonged here.

After dinner, Tao and Fang both went out with friends, leaving Hu Nü in the dormitory to unpack her luggage. It didn't take her long to make herself at home. Her bed was made and her small desk top was occupied with a lamp, a pencil box, a pile of high school English textbooks, and an English-Chinese Dictionary. Hu Nü sat down in her chair, stared at the white wall in front of her for a while. Recalling her job transfer, she couldn't help but smile at her fate.

Her job transfer from the Passenger Transportation Department to the Education Department came totally unexpected. As the new railway was expanding further and further into the northwestern part of the province, new schools for railway employees' children had to be established. "There is an urgent need for more teachers!" She heard this from a passenger sitting in her car, who happened to be an education officer at the Railway Bureau.

"What are the qualifications?" she asked timidly. Knowing her family background had made her politically handicapped, she had watched other stewards being transferred to better and more interesting jobs in the last two years.

"Railway employees with a minimum education of senior high school level before the Cultural Revolution, and of course a passion for teaching," the education officer said. "Are you interested?"

"Me?" Hu Nü couldn't believe he was addressing her. "I'd love to be a teacher, in fact I wish I could have more education myself," she cried. "But my formal education stopped at junior high when the Cultural Revolution broke out. Then I never had a chance to enter senior high school, not to say university."

"What school did you attend? And what subject, or subjects, did you like?" asked the education officer.

"Wuhan No.2 High School." She answered. "My favourite subjects were algebra, geometry, and English."

"But No.2 was an elite school for boys, wasn't it?" The education officer looked at Hu Nü suspiciously. "Oh, oh, I remember now, you must be one of the few smart girls who were selected by No.2 one year as an experiment?"

"Yes, you are right," she blushed.

"Now listen, would you be interested in becoming an English teacher? I can make an exception." The man's eyes were shining at her. "We need English teachers more than others, desperately. Right now several schools with high school divisions have to share one English teacher. He travels from school to school every week."

Hu Nü couldn't believe her ears. "Would I be interested in becoming an English teacher?" she repeated the question. "ABCDEFG. . ." The English Alphabet Song came popping out of her mouth as if someone had just switched on a hidden musical box. "Teaching English everyday, that would be wonderful! Of course, I am interested."

By the time the train arrived at its destination, Hu Nü knew her future was about to change. The education officer said that he would look into her job transfer right away. Since few wanted to become school teachers, and even fewer wanted to teach foreign languages, he didn't think there would be any problem for Hu Nü's transfer. Hu Nü was worried about her family background, which had disqualified her before, but she was told there were no obstacles this time due to the severe shortage of teachers. Qualified, willing candidates from all walks of life would be welcomed and immediately accepted.

Indeed there was no problem at all this time. The Passenger Transportation Department was more than willing to give her to the Education Department. But most of Hu Nü's friends and colleagues were shocked to hear that she wanted to leave the glorious working class to join the condemned bourgeois intellectual class. "Now look, do you want to be called a Stinky Old Number Nine like your father?" her friends asked her directly, trying to persuade her to stay.

Stinky Old Number Nine was a derogatory nickname invented lately for bourgeois intellectuals, teachers included. Stinky Old Number Nines had to submit themselves to the working class for re-education. Hu Nü thought she wouldn't mind submitting herself for the sake of being able to teach English.

Three Brides

Fang was a local woman. Born and raised in a working-class family with five children, she was very happy to be employed by the Railway Bureau and guaranteed the famous iron rice bowl. She had two years' senior high school education before the Cultural Revolution, but she didn't mind teaching Grade 3 arithmetic now. "An iron rice bowl is an iron rice bowl is an iron rice bowl," she said to me. "Why do I want to do more work?" Fang stayed at school during the week, but she routinely went out with her boyfriend every other evening after dinner. Occasionally she came back before ten o'clock, but most of the time after we went to bed. That was why, she said, she had chosen to live in the additional part of the unit, the kitchen area as I called it.

Tao, who shared the larger room with me, came from a teacher's family. "Is that why you decided to become a teacher yourself?" I asked her.

"Precisely," she said with a nod. She then told me about her mother, a high school principal, who committed suicide during the Cultural Revolution when being criticized as a capitalist roader. "My parents both loved teaching. I remember my mother used to say 'teachers are the spiritual engineers of mankind'. But it was not that romantic when she killed herself because this mankind had lost its spiritual quality." Tao paused, waiting for my response.

"I'm sorry." I admired her coolness when talking about her mother's suicide. Tao had one year of senior high school education before the Cultural Revolution, when she was assigned to teach junior high mathematics at our school.

"The image of teachers as spiritual engineers is way out of date. Am I right? What do people call us now?" I asked Tao, trying to remember the new nickname for intellectuals. "Oh, I have it, we are called the Stinky Old Number Nine, aren't we?" I remembered how upset my fellow stewards were when they heard I was going to be a school teacher.

"Hu Nü, you're not a Stinky Old Number Nine. That stinky honour belongs to those with university education, and especially to Ms Li and Ms Liu in our office who were educated abroad. They deserve it, we don't." Tao shook her head and laughed.

Tao said her boyfriend was a Stinky Old Number Nine. Pointing at a framed photo on her desk, she said he was a professor of mathematics at Hunan University in Changsha, a city at least seven hundred kilometres south of Xian Fan. They saw each other only twice a year, during the summer and winter vacations. "This is the main reason why I am staying in teaching, because of the two long vacations each year. But after we get married, he will apply to be transferred to Xian Fan. And then maybe, I'll change my job to something else." Tao's big eyes were shining.

Next door to us lived the other two young teachers: Big Sister Yang and Xiao Zhang. I heard that Big Sister Yang had the highest education among the young teachers. She had finished her senior high school prior to the Cultural Revolution, and she taught junior high Chinese at our school. At the time of my arrival, she was in Wuhan on maternity leave.

Like myself, Xiao Zhang had only junior high school education before the Cultural Revolution. She was teaching Grade 1 Chinese and arithmetic. I decided to visit Xiao Zhang one evening. She lived in the attachment, the kitchen area of their house. So I went to the back of the house; surprisingly, before I put my knuckle on the door, she had already opened it from inside. "Come in, Hu Nü." A smiling Xiao Zhang, stepping back, let me in. "Sorry it's such a tiny place," she apologized.

I stepped inside and she closed the door gently behind her. Immediately, I felt the walls, the two doors, and the sloping roof caving in. This attachment was no proper living quarter: under the roof was her bed. She had to be very careful not to hit the roof with her head when sitting up. I sat down on the edge of her bed and she sat on the chair at the desk. On top of her desk was a photo of herself "Nice picture," I said, admiring the pretty girl in it. Her large black eyes were clear and innocent, the dimple on her left cheek enhanced the innocent smile. Her thick black pigtails were braided tightly and hung behind her ears.

"That was taken last year," she sighed, "when I first came to this school." She leaned back on her chair.

Looking at this woman in front of me, I couldn't believe how she had changed! Had she not mentioned it, I would have said the girl in the photo was at least five years younger. Now there were lines across her forehead, and around her eyes, her dimple enhanced a helpless grin, her long black hair had lost its rich lustre. Where was that freshness and innocence of the young woman in the photo? Was the weather too harsh here? Was the job too demanding? Or was the food not nutritious? One year only, but what change! Xiao Zhang poured hot water from a tall thermos into two mugs.

Both Fang and Tao started shopping for their weddings. There were daily discussions of what they had bought. I heard for the first time that it had been an established custom that the bride was expected to get the bedding and the groom the furniture. So, one by one, Fang bought five different silk duvet covers: golden dragons embroidered on red background, silver phoenix on green, pink peony blossoms on lemon yellow, nine energetic fish swimming on ocean blue, and snow-white, long-legged cranes taking off into baby blue sky. One evening she displayed all the silk sheets, to see how she would pile them on top of each other on her wedding night. Under the light, the silk was shimmering, rich and soft, and looked almost too extravagant for the crude environment.

"Wait, there are pillow cases and bed covers." Fang pulled out more stuff from wrapped packages. I was surprised to see she had bought so much bedding. "Why do you need so many sets of everything?" I asked.

"Five sets are nothing, many brides prepare eight sets. You see, after the wedding you have other priorities, you may not have money to buy things for a long time. So you stock up now." Fang spoke seriously, looking to Tao for support. Tao said she had only bought three sets, because she wanted to have a honeymoon trip to a scenic spot.

"Now, what about you, Hu Nü, do you have a boy friend?" Tao asked.

"And where is he?" Fang added.

"We broke up," I tried to sound casual. "He works in a military factory in the deep mountains."

"Oh, that's too far anyway, forget it, you don't want to waste your life in the wilderness, find somebody else," Fang said rapidly.

"That's right, find someone else, we'll help you," Tao agreed.

Big Sister Yang next door came back from her maternity leave with a one-hundred-day-old baby girl. We rushed over to see them. She was a stoutly-built chubby woman, her round smiling face highlighted by fine hair. On the right side of her cheek was a dimple, reminding me of her roommate Xiao Zhang, whose dimple was on the left cheek. Visitors passed the baby around, complimenting Big Sister Yang on its weight and size. As I was carefully holding the baby's soft body in my hands, the cotton diaper suddenly became hot and damp, and my hands were dripping wet. I screamed and didn't know what to do, which scared the baby. It started crying, but everyone else burst out laughing. "Hu Nü is the lucky one!" They said together.

"Why am I lucky?" They looked at each other, only laughed more.

The baby was still crying. Sitting down in the chair, Big Sister Yang unbuttoned her shirt, pushing up her bra, revealing her two big full breasts. With all of us watching her, she gently rubbed her right breast all over, pressed the area round the nipple to create a spray, and then pushed the nipple into the baby's month. I was breathless, too embarrassed to stand there and watch, but nobody was moving or leaving. The married women continued to comment, now of the nutritious quality of Big Sister Yang's thick milk.

That night I dreamt of myself and Xin bowing to guests at our wedding, and then jumping into our wedding bed on top of eight sets of silk duvets to make babies. At twenty-two, marriage seemed a conspiracy to me. It was a secretly coded ritual that was shared by grown-up men and women to do things that otherwise would be simply too embarrassing or totally forbidden.

Fang's wedding was scheduled for October 1 to coincide with the National Day. A newlywed was entitled to take two days off from work, plus the holidays, so she could have four days off. Nobody from school was invited to Fang's wedding banquet. She said her husband's family was paying for the meal, and since her own family was rather large, he couldn't afford to invite more people. The Teachers' Union at school asked everyone to chip in 50 *fen* (8 cents Canadian) towards a wedding present. Tao was trusted with the task of choosing a present. She bought a small kerosene stove, which was sufficient to stir-fry a bowl of vegetables or to cook a bowl of noodle soup for singles living in a dormitory.

The day after the National Day holidays, to everybody's surprise, Fang came back to work like everybody else. She said she wanted to save the other two days for later. Like all newlyweds, she distributed candies and cigarettes. Everyone at school was given a small red paper bag containing ten candies, and each office received a package of cigarettes to share.

"Congratulations!" Everyone said the same greeting to Fang with a smile, except for a few male teachers, who said, "Is our slim bride going to become as chubby as Big Sister Yang?" I knew this was a dirty joke, meaning, if she would get pregnant. When Fang stuck her tongue out at them, they all burst out laughing.

In the afternoon I ran into Fang in the women's washroom. I wanted to ask her about the wedding banquet, but I swallowed my question. From her haggard look, I knew she must be exhausted, having replied to greetings and questions about her wedding all day. I decided to wait until after school, perhaps I could catch her in our dormitory before she left for home.

To my utter surprise later, when I came back from the canteen with my dinner in my hand, Fang was still in the dormitory. She was cooking on the small kerosene stove, our wedding gift to her.

"Hi, Mrs Long, why are you still here?" I tossed my question at her.

"Stop it, Hu Nü, it's not funny." She sounded more annoyed than entertained by the greeting.

"But you're Mrs Long, according to the English custom," I said. "Now that you are married, shouldn't you be going home instead of staying at our single female teachers' dormitory?"

Fang raised her head from the boiling pot. "He is a shameless pig! That's what he is. He makes me sick." Fang was angry at her husband, who had wanted to remove her panties on their wedding night.

"So did you?" I was surprised by Fang's complaints. "Did you tell him why you didn't want to?"

"No, I didn't. Would you, Hu Nü, would you let a man take off your panties? What does he want?" Looking at her, my mouth gaping open, I saw a child in front of me instead of a grown-up woman who had got married two days ago. Her innocence and ignorance shocked me. Did they ever touch each other before their wedding night? I tried to recall my own experience, whether I had fear or desire when Xin first touched me. I could only remember I wanted him to feel me as much as I wanted to feel him. "But he is not just any man," I said to Fang, "he is your husband. You love each other, so you decided to get married, right? And marriage means sharing everything including each other physically. Fang, didn't you know all this before you got married?"

Suddenly realizing I was actually talking to a colleague of mine, I changed my tone. "Tell me how was the wedding banquet?"

"Oh, that part was fine. We had six tables all together in Xian Fan Da Sha, you know, the best restaurant in the city. I can't even remember how many courses were served, the dishes kept coming. It must have cost his family a fortune."

"So the dinner was good. Did the guests come home with you after dinner?" I asked.

"Oh they did. All of them came." Fang was excited again. "They admired my decoration of the room, especially my bedding, they said that I have an artist's taste for colours." I remembered Fang's five sets of silk duvet covers and matching pillow cases.

"But after the guests left, suddenly he took off all his clothes and started to caress me like mad. I didn't even dare to look at him. Then he wanted to remove my panties. I thought he was joking. Maybe he was drunk. So I refused. We were both upset. We didn't go to bed at all, we sat on the bed all night." Fang yawned. She said she had no idea that married couples were expected to do these sorts of things with their bodies. So right now she was taking a break from her husband. She had told him she wanted to keep her old routine, and every other day she would stay at the single female teachers' dormitory.

At the end of the winter vacation in 1972, Tao came back to school with a tall young man. She made an immediate announcement that she was married, and right away started distributing candies and cigarettes to every office. During the holidays, the newlyweds took a honeymoon trip to Kunming, a year-round spring city in Yunnan Province. After work, teachers and senior students flocked into our dormitory to greet them and look at their honeymoon pictures.

"Why didn't you tell us earlier about your wedding plan?"

"How was the trip?"

"What does Kunming look like?"

After a few busy hours, I could see Tao's big eyes were no longer shining with enthusiasm. Her husband, Professor Wu, was yawning and droning, "Fine, fine. Thank you."

Big Sister Yang came over with her baby. After asking the routine questions, she excused herself. Before leaving our crowded room, she gestured to me to come out with her. "Hu Nü, you're a sensitive young woman, don't you think you should find another place to sleep tonight?"

"Oh, you're right. I was thinking about it myself," I answered.

"You can move to my room," Big Sister Yang offered, "there is an extra single bed there."

"Thanks, Big Sis, I'm sure Tao and her husband will appreciate this." I was grateful to her for making me look considerate.

Rolling up my bedding and picking up a few things, I moved to Big Sister Yang's room next door.

In the evening, I usually studied English for two hours before going to bed. But Big Sister Yang pushed the baby carriage towards me. "Stay with Aunty Tiger for a while, Mummy is going to have a shower." She was smiling at me and the baby at the same time. The baby had certainly grown, she could smile and make various sounds now. I put my book down and started to play with her. Big Sister Yang took a washing basin. "Thanks Hu Nü."

During the winter season, we showered in the Railway Shower House, which was open three times a week for its employees and their families. After coming back from shower, Big Sister Yang put a big load of clothes in a wooden wash tub; sitting down on a short-legged stool, she started rubbing and scrubbing the clothes on the washing board. "I'll be able to put them out first thing in the morning," she smiled at me. At about nine o'clock, she finished her washing. After feeding the baby again, she put her to bed. I felt a little tired and decided to read a novel in bed.

"Enjoy yourself before it's too late," Big Sister Yang said to me. "For years after the Cultural Revolution, I remained single, hoping to go to university. When I was twenty-six, I realized I just couldn't go on waiting for something that was never going to happen. My peers had all been married and started to have children."

"So are you happier now that you are married and have a child?" I asked her.

"I can only say now I am too busy to think about such a question. You have seen my daily routine, it doesn't matter whether I am happy or not, duties must be done." Big Sister Yang's husband was an electrician in a factory in Wuhan. Like many married couples, they were in different cities because of their jobs. Women, in most cases, raised children alone.

I was dozing off when I felt a push on my elbow. It was Big Sister Yang. She was standing on the cold cement floor in her underwear. "Shhh," she put a finger on her lips.

"What time is it?" I whispered.

"Eleven-thirty," she moved her lips without making a sound. She pointed at the door that separated our room and the attachment, the kitchen area, where Xiao Zhang lived.

"What?" I was scared.

"Listen."

Holding my breath, I listened attentively. There was light movement of footsteps, but no talking.

"Maybe she just came home from outside?" I whispered. After all, it was her dorm, she lived there. But did gentle movements like that disturb Big Sister Yang? She should have been pretty tired at the end of the day.

"Listen," Big Sister Yang whispered to me again, still pointing at the door behind her.

"I can't hear anything." And was too sleepy to be bothered. Closing my book, saying "Good night," I pulled up my duvet and went back to sleep.

"Aunty Tiger sleeps like a baby," Big Sister Yang was smiling at me while putting her baby on my lap. "I am going to hang the washing on the clothesline outside." When she came back, I went to the canteen to buy breakfast for us. Breakfast was usually rice porridge and steamed bun. Over breakfast, I vaguely remembered what had happened the night before. "So, Big Sis, what disturbed you last night?" I asked.

"Hu Nü, you're so innocent. Didn't you hear anything at all last night?" She looked at me.

"No, nothing," I shook my head.

"Haven't you heard any gossip about Xiao Zhang since you came to this school?" she said slowly, watching my reaction.

"Gossip? No, I haven't." I shook my head again.

Putting down her porridge bowl, she came over to me; pushing my hair aside from behind, she blew hot words into my ear: "She is a *po xie*."

"Really?" *Po xie*, literally a worn-out shoe, was a derogatory term used to describe or insult a sexually promiscuous woman.

"Who does she prey on?" I asked.

"When she first came to this school, she had a relationship with the physical education teacher, Xiao Pan, then with the music teacher, Xiao Li, and now, I heard, with someone in the Transportation Department." Big Sister Yang said with a sneer. "She has no sense of morality or dignity, she sleeps around."

As she was talking, I remembered an incident in the canteen one evening. Xiao Zhang and I were lining up to buy dinner, when suddenly some housewives from behind us threw their shoes at her. Looking around, I saw three women, each with only one shoe on. They were laughing hideously at her. Xiao Zhang didn't say a word, she simply left the line without buying her dinner. I bought an extra portion and brought it to her dorm. When she opened the door for me, I could tell she had been crying. "Thanks, Hu Nü, I hope you don't look down upon me." Tears came down her face, pausing at the dimple on her left cheek before rolling down her chin.

All day Tao's eyes were red. Professor Wu was leaving for Changsha the next day. In the evening, Big Sister Yang, Xiao Zhang and I came over to bid our goodbyes and to wish Professor Wu good luck with his job transfer.

"Where is Fang?" Big Sister Yang looked around and asked. "Is tonight Mr Long's lucky night?" We all laughed.

"No, no. Your gossip is out of date," Tao interrupted. "Fang has been going home everyday ever since my husband's been here. The notorious cold bride has been turned into a hot cake," Tao said cheerfully.

"Ah, you know what," Big Sister Yang said loudly, "I noticed Fang's appetite has changed. Recently, instead of having big lunches, she bought cold cucumber and sometimes sweet and sour turnip. Maybe she's had it." Big Sister Yang paused, looked around as if she had just made an important discovery. Xiao Zhang and I sat on the edge of Tao's double bed giggling, pretending we were admiring the honeymoon snapshots on the wall. By then, I understood a few euphemisms used by married men and women regarding pregnancy.

The next day, Tao separated the double bed in our room back into two singles, and I moved back to my own bed in the evening. The day after Professor Wu's departure, Tao's chronic insomnia came back. I usually slept like a baby, but Tao's tossing in bed had kept me awake for hours the first night.

"This Cowherd and Weaving Girl separation has to end, or I'm going crazy," Tao sighed, talking to Fang in the morning. "See how lucky you are."

Fang smiled.

"Are you hiding a big secret from us, you bad girl? So have you had it?" Tao was speaking that allusive language again. Fang nodded with a mischievous but content expression on her face. "So Big Sister Yang was right." Tao rushed out to report the news next door.

Tao's insomnia became so bad that sometimes even sleeping pills didn't work. A Chinese medicine doctor said she had too much fire in her system. Tao said indeed she had far too much energy. She stayed in the office in the evening until late at night, but she still couldn't sleep after coming back to the dormitory at midnight. Sometimes she took a long walk around the residential area, hoping to get physically tired. I never heard her getting up or going out at night, she usually used the back door in the kitchen area, since Fang didn't sleep there any more.

But one night I woke up, so did the whole neighbourhood. It was the noise next door.

It must have been around midnight, a woman's screams together with a door banging had woken me up.

"Tao!" I yelled. She should have been awake by now, with such racket going on.

"Tao! Wake up!" I sat up in bed. Tao was not even in bed. Her overcoat, which usually hung behind the door, was not there. I quickly got out of my bed, put my padded cotton jacket on, and slipped on my boots. The banging had stopped. I heard Big Sister Yang's baby crying and then her hoarse sleepy voice asking "Who is this?"

Outside her door, stood a few neighbours in their long underwear, with an overcoat or a padded jacket over their shoulders. They were stamping the ground to keep warm. January chill had enclosed the row homes in a gray foggy mist. Under the dim street light, I saw Big Sister Yang leaning on her door talking to a middle-aged woman I didn't recognize. "What's the matter, Sister Li?"

"My husband, Party Secretary Li, has been stolen by the *po xie* living here!" The woman was pointing her finger at the door of the attachment where Xiao Zhang lived.

"Sister Li, you mustn't say things like that, unless you have evidence," Big Sister Yang challenged the crying woman.

"Of course, I have. I saw her sitting on his lap in the office. I hid myself in the dark corridor. She left the office first and then he did. I followed him at a distance. Suddenly he disappeared near the back of this house. Shameless *po xie*, she's stolen my husband!"

Big Sister Yang looked at the neighbours, by now more of them had arrived and were standing around her door. Nobody said anything. Why should she help this betrayed wife hunt down her husband who happened to be the Party Secretary at her school? Big Sister Yang shrugged her shoulders. "Go ahead, do whatever you like," she said.

The woman rushed inside and banged on the door to the

attachment. To our surprise, Xiao Zhang opened the door instantly. She was fully dressed. The duvets on her bed were still folded into rolls, with pillows sitting on top. It looked like she had not even gone to bed yet.

"What do you want? Who has your husband? If you think your husband has come here, why don't you go home and ask him?" She slammed the door shut, leaving all of us standing there gasping for words.

Tao was getting ready for bed when I returned. "You missed a big drama just now." I wondered whether I should recount the whole event to her.

"If Sister Li wants to know the truth, she should hire Detective Tao to solve the mystery."

"What? So you know the truth?" I asked curiously.

Tao gestured to me to come closer. With her big eyes looking into mine, she whispered, "I saw him sneaking out from her back door like a ghost when his wife was banging on the front door. I happened to be coming back home from the office."

"So he did come here?" I couldn't believe this. "Then it must be true that his wife did see him enter her room from the back door."

"Most likely, then she went up to the front. Of course, we don't know how long it took her to make up her mind to knock on Big Sister Yang's door. But when she did, it was the time I just came home from the office." Now the scenario was complete, with Tao's important details.

"It seems strange, why didn't she bang on Xiao Zhang's door directly and capture her husband red and hot? Instead, she went around to the front to knock on Big Sister Yang's door, waking everyone up, and giving her husband enough time to escape from the back!"

"I'm wondering about that myself," Tao said, after a pause. "The only reason could be that she didn't really want to catch her husband red and hot in Xiao Zhang's bed. She just wanted to teach him a lesson, to show him her power, but she didn't really want to publicly humiliate him. She doesn't want to divorce him yet."

"Though it does seem humiliating enough for herself, but maybe it doesn't matter." I agreed with Tao's analysis. We felt like two private detectives working together to solve a mystery. "Sister Li is a clever, but pathetic woman. On the other hand, why is Xiao Zhang so dumb? What does she want in this relationship?"

"I don't know." Tao yawned widely. Perhaps solving the case had tired her. I let her go to bed straight away.

The next morning the school bell rang at eight o'clock sharp just as it did every morning. Walking past the teachers' offices on different floors was part of Party Secretary Li's daily morning routine. He greeted everyone briefly and asked if everything was fine. There was hardly any noticeable change in his manner.

"I wanted to say to him, you knew very well, Party Secretary Li, we didn't sleep well last night, there was adultery going on in the neighbourhood," Tao said to me afterwards. We laughed.

"Indeed," I said, "but I didn't see any fingerprints, or bruises on his face, did you? That means our analysis is correct, his wife spared him last night."

Life went on. Gossip went on in the canteen corners, in the offices, and in the homes in this neighbourhood.

"Hu Nü, could you get me a dish and a steamed bun please?" Xiao Zhang handed me a bowl and a twenty-cent canteen coupon on the way back from school. Her eyes were red, swollen, and downcast, her face pale and dull.

When I came back to her place with her dinner, she had left the back door ajar for me. I thought she probably did the same for Party Secretary Li. Once inside, I was amazed again by how small the place was even for one person; it would be almost impossible for a big guy like Party Secretary Li to turn around without knocking things over. The walls, the doors, and the sloping roof all seemed to be closing in. I lowered my height and sat down on the edge of her bed. Xiao Zhang sat on her chair, we ate our dinner silently for a while.

"Xiao Zhang, I want you to know that I didn't come here to ask you about your personal life, but since you invited me over tonight, I thought you might want to talk about it." I was trying to show my concern.

"I do want to. I know you probably look down upon me too, like everyone else, I don't blame you, but I still want to tell you about what has happened." Xiao Zhang's voice was shaky.

I nodded, waiting for her to start.

"You probably know, I do a lot of preparation in the office at night. Party Secretary Li started dropping by. We began to talk about things, first just about school events, then about personal lives. I asked him why he came to school every night, while he should be spending time with his family. He told me he had no children, and that there was not much in common between him and his wife. Their marriage was arranged by their families while he was in the army." Everyone at school knew Party Secretary Li was a veteran, he wore old army uniforms all year around.

Xiao Zhang dropped her eyelids and lowered her voice. "Perhaps it is partly my fault that I showed sympathy towards him. He was grateful to me for listening to him; he said everyone else at school keeps a distance from him because he is the Party Secretary. He is expected to solve other people's problems, while he himself is not supposed to have any problems, and definitely not family problems. This is how we started, I, an elementary school teacher, a nobody, giving him, the Party Secretary, a little emotional support."

Xiao Zhang, looked at me and laughed sadly. "I thought he was a human being like everyone else, who deserved love and understanding. Quite a few times, he spoke to me about getting a divorce, and about the two of us going to a remote school along the new railway line to start afresh."

"And you believed in him?" I asked. Xiao Zhang nodded. "I could see that possibility."

"What are you going to do now?" This was my major concern. Everybody knew that Xiao Zhang couldn't go on teaching at the school and living in the residence much longer. Since that night, she didn't dare go to the canteen by herself, because Sister Li, who worked there as a kitchen help, had the whole canteen staff on her side, and no one would sell food to Xiao Zhang. Housewives called her *po xie*, instead of Teacher Zhang, sometimes even in front of her pupils. Quite a few parents came to see the principal to have their kids transferred from her class to other classes.

"Next week, I'll be transferred to a new school along the new railway line, the principal told me this afternoon." This was the reason why her eyes were red and swollen when I met her in the afternoon.

"What about Party Secretary Li?" I asked sarcastically.

"I heard he will be stripped of his Party position and transferred out of the school system entirely," Xiao Zhang said. "I guess that is fair."

"Is he still going to get a divorce?" I wanted to know.

Xiao Zhang clicked her tongue. "I don't know, it's up to him now. It's not difficult for him to find out where I'll be teaching."

She sounded hopeful.

Six months later I noticed Sister Li about six months pregnant. "How is your husband? Where does he work now?" I asked her curiously.

"Don't you know he is the Party Secretary of the Transportation Department?" she announced proudly.

Two years had passed since Xiao Zhang was transferred out of our school. I visited her once at her new school. I never told her about Sister Li's pregnancy or Party Secretary Li's new job. I was relieved that she didn't ask me any questions.

In the summer of 1973, I received an invitation from Xiao Zhang. It said: "To Hu Nü (and her boyfriend if applicable): You are cordially invited to our wedding banquet."

Who was her groom? I couldn't wait to find out.

The wedding banquet was held in the Four Seasons Restaurant, one of the most reputable restaurants in Wuhan. Under the large red character of double happiness on the wall, the guests were told that the groom and the bride were childhood sweethearts, but had lost contact with each other for nearly a decade after he joined the army. He had found her again after being discharged from military service a few months ago. I found it amazing that Xiao Zhang had to marry a veteran.

I was the only guest from her side beside her family members. When it was time for the bride and groom to make a toast at every table, the groom came up to me, raising his glass high. "Hu Nü, I'm so glad that you came to our wedding today. Xiao Zhang said if Hu Nü can't make it, we have to postpone our wedding date. She said you are her best friend, let's drink to that, I hope we'll be best friends in the future."

Xiao Zhang raised her glass to me. Her eyes filled up, tears rolled down her face like pearls from a broken string; they made a stop at the dimple on her left cheek, then streamed all the way down her neck.

Liberation Park

"So who is your boyfriend, why didn't you bring him today?" Xiao Zhang asked Hu Nü at the end of her wedding party.

"To tell you the truth, I am not sure about this relationship," said Hu Nü. She was involved in her first serious relationship after breaking up with Xin. "I think I should wait a bit longer, maybe my crown prince will eventually arrive, riding on the back of a white horse, as has yours. How long did it take you to find your true love? A decade, is it? I can wait. I am only twenty-three."

"Stop joking, Hu Nü," Xiao Zhang interrupted.

"Why not?" said Hu Nü, laughing. She was thinking about Xin and her childhood sweetheart Hua. Maybe one of them would eventually show up after ten years. But right now her mind was preoccupied with the many English words she had learned recently, as well as the English teacher who taught her in the six-month training course she was taking.

"So who is it? Let's hear about him." Xiao Zhang sounded anxious.

"It's my English teacher at the Railway Teachers' School," Hu Nü said, "he must be in his thirties."

The lack of English teachers had severely handicapped the railway educational system. In order to open the much needed high school divisions along the new railway line, the railway bureau had decided to train its own English teachers. Hu Nü and thirty others were selected to be future English teachers; they were sent to a hastily organized Railway Teachers' School. They had classes six hours a day, six days a week for six months.

On graduation day she went to say goodbye to the teachers before leaving school. Teacher Wang was the only one in the office. He was delighted to see her, she was his best student. He said he would be available if she needed more help with her studies in the future. Near the end of their conversation, he even lent her his own text books from Nanjing University where he had attended before the Cultural Revolution. Hu Nü was overjoyed.

She started studying these old university textbooks by herself eight hours a day, seven days a week during her summer vacation. Near the end of August, she had finished both Book One and Book Two, and she was ready for Book Three. She went back to school to see Teacher Wang and found him in a bedroom shared with two other single male teachers on campus. He offered to walk her home, because his room was too hot to invite her to sit down. They walked along the quiet Riverside Boulevard, which Hu Nü knew so well from childhood. When they got closer to the gate of the Big Yard where she had lived for more than a decade, she said goodbye. He asked her timidly if she would like to come out for a walk the next evening.

"So far we have been meeting almost everyday after dinner and taking a long walk in Liberation Park," Hu Nü told Xiao Zhang. "And the rest is to be seen."

"Do you like him?" asked Xiao Zhang.

"He is not the kind of hot-blooded young men like Xin or Hua, my old boyfriends. He is nine years older than me and quite reserved. But when I think about my future English studies, I'd appreciate his help for sure," Hu Nü said honestly. "So if I decide to keep dating him, it will be more of a rational decision than an emotional one."

"Hu Nü," Xiao Zhang interrupted, "you always use reason, reason. Sometimes you need to listen to your heart, I mean feelings, especially when it comes to love." Xiao Zhang looked serious.

Hu Nü thought her friend was right, she didn't have much feelings for Teacher Wang, at least not yet. Taking a second look at Xiao Zhang, Hu Nü realized her friend was actually a very sensitive woman.

In September, Hu Nü went back to her own school in Xian Fan. She found that amazing changes had occurred in her friends' lives during the six months she had been getting her training in English. Fang was now the mother of a three-month-old baby boy. Like Big Sister Yang, she didn't hesitate even a moment before unbuttoning her shirt to feed the baby in front of her colleagues. Tao was four months pregnant. Her husband, Professor Wu, had finally been transferred to Xian Fan to teach at its only Technical College. Big Sister Yang was pregnant again, with her second child. Her first baby could now walk and talk. The female teachers' two dormitories had been assigned to Tao and Big Sister Yang, since Fang and her husband lived at his residence.

Hu Nü was the only single female teacher at the school. For her safety, the school Party committee gave her a small room on the third floor of the school building as her dormitory. As the only English teacher at school, she was assigned all the English courses in the junior and senior divisions. She didn't mind the heavy load. "I need more practice," she smiled. Now that she lived on the same floor as her office, she spent almost every evening working in the office.

She enjoyed her new life as "a workaholic." One afternoon, the Party Secretary asked to see her in his office.

"Hu Nü, how is everything?" A smiling Party Secretary Zhang asked her. He was in his late fifties.

"Fine, everything is fine, just fine," she answered, wondering what this meeting was about.

"Hu Nü, I don't know how to talk to you about this." Party Secretary Zhang was struggling for words.

"Did I do something wrong?" Hu Nü asked cautiously.

"No, no, no. Nothing of that sort. You're a good teacher. This is about something else. Let me tell you what it is." Using a lighter, he lit a cigarette. "Do you happen to know a Teacher Wang in Wuhan?" he asked.

"Yes," she answered, wondering what had happened to her new boyfriend. But nobody at her school should have known about him yet, because she had not told anyone.

"He wants to marry you." Party Secretary Zhang was looking anxiously at Hu Nü.

"What?" Hu Nü was completely shocked by the blunt statement from the mouth of her Party Secretary. "Party Secretary Zhang, are you joking with me? I don't understand what you have just said."

"I don't understand it either. Let me tell you the truth. This morning when the Railway Bureau Party Committee called me, they wanted me to talk to you about this. I thought they were joking. I told them I can't have such a conversation with a young teacher, and they told me that it is exactly my responsibility to have such a conversation with you." Party Secretary Zhang laughed. Now Hu Nü was even more puzzled.

"The whole story is this: this Teacher Wang, I assume you two have been dating, has been chosen recently by the Ministry to be sent abroad. He will be working as an interpreter on the new railway between Tanzania and Zambia. According to the regulations, everyone sent abroad has to be married at home. Teacher Wang gave your name as his girlfriend, now the upper level Party committee wants to know whether you will marry him before he can be sent abroad."

Having unloaded his burden, Party Secretary Zhang looked somewhat relieved. In front of him sat Hu Nü, whom he liked a lot. As an old educator himself, he had fatherly feelings for these young women who chose teaching careers over others in a difficult time when nobody respected education. In the last two years, watching one after another of them getting married and becoming burdened too soon with families and children, sometimes he wished he could talk to them about putting off their personal commitments for a few years and getting ahead with their own careers first, because he firmly believed that education should regain its former high status.

But looking at Hu Nü saddened him: this lively young person was unusually quiet, her big shiny eyes were clouded and downcast. What had he done to her? He could tell she was not ready for marriage yet. He had heard from other teachers that Hu Nü spent her entire evenings studying and working in her office. She was the kind of young teacher whose example he would want others to follow. She had been on the right track until he called her into his office ten minutes before. Now he could see what a burden he had given her.

Hu Nü closed the dormitory door behind her. She noticed a shaft of bright sunshine coming in from the window near the ceiling, casting a long shadow on the cold cement floor. She seldom came back to her bedroom in the middle of the day, it was perhaps the first time she had noticed that her bedroom window was so small and totally unreachable up there. Did the window make the room look like a prison cell? And the long narrow shaft of sunshine looked so precious and transient. She looked around her small bedroom: a single bed, a school desk, two chairs, a washbasin stand, and a small square table, on which she kept her hot water thermos and eating utensils. Her clothes were inside her pillow case or underneath her pillow. On her desk were a few recent issues of *China Reconstruct*, an English publication from Beijing. This was her home! She had been happy to be here until half an hour ago. She hadn't felt lonely at all until this very moment.

She felt tired now, so she lay down on the bed and closed her eyes. She tried to visualize Teacher Wang or Wen, her boyfriend. He was an introverted person with few words, wearing dense spectacles, though he had a pair of good-looking eyes under his glasses. His face was a bit long, his lips were thin, and his skin was smooth and pale. There was a slight beard on his face. This was the man who wanted to marry her in order to go abroad. Or rather the Party wanted her to marry him, so he could be sent abroad. But did she know Teacher Wang well enough to marry him yet? They had just started dating a month ago. She remembered the walks they had taken in the Liberation Park in the evenings, touching upon bits and pieces of each other's lives and interests. They also spent time correcting her English exercises. Since her return to Xian Fan in September, she had hardly ever thought about him except when receiving his letters. She pulled out his recent letter from under her pillow.

My dearest,
Classes started today at the Teachers' Training School. I am teaching two large classes this term. Among the fifty trainees this year, no one has a pair of large shiny eyes like you have. I keep hoping to see you sitting in the last row whenever I enter the classroom. I know now why I went to the classroom so many times everyday last year.

I have been thinking about our last walk in Liberation Park. I am sorry that you were insulted by the park staff. I hope this experience won't cast any shadow on our relationship. I love you, Love, I miss you.
Wen

Hu Nü felt a sour taste in her mouth. She wished he hadn't mentioned the last walk they took in Liberation Park. It was their last evening together before her departure for Xiang Fan; and it was the walk that could have ended all future walks in that park.

It had started out as a beautiful evening. They set off for a long walk in Liberation Park; this had been their evening routine for more than a month. The park was the largest in the city and the closest to where they both lived. They usually entered the park from its eastern entrance and exited later from the western entrance. They walked through the green bamboo bushes and a fragrant rose garden, past the Memorial Monument for Soviet Pilots who died in Wuhan fighting the Japanese, then through a leafy apple orchard, and finally climbed a few spongy pine-needle-covered hilly mounds and came down to a clear pond with a lot of goldfish. "Did you have girlfriends before?" she asked cautiously.

"Yes, a girl growing up in the same neighbourhood in my

hometown," he murmured. "And you, any boyfriends before?"

"Two," she answered quietly.

In the hazy twilight, they saw a park bench available by the side of the pond. They ran towards it hand in hand and sat down on it simultaneously. "Oh, my legs," she cried out. He put his right arm behind her back for her to lean on. "Just a few minutes' rest. It's nine-thirty," Hu Nü said. She was scheduled to leave the city the next morning, so she should be in bed by eleven. Realizing that Hu Nü was leaving the next morning, Wen pulled her closer to him and started caressing her. His left hand caressed the shape of her face, her neck, her shoulder, and it went under her blouse to cup her breasts. She was embarrassed at first; after all they were outside in a park. But it was already dark, nobody was around except the goldfish in the pond. She leaned on his shoulders, closing her eyes, listening to the quiet of the night and feeling his hands moving up and down her breasts and then going under her skirt.

"Hands up!"

"Hands off her!"

The shouts had come from behind the bench. Instantly flashlights were pointing at their faces and then sweeping up and down at where they were sitting. Wen quickly pulled back his hands.

"We are park patrol staff," said the man and woman in uniform who were facing them. "What were you doing to her just now?" The man asked Wen.

Wen must have thought this was a funny joke. "Nothing," Hu Nü heard him answer calmly.

"He is not honest," said the female guard, "you two have to come to the office with us."

Hu Nü wished she had stopped Wen earlier. Now that they were caught, what would happen to them?

Once they reached the office, they were separated. The female guard took Hu Nü to a small room with bare walls and a single light bulb hanging down from the ceiling. There was a desk with two chairs; a telephone, a clock, and a sheaf of papers were on the desk. The guard took down Hu Nü's name, address, date of birth, and occupation, and then she asked her for details about Wen and their relationship. Hu Nü told the woman they were dating. The woman made a phone call to the local registrars security office, checking the information Hu Nü had provided. Then she went out. Hu Nü believed she was going to compare notes with her colleagues. It was already eleven o'clock. She knew her mother would be worried about her if she didn't get home before midnight. After quite some time, the two uniformed staff returned and brought Wen with them. "So, what were you two doing in the park at this late hour?" the male guard asked.

"We had a long walk, we were taking a rest before going home," Hu Nü explained.

"And where was your hand before we caught you?" the woman asked Wen.

"I know I was wrong," Wen mumbled, "my hand shouldn't have been where it was." He lowered his head.

The man and the woman made eye contact. "What else did you two do?"

"Nothing else," Wen said. Hu Nü nodded.

"But we can't trust you, because you were not honest with us in the first place," the man said. "We need to check her out to see whether you two had intercourse."

"No! You have no right to check me physically!" Hu Nü shouted. "What we have told you is true, I can guarantee you in the name of my family."

"If you don't want to cooperate, you're not going home tonight. We also have to inform your work places tomorrow morning and expose your indecency in the park," the woman said coldly, looking at Hu Nü and Wen.

Wen looked at Hu Nü, "Please, please let them examine you, so we can prove our innocence."

Hu Nü said furiously. "No! I didn't do it, I've told all of you. I have my dignity!" Turning to Wen, she said, "Why don't you ask them to examine you if you are so earnest to prove your innocence?" Hu Nü sat down in the chair, crossed her arms on the desk and lay her head down upon them. She was prepared to stay here overnight if she had to.

The two uniformed staff made eye contact again. Then they went out of the room, leaving Hu Nü and Wen on their own.

"Hu Nü, please don't misunderstand me, I just want to get out of here. Especially, I don't want anyone at work to know this," Wen said quickly. Hu Nü had no interest in talking to him.

Five minutes later, the male guard returned. He announced, "OK, considering this is your first offence, we decided to let you go home this time."

Wen thanked the guards for their kindness.

Hu Nü stood up and walked out of the office without a second's delay.

Once outside, Hu Nü took a few deep breaths to let out her anger. Looking up at the starry sky, she saw the Milky Way, which appeared to be unbelievably clear tonight. She recalled the fairy tale about the Cowherd and the Weaving Girl. The Weaving Girl is a fairy from the Heavenly Palace. Peeking through the clouds, she falls in love with a kind, handsome, hard-working cowherd on the earth. She sneaks down from the Heavenly Palace to become a Weaving Girl in order to marry him. A few years later, the Queen Mother of the Heavenly Palace finds out one of her granddaughters has gone missing. She sends down her heavenly troop to look for the escaped fairy. By then, the happy young couple has already had two children, a boy and a girl. The heavenly troop finds the Weaving Girl and drags her back to Heaven. When the Cowherd sees his wife being taken away from home, he quickly picks up their children and puts each in a bushel. He carries the two bushels on a shoulder pole and runs after the heavenly troop. As he is about to catch up with the troop, the Queen Mother, who is watching from above, throws down her hair-pin, which instantly becomes a river of stars. That is the Milky Way, which forever separates the Cowherd and the Weaving Girl. Once a year, on the seventh day of the seventh moon in the Chinese lunar calendar, all blackbirds on earth gather over the Milky Way, forming a bird bridge for the Cowherd, the Weaving Girl, and their children to be reunited.

Hu Nü didn't know why she recalled this fairy tale at that

particular and definitely unromantic moment. Wen was only a few steps behind her. "I am very sorry for what happened tonight." He tried to hold her hand; she shook it off resentfully.

Honeymoon

The Chinese say there are three important things in a person's life: birth, marriage, and death. If marriage is that important, how come I don't have any recollections of the day I agreed to tie the nuptial knot with Wen? I recall a two-month period during which I was on sick leave from teaching due to a lung infection. Wen came to see me everyday, keeping me company, correcting my English exercises, washing my clothes, and walking me to the hospital for my daily antibiotic injection. My parents were touched by his kindness. However, during that period Wen had never mentioned marriage or the possibility of going abroad.

It was near the end of my sick leave, Wen's father had come to Wuhan on a business trip. His parents lived in Wuxi, Jiangsu province. Old Wang was in his sixties, short and slim, with a slightly bent back. At that age he was anxious to see his only son settle down and grandchildren gather at his knees. Having been a shoemaker all his life, he had designed and made enough shoes for many Chinese celebrities, and even foreign celebrities, such as the Cambodian prince during the latter's exile in China. Now he hoped he had time to make a few pairs of shoes for his daughter-in-law before his retirement. So when we met for the first time, Old Wang measured my feet. "Your new leather shoes will be waiting for you this summer," he said. I didn't realize that Old Wang had come to Wuhan to make sure his future daughter-in-law was not too sick to bear him grandchildren.

Three months later my miraculous recovery from lung infection surprised my doctor. This was before my twenty-fourth birthday, and Wen asked me to marry him. "Now, you can pass the premarital medical check-up,"he said, smiling. He said people with lung diseases were considered unsuitable for marriage. "And, if you add our ages together, we get more than fifty. You see, we meet the government requirements for a marriage certificate. So let's get married."

Our honeymoon cruise left Wuhan Harbour on July 20, 1974, with my parents and sisters waving us goodbye on the dock. The ship went downstream along the Yangtze River and landed in Nanjing the next afternoon. Like Wuhan, Nanjing is famous for its heat and humidity in the summer. Wen had gone to Nanjing University before the Cultural Revolution and knew the city well, and so we found a small downtown hotel within an hour. After checking in, I was disappointed that it didn't even have a proper shower. The staff told me I would have to get a pail of water and wash myself in an empty room in the backyard. "Make sure nobody peeks at you," a male voice came out from the reception window.

I was shocked. "Are people in Nanjing so vulgar and offensive?" I asked Wen.

"Let's not worry about these people's morality. It's our honeymoon, I don't want anything or anyone to ruin our mood today." Wen put his arm around me. "I'll watch the door for you while you wash. Let's go." Wen took a pail of warm water for me to the back yard. We found the empty room, which had a cement floor and drains in the corners. There were no curtains on the windows, and there was not even a table or a shelf for people to leave their clean clothes on. What a place! I felt disgusted that Wen would take me to such a filthy place for the first night of our honeymoon.

"Trust me, Hu Nü, it's going to be all right here," he said defensively, when I suggested that we move to a better hotel. "I don't want to waste money on hotel decor, besides we've already paid them for tonight, I don't think they'll refund. And I'd rather spend more money on our dinner."

I knew Wen was always pragmatic, but I didn't think he would be counting costs during our honeymoon. But he was right, we didn't want anyone or anything to ruin our mood today. "OK, let's not worry about it. We can go for dinner soon," I said.

We stepped into a fancy downtown restaurant for dinner. I could tell from its cleanness and the number of waiters standing by that it was not the kind of eating counter where we sometimes had a quick meal in Wuhan. When a waiter put a two-feet-long flat plate in front of us, I was astounded: it contained a big fish with its meat cut like scales, fried crispy, and coated with many delicate ingredients and mixed with sweet and sour sauce. "What do you call this dish?" I asked Wen.

"This is the famous sweet-and-sour squirrel fish," said Wen, "my favourite dish from university days when I couldn't afford it!"

"I see."

The crispy scalelike presentation was meant to resemble a pine nut shell instead of a squirrel that eats pine nuts. "Open your mouth," said Wen, breaking up a big piece with his chopsticks, and held it up over my face.

I opened my mouth wide, he dropped the piece inside and waited for my response. "Mmm," I exclaimed. Other customers in the restaurant were watching us. I was a little embarrassed. "I can help myself now," I whispered. Another seafood dish came: slices of eel stir-fried with onions and ginger. Later a plate of steamed green cabbage hearts coated with crab meat. "Oh, look at these lovely baby cabbages, they look like jade, don't they!"

After dinner, we decided to walk back to the hotel. Wen told me the dinner had cost half of his month's paycheck, but he was glad to make me happy. He also told me street names and local gossip he remembered from more than ten years ago. It was about eleven-thirty when we finally got back to the hotel. Wen picked up the key from the night staff at the front desk. There was nobody in the lobby.

Though midnight, it was still impossibly hot and humid in our room. We wiped our sweat with warm water from a thermos and then cleaned the straw sheet on the double bed. Wen fanned the straw sheet with a bamboo hand fan. We were both pretty tired by then, but realizing this was our first night together, we were excited again.

Wen picked me up and gently put me down on the bed. "My dear wife from today on," he whispered in my ears. "My dear husband," I said softly, closing my eyes. I let him put kisses all over me, unhook my bra, and take off my panties. He was sitting on the edge of the bed, gently stroking my body. I forgot it was the first time that I was completely naked in front of a man. Opening my eyes, I saw him naked as well. Placing his caressing arms underneath my neck, he lay down beside me and turned off the light. In darkness, I felt the movements of his hand more accurately and the volume of his manhood more sensitively. We probably didn't even say goodnight to each other before falling asleep in each other's arms.

"Open the door! Open the door!"
"Open up! Open up right now!"
"Policeman is here, checking registration!"
I woke to up to hear heavy footsteps coming upstairs.
Quite a few people were banging our door with their fists, a strip of light was visible underneath the door.
"Tao! Wake up! Wake up!" I screamed. I recalled Party Secretary Li's wife banging on Big Sister Yang's door in Xian Fan. But quickly I realized that this was my honeymoon night in Nanjing, and I burst out crying.
Sitting up in bed and pulling out his glasses from underneath the pillow, Wen rapidly covered me up with a cotton sheet. "Don't worry, I'll get up and see what they want." He stepped into his underwear while walking towards the door.
"Open the door! Or we'll have to kick it open!" Heavy boots started landing on our door. Wen opened the door from inside before he could find the light switch.
"Hands up! You! Put your hands up!" someone yelled at Wen. Strong flashlights swept across the small room. I couldn't even open my eyes. Someone turned on the light, I saw five or six big guys standing at the door. Wen was standing in a corner with his hands above his head like a fugitive. My naked body was shivering under the single cotton sheet.
"Who is she?" a man in a police uniform asked Wen, pointing his

finger at me.

"My wife," Wen said loudly.

"How old are you?" the policeman questioned.

"Thirty-three."

"How old is she?"

"Twenty-four," Wen answered.

"Show me your documents."

Wen walked over to our luggage, still holding his hands above his head. He handed our new red marriage certificates to the policeman together with our identification cards from the Railway Bureau. To my surprise the policeman didn't even give a second look at the standard marriage certificates. He only looked at the photo ID and then at us several times before handing all the documents back to Wen.

The policeman waved at the rest of the people, the invading troop quickly withdrew from our room without an apology. I heard the policeman's voice going down the stairs, "Bad information, wasting time."

After Wen closed the door, I couldn't help but cry out loudly and angrily this time.

"Shhh, other guests can hear you," Wen put his hand on my mouth.

"They have already heard everything anyway, did the policeman search other guests as well or just us?" I wanted to rush out of the door to question the policeman, who didn't even show us his ID.

"Did you see the day staff, the man who checked us in this afternoon?" Wen said. "Remember you said he was vulgar."

"What did they think we were?" I asked Wen.

"They think you're too young to be my wife, and that we're committing adultery here," Wen said with certainty. I couldn't believe this was how the people viewed us, but, I was convinced because Wen often claimed that he knew Nanjing well.

Neither of us ever wanted to talk about our first night in Nanjing. It put a curse on our marriage from day one.

Three months later, Wen was called to Beijing for a month of training before being sent abroad. The order came when I had just found out that I was pregnant. I decided to go to Beijing with him, so we could spend a few more nights together before his departure for Africa for a period of two years.

In Beijing, our request was turned down by his superiors immediately. He was told that we could only see each other between six and seven in the evening. So I spent the rest of each day wandering in the streets by myself. After walking up and down the main streets and in and out of the shops by myself for a week, I decided to return to Wuhan before he set off for Africa. The day before my departure, Wen asked his superiors at the Foreign Affairs office again to be excused for the night. He believed his leader would make an exception and grant him a single night with his wife. But to our total disappointment, his request was rejected again. No excuse or exception could be made for people who were being sent abroad.

I left Beijing by myself the next morning.

Wen and I didn't see each other until two years later. After completing his two-year term in Zambia, he came back to Wuhan happily loaded with what he had bought with his stipend: a camera made in Shanghai, a powerful Phillips short-wave radio, a Swiss watch, and an electric rice cooker. He had also accumulated a lot of food during the two years abroad: bags of sugar, tins of milk powder and hot chocolate mix. He said he bought the valuables in the Friendship Store in Beijing upon his return; the food had been shipped from Africa. Wen was happy to be back. But unfortunately, he returned a total stranger to me and our child.

Funeral Rites

At sixty-eight, my father-in-law was diagnosed with late-stage liver cancer. The news didn't come to me directly from him, it came from Beijing.

I was called to the Party Secretary's office one morning. He showed me my father-in-law's letter. It was written to his son, begging him to come home from Zambia for just a few days. "My days are numbered, please tell your leader you don't need to stay long. I just want to see you one more time. You can return to work right away," the old man said in the letter. The letter had been intercepted in Beijing.

"The Ministry has decided to send you to see your father-in-law instead, and to deal with the funeral. Our school has decided to send Dean Liu to go with you. You have a baby, we think, you can use her help on the way. Your trip will be covered by the Ministry."

Everything was prearranged, the only thing I had to do was pack my luggage. The next morning, we boarded the ship going down the Yangtze River to Nanjing. In Nanjing we checked into a big downtown hotel with a proper bath and shower, not too far away from the unforgettable small hotel where Wen and I had been raided by the police on our wedding night.

We arrived in Wuxi in the early evening of the second day and went to the hospital right away. In a ward shared with seven other patients, I saw my father-in-law lying in a bed facing the door. He was already a skeleton, his skin had turned yellow like wax, tubes were stuck all over him from his nose to his ankles. He was wearing nothing except loose homemade long underwear covering his bony crotch. He was in coma when Dean Liu and I walked in with my baby in my arms.

"Papa, papa," I leaned over his bed. "I'm here. Open your eyes, your granddaughter is here." I started to cry at the sight of my father-in-law reduced to a human wreck, still waiting faithfully for his son's return.

The old man was motionless. Dean Liu gestured to me to pick up his hand. I held his bony hand in mine, feeling the protruding knuckles, which had been shaped by a lifetime of making shoes for other people. "Papa, wake up, papa, wake up please."

His eyelids twitched and separted by a hairline. "Papa, this is your grandchild," I put the baby in front of him. The old man opened his eyelids another hairline, his lips were twitching, but no sound came out. I held his hand on the baby's head for a few seconds. His eyes seemed to have opened a bit wider, his lips formed a smile.

"Wen can't come home yet, the Party has sent Hu Nü here to see you," Dean Liu said.

The old man didn't respond. His eyes were partially open and his lips were set apart a little. Holding his hand, warm but motionless, I hoped to transfer all my strength to him. Five minutes passed silently with all of us watching him and waiting for him to say something. Suddenly his hand dropped. I picked it up quickly and held it tightly in mine.

My mother-in-law, leaning beside me all this time, cried out. "He's gone," she mumbled. "He was waiting for Wen. He didn't wake up for two days. He was saving his last bit of energy for his son. But Wen couldn't come home, and now he's gone."

I continued to hold my father-in-law's hand. It was still warm, it was hard to believe that life had withdrawn from him in front of my eyes. I didn't want to let go yet, until the nurse came over to cover his body with a white sheet.

It was the first time for her to face a relative's death. Hu Nü was shocked; she didn't know what to think, but she couldn't cry. Leaving the hospital with her mother-in-law and Dean Liu, she decided to take a long walk home by herself. It would give her the half hour she needed to adjust to the shock. Dean Liu offered to take her baby home.

Hu Nü set off in the evening haze, down the long boulevard. She remembered that the previous time time she had come here on her wedding, and her father-in-law had brought out two pairs of leather shoes he had designed and made for her. She tried them on, one black and one white, different styles, and they fit her like her own skin.

Stepping into the courtyard of her in-laws' house, Hu Nü heard a woman wailing. Was that her mother-in-law? she wondered. Her ears were full when she got closer to the unit. Some neighbours were gathered at their doorstep; from inside, her mother-in-law's sharp, high-pitched cries came out.

"You'd better go in and comfort your mother-in-law," said Dean Liu. "If she takes it too hard, she might get sick, then you and I will have more problems to face." Hu Nü agreed.

Her mother-in-law was a short chubby woman in her late sixties; even with the best shoes designed for her feet, she wobbled as if she needed a cane. Like many women of her generation, she couldn't even read a local evening newspaper. Between mothers-in-law and daughters-in-law, there was a gap in culture, and Hu Nü didn't speak the local dialect. The two women hardly spoke directly to each other.

Mrs Wang disliked big-city girls in general, and this daughter-in-law was one of those big-city girls who were spoiled from childhood. She had got annoyed the last time when Hu Nü and Wen came visiting soon after their wedding. Hu Nü didn't get up in the morning at all to greet the in-laws or cook their breakfast. It was her son who had to do all the womanly work in the house. Now that her old husband was gone and her son was abroad, Mrs Wang felt even more lonely and desperate. She knew right now a group of neighbours were gathering outside her unit, it was time for her to cry. Taking a deep breath from the bottom of her belly, she wailed.

Hu Nü came in, put an arm around her mother-in-law's shoulder. "Mama, take it easy. Papa has gone now, you have to take care of your own health," she said. "Would you like something to drink?" Her mother-in-law pushed her away. "Go take care of the baby, you," she sobbed. "I know how to take care of myself." She let out another long cry.

Hu Nü knew her mother-in-law disliked her. It seemed as if she wouldn't be able to provide the kind of support required. Perhaps the old woman needed to cry a bit, she must miss her husband of so many years. How would she live without him? Hu Nü decided to leave her mother-in-law alone. She herself couldn't cry aloud, her tears dropped silently whenever she remembered her father-in-law's waxen face. It was not easy to express her sadness for losing such a loving, caring father-in-law, whom she only wished she could have known better. She knew that Old Wang had liked her in the same way as she had liked him. But still she could not cry out tearfully and mournfully in front of others. If this was a custom here, she wouldn't be able to fulfil the duty of a daughter-in-law. She thought she would just tell Dean Liu that her mother-in-law needed to cry aloud and they should leave her alone.

During the evening, Hu Nü was relieved to see that in between the visits of different neighbours, her mother-in-law took breaks, going in and out to the kitchen to get something to eat or drink. But as soon as she heard someone stepping into the unit, no matter who it was, she would start bawling. This went on until ten o'clock when the last group of visitors left and Hu Nü and Dean Liu could finally go to bed.

At daybreak the next day, before Hu Nü and Dean Liu had even stirred in bed, a sharp cry came from the attic, followed after a while by more of the same. The ten-family courtyard woke up to another day of Mrs Wang's grief.

In the morning, leaders from Old Wang's shoe company came to console the widow. Mrs Wang shed a lot more tears than the day before. Dean Liu said she had participated in a meeting to discuss the widow's monthly living costs. The shoe company requested the Railway Bureau to make an equal contribution towards a monthly widow's benefit because her son was not available to take care of her. In China, a husband's pension stops when he dies. In this case the two companies made an exception to create a pension fund for the surviving widow. When Hu Nü heard the good news from Dean Liu, she rushed over to tell her mother-in-law. The old woman, who was still wailing at the top of her lungs, thinking the leaders were still there, smiled at her daughter-in-law and then began another series of moans and chants. "I am an old widow, my poor husband is dead, I have no one to rely on."

Hu Nü was puzzled. This time Dean Liu told her not to worry about her mother-in-law. "The old woman is crafty. She knows when and how to cry. Let her perform."

Hu Nü started to understand the Chinese saying about the three important events in life: birth, marriage, and death. This was Old

Wang's last important event. In this part of the country, the last event could be as ceremonial as the first two, and more dramatic, especially if the deceased was over sixty-five years old.

Just as at a new birth or a wedding, neighbours brought gifts. Hu Nü watched her mother-in-law thank them and quietly take in all the wrapped parcels. Most of the gifts were embroidered silk duvet covers. Hu Nü wondered in what part of the funeral rituals these colourful silk pieces would be used. She remembered neighbours had brought similar gifts at her wedding, her mother-in-law showing her one beautiful piece after another, and Hu Nü thought she would never have to buy duvet covers for the rest of her life. Later Wen said if she really wanted to, she could have one of these duvet covers. Otherwise, his mother would keep them, because his family had to buy gifts for the neighbours' big events. Now Hu Nü realized those silk duvet covers were genuine all-purpose gifts, going in and out of different households in the neighbourhood for the big family events of birth, marriage, and death.

Besides duvet covers, Old Wang's shoe company, the Railway Bureau, and the neighbourhood committee each sent in a memorial wreath made of white and pink paper flowers. Written on strips of paper, which hung on the sides of the wreath were wishes for the deceased's eternal life on one side and the mourner's name on the other. Five mourning days passed; there were enough wreaths around the doorway, and along the walls, creating an overwhelmingly sad atmosphere.

On the sixth day, Hu Nü was woken up in the morning by a noisy group of women inside the unit. Her mother-in-law called her to get up and get dressed. Shortly after she left the inner bedroom, the noisy neighbours rushed in, bringing in an armful of white handwoven cotton pieces that looked like cheese cloth.

"We are going to dress you up a bit," one of them said cheerfully. Hu Nü was amused. The woman started putting pieces of material over Hu Nü's shoulders. The other two women worked around her to tie up the knots. The first woman asked Hu Nü to put on pants made from the same material. Hu Nü could see now those garments were not stitched together; they were tied together by loose strips at the end of each piece. The pieces looked as if they had been torn up rather than cut with scissors. A head cover was put on Hu Nü's hair; there was also a pair of white cotton shoes. Hu Nü tried on the shoes, they were at least one size too wide and too long. Someone had made her a pair of sloppy loose shoes. And it was her responsibility as a daughter-in-law to wear them to the funeral rites of her father-in-law, the best shoemaker in the city.

Standing in front of the mirror, Hu Nü didn't recognize herself. She looked bulky and foreign, like the old movie character Xiang Linsao, a miserable country wife whose entire life was depicted in mourning first her husband's death and then her son's. Dean Liu was standing by; she wished she had brought her camera, at least she could take a picture to show it to Wen later.

At about ten o'clock that morning, the funeral troupe set off in two pick-up trucks for the crematorium in the suburbs, carrying the wreaths and all the neighbours who wanted to come. On the way Hu Nü was given a written speech prepared by a neighbour, also a school teacher. She quickly browsed through it; it was written in the kind of unemotional official language used to mourn in public someone unrelated to the speaker. Hu Nü knew the tone of the speech would distance herself from her father-in-law, especially if she delivered it in standard Mandarin. But this was not what she wanted to do. She wanted to tighten up the relationship and fulfil her duty to her father-in-law in his last need.

As soon as they arrived at the crematorium, a memorial service was held in a solemn hall. At least forty mourners participated, filing in a single line to say goodbye to Old Wang lying peacefully in an open casket. Hu Nü thought it would be more appropriate for any one of the old folks to talk about Old Wang in their local Wuxi dialect. But the service proceeded too quickly for Hu Nü to make a suggestion. It was her turn to deliver the speech. She gave her baby to Dean Liu and walked up to the microphone. After reading the first few sentences from the prepared speech, she decided to let her own memory of her father-in-law take over. Knowing her Mandarin would alienate most of the folks there, she hoped the universal experience between a daughter-in-law and a father-in-law would help her audience understand her feelings. She talked about their first meeting, about their regular correspondence, and about the shoes he had designed and made for her after one measurement, which all fit her comfortably like her own skin. "I will miss him."

The rest of the day proceeded like an outing for the city folks. Some mourners went for a long walk to the nearest small town, others went up to the temple on the hill to look at the varieties of ash urns. In the afternoon, someone heard Old Wang's name called over the loudspeaker. It was time for his relatives to pick up his ashes.

The mourners were pretty tired by then, most of them hadn't had anything to eat. Hu Nü just wanted to get home, she needed to put her baby to bed. Finally the pick-up truck entered the familiar laneway of her in-laws' home. Suddenly it stopped at about one hundred feet away from their courtyard. Everybody jumped down from the truck. Hu Nü thought the truck had broken down, but thank God, at least they were close to home. As soon as she got down, the teacher neighbour came up to her, giving her her father-in-law's framed picture and the urn containing his ashes.

"Hu Nü, your father-in-law's last hundred steps have to be completed by his son, but since Wen is not here, it's your responsibility to help him complete the final journey," he said.

Hu Nü didn't quite follow this instruction. Passing her baby to Dean Liu beside her, she took over her father-in-law's ashes and the picture.

"No, no," another neighbour said, putting her baby back in her arms. Knowing Hu Nü didn't understand the funeral rituals, the teacher neighbour explained in Mandarin, "You need to carry the baby and your father-in-law, because that's three generations coming home." He helped her arrange the baby on her left arm, and placed the box of ashes on her right arm, and then placed the framed picture standing atop of the box leaning against her chest.

"I'm not sure she can carry the baby and the rest," Dean Liu said.

"But she has to, because Wen is not home, she is fulfilling Wen's duty," the teacher neighbour said firmly.

"OK, if I have to do it, let's go," said Hu Nü. She just wanted to get home.

Hu Nü at the head, her mother-in-law behind her, then Dean Liu, followed by neighbours and fellow workers from the shoe company, a long home-returning procession proceeded towards the gate of the courtyard. Half way down, Hu Nü felt a nerve in her right wrist twist and shake. She tried to hold the box even more tightly with her hand because of its fairly large size. She pressed her chin down on the top edge of the framed picture. She knew she had to walk fast without dropping anything.

In front of her, on her path, suddenly she saw people as if playing with a fire, or trying to make a fire. Why had they picked the spot in front of the courtyard? What was she supposed to do now? Should she yell at them to get out of her way? Before she could ask her mother-in-law or the teacher neighbour, she heard people ahead of her chatting, "Wang *xiansheng* coming home! Wang *xiansheng* coming home!" She began to understand the ritual now that the neighbours were calling Mr Wang's soul home. Her mother-in-law and those behind her answered in unison, "I'm coming home! I'm coming home!"

Hu Nü continued to walk towards the gate, holding herself up, her sleeping baby in her left arm, and the box and the picture in her right arm. The fire in front of the gate seemed to get bigger, and crackled. Wisps of blue smoke rose above the orange flames. She could see neighbours burning paper. She knew burning paper money was also part of the funeral ritual; it was for the dead to use in the underworld.

She heard the neighbours yelling at her.

"Hu Nü, jump over the fire!"

"Jump over the fire! Jump!"

"Jump over the fire? Not me." Hu Nü couldn't believe what they were asking her to do. She looked around, people behind her had already caught up, they had surrounded the fire, leaving the space in front open for her to jump.

"But I can't jump, not in these shoes?" Hu Nü said. "These shoes are too loose to jump over anything, especially fire," she said, asking for understanding.

"Hu Nü, jump over the fire!"

"Jump over the fire now!"

Neighbours were shouting and making gestures to her to understand. Her baby was waking up, stirring in her left arm. Hu Nü knew very soon she would not be able to hold everything in place in her two arms. If she had to jump before she could get home, she should jump right now.

"Hu Nü, you must jump over the fire so Mr Wang can return home!"

She heard the teacher neighbour's voice in Mandarin. She thought she wouldn't put up with this rubbish any more had it not been a rite for her father-in-law. Tightening up both sore arms and painful wrists, closing her eyes, she made a leap over the bonfire.

"Wang *xiansheng* is home! Wang *xiansheng* is back home!" Neighbours cheerfully held the gate open, right away someone took the ashes and the framed picture from Hu Nü. Hu Nü walked in the courtyard like a hero.

She and Dean Liu went straight into their room, Hu Nü put the baby down on the bed and went to the kitchen to fetch baby food. To her surprise, inside the large kitchen and its big eating quarters in the courtyard shared by the neighbours, several round tables were set up. The mourners were helping themselves to the seats at the tables. With bowls, spoons and chopsticks in their hands, there was a lot of clattering.

"It looks like they are having a feast to celebrate my father-in-law's death or something." Hu Nü described the scene to Dean Liu when she came back with a baby bottle in her hand.

"Of course it's a celebration, because your father-in-law lived over sixty-five, so his passing away is not viewed as a sad thing." Dean Liu explained. "Instead, it's called a white happiness, while wedding is a red happiness, but, they are both happinesses to be celebrated, like a birth."

Hu Nü's true relief came the next day, when she woke up by herself at noon, realizing she had actually slept.

Her mother-in-law wailed no more.

Three Divorcees

"Who's that beautiful middle-aged physician at the clinic?" I asked Xiao Jin, my friend.

"Oh, you probably mean Dr Tan," she answered, "she has just moved into the ground-floor apartment." She pointed downstairs.

Lao Tan was a graceful, middle-aged physician: her pale face and large, beautiful, deep eyes, her thick black hair down to her earlobes like a stylish curtain, and her long white neck stretching out from a loose black turtleneck sweater gave her the appearance of a marble bust on a museum pedestal.

"Just so that you know, she's divorced. I heard she married two brothers and divorced them both," Xiao Jin said.

"So, should we stay away from her, or talk to her?" I asked playfully. Since we both were divorcees, we were sensitive to other women's marital status.

"Both," she said, "you don't want people to gossip about us too soon, saying 'like attracts like.'"

Xiao Jin had been married three times and divorced twice, to the same man. He was a Peking Opera actor trained to perform the role of the male scholar in traditional plays. The scholar was usually paired with a beautiful maiden and they secretly fell in love. Obstacles had to be overcome before their happy union at the end of the play.

"Can you believe my husband is in love with another young actress in his troupe?" She sounded irritated. "Again they became lovers on stage first, then off stage. So I am an obstacle to be removed."

"Indeed, why don't you quit playing the generous first wife?" I said, following the same old plot. "He wouldn't have done it the third time if you hadn't given him his second opportunity."

"But I won't this time, you watch me, Hu Nü, nothing passes the third time, according to the old Chinese saying."

Shortly after we met, Lao Tan, Xiao Jin and I became friends. I told them I preferred an English proverb to the old Chinese saying about our friendship. "Birds of a feather flock together," presented a beautiful image of us three divorcees.

"Teach me some spoken English, Hu Nü," Lao Tan told me earnestly," a month today, I'll have an interview with the American Embassy in Beijing."

"What for?" I was surprised.

"My aunt in New York has sponsored me to go to America," she answered. "My spoken English is so pathetic that I am afraid I won't pass the interview."

"Are you going to leave China for good?" I asked. In the early 1980s, Chinese people knew little about the outside world.

"I don't know, my aunt is in her seventies, I don't want to be a burden on her," Lao Tan said. "I heard Americans have started taking Chinese herbal medicine seriously. Maybe I'll open a Chinese medical clinic in New York, wouldn't that be nice?"

Lao Tan came back from Beijing disappointed. Her interviewer told her she had to improve her English; her aunt, a pensioner, couldn't possibly support another person financially. But Lao Tan could reapply after half a year's interval.

"Do you think there is hope for me?" she asked me.

"Of course, otherwise the American Embassy would have told you straightaway that you needn't apply in the future," I told her. Our English lessons continued with a new textbook I borrowed from the university library, *Introduction to American English*. This book taught both English and lifestyle. When we first read about shampoos, conditioners, dishwashing detergents, we had no idea what they were. In China, we used soap to wash our hair in those days. If the dishes were greasy, we just used hot water.

Lao Tan was much better prepared for her second interview. But, to our total disappointment, her application was rejected again. She was told that her English was much improved, but it took more than English to find a job in America. Her medical qualifications were not accepted unless she planned to redo all the university medical examinations in English and get her license. But meanwhile, who would support her?

On a rainy Sunday morning, I found Lao Tan not in. As this was rather unusual, I decided to go upstairs to visit Xiao Jin instead.

It took her a good three minutes to open the door. "Come in," she whispered.

"What are you doing?"

"Nothing, nothing much," she mumbled. After I had sat down on the couch in the sitting room, she asked me seriously, "Hu Nü, did you ever ask yourself where the good men in the world are? You know what I mean, the successful, handsome, romantic, passionate, understanding, supportive men, where are they? Perhaps they don't exist, except in our imagination."

I laughed loudly. "I see, this is what has kept you busy on Sundays, dreaming about ideal men."

"Because I need to ask myself whether it's worth the pain of getting another divorce," Xiao Jin answered.

"Now, don't you forget, getting the divorce is for yourself," I reminded her. "To free you from this unhappy marriage."

"Yes or no, society looks down on divorced women, and no good men want to have anything to do with us because divorcees are considered secondhand goods. And later we ourselves might regret getting the divorce." Pausing, she continued, "But I don't understand why it is like this."

I thought for a while. "I think the reason is that so far all Chinese men have grown up in more or less the same male-centred feudal culture. That's why it's hard to find an exception. Do you agree?" I noticed Xiao Jin's eyes were avoiding mine. "What's wrong?" I asked, "you are not hiding a wild man inside your apartment, are you?" I joked with her, knowing she wouldn't mind.

To my utter surprise, she nodded, her eyes gazing at me ever so seriously.

"What? You're kidding, you bad girl, where is he?" I jumped up from the couch.

Xiao Jin burst our laughing.

"But I am not joking, actually there is someone inside." She was serious again. "My hidden man! Would you please come forward? Hu Nü wants to see you." She pitched her voice towards the direction of her bedroom. I thought she was still teasing me. So both of us turned around to face the bedroom door, and again she spoke aloud. "Where is that bold wild mam - come out, don't be shy to identify yourself!"

Xiao Jin went inside. I thought this couldn't be true.

There was motion inside her bedroom, and suddenly a middle-aged man appeared at the bedroom door. Xiao Jin was behind him, pushing. "Here he is!" she said excitedly.

Instantly, I knew who he was. According to local custom, I should call him Uncle Tin, because he was my father's colleague.

"Hu Nü, you've just made an incredible point, I want you both to hear this—I want to be an exceptional Chinese man." Behind his glasses, Tin's eyes were shining emotionally.

When I saw Xiao Jin again, I chanted an old Chinese saying, "In front of a widow's house, there are troubles." A "widow" refers to a woman whose husband has passed away or who has been divorced by her husband. The word in Chinese is *guafu*, and it sounds as awful as the word for a leper. For that reason, we called ourselves divorcees; we had divorced our husbands to get out of failed marriages.

"How long have you hidden Uncle Tin in your bedroom?" I asked.

"Nonsense, Hu Nü, he is no Uncle Tin, Old Tin, call him Lao Tin," Xiao Jin corrected me, laughing. "It was six months ago last Sunday," she answered. "He is trapped in an unhappy marriage with an ever-critical wife and a disabled teenage daughter. Last year we went on an errand together, on the train, we talked widely about family, marriage, parenthood, and personal happiness. I have never met a man who is so communicative," she reminisced. "Then after we came back to the office," Xiao Jin looked at me frustratedly, "we could not talk to each other because we were married to other persons. So Lao Tin lied to his wife about doing overtime on Sundays, he came early and sneaked into my apartment. We stayed in all day, until he could sneak out in the evening." After pouring out her story, Xiao Jin waited for my response.

"What are you going to do next?" I asked. "Sooner or later his wife will find out about this. And you're going to lose him."

"He said in half a year his daughter will finish her junior high school. She will go to a school for the disabled, and he only needs to come up with the tuition. Then he will ask his wife for a divorce," Xiao Jin said.

"You believe that?" I was not convinced.

"Yes and no," Xiao Jin said slowly and thoughtfully. "That's why I was glad you came knocking at the door last Sunday, so we have a witness."

"I see. So it's good that we said what we have said." I was still uncomfortable that Lao Tin had overheard our conversation.

"Oh, definitely," Xiao Jin gave my hands a firm shake.

Lao tan's son was arrested by the police for a bicycle theft. He was sent immediately to a provincial labour camp for juvenile delinquents. This was why she was not available that rainy Sunday morning. She had gone to the camp.

"It is set in a totally outlandish place," recalled Lao Tan. "First train, then bus, and then a five-kilometer muddy country road with no vehicle service at all."

"How is the boy?" I asked. "Why did they take him there without a trial?"

She sighed, shaking her head tearfully. "My son is ashamed of himself, he kept apologizing to me. He said he didn't touch the bike, but he did watch his friends steal it, and he didn't report them to the police because they were his friends. Now he has been given three years. They will teach him a hard lesson, perhaps something good will come out of it."

"Hu Nü, tell me the truth, do you really think I have a chance to go to America?" she asked.

"I honestly don't know," I said. "I've never been inside a foreign embassy. I have no idea how they select people to go to their countries."

"You see, now I am caught in an even worse dilemma. With my son in juvenile jail, he will never be able to pass the security check. In the application form there is a question about whether one has ever been jailed in one's own country. So my son has done us both in now and forever. If there was a little chance for us to go to America before, there is zero now." Lao Tan looked at me, as if asking for an opinion.

I didn't know her son was also an applicant for immigration to America. I agreed with her, "It doesn't look promising, Lao Tan. After two rejections, you have built up a negative record. All systems, I think, either socialist or democratic, keep files on people. So unless your situation changes completely, your old file stays intact. Maybe, you know what, maybe you need to look for a rich American husband to replace your poor old aunt as a sponsor."

As I finished my imagined scenario, Lao Tan burst out laughing. "Hu Nü, I love you for your playfulness, no matter how depressed I am, you can always cheer me up. Now it will be your task to find me a husband!" We laughed together.

Another evening, after we sat down to study, I noticed Lao Tan's eyelids were drooping. "Lao Tan, you look a bit tired, why don't we take this evening off? We can read about what Americans do in Las Vegas some other time."

To us, Las Vegas was only a dot on the world map, where crazy Americans went to blow their money. It was hard to imagine that a place was famous simply for its extravagant hotels, sensational shows, big-time gambling, and quick marriages and divorces.

"I want to tell you, Hu Nü," Lao Tan interrupted my train of thought, "I want to let you know that I am gradually giving up my American Dream, the one you said is for every immigrant in America to share, going from rugs to riches."

"From rags to riches," I corrected her with a smile.

"I have more or less stopped dreaming about America. I think I need to face my reality here and make it work for me and my son, especially when he comes out of jail in two and half years. What do you think?"

Outside, spring showers splashed the ground; from the poorly insulated door frame and cracks under the windows, wind and rain leaked in. I looked around her one-bedroom apartment. In the tiny sitting room where we were, there was a single bed, her son's. A round table and three chairs occupied a corner close to the kitchen, a narrow desk with three drawers and a chair stood under the window. Her homemade flowery window curtains were dripping with water. Nothing on the wall. And here was this middle-aged woman who, weighted down by her life's struggles, was looking for a solution, struggling to change her nightmare reality into a liveable dream. I looked at her with admiration.

"Hu Nü, I know you won't laugh at me," said Lao Tan slowly, "but do you happen to know a middle-aged professor of English, a widower, or divorced?"

I did a quick search through my mind of all the male professors of English I knew. Was anyone single? But why did Lao Tan seek a professor of English? Now that she had given up her American dream, English should become secondary.

"I always wanted to meet a man who could speak English as fluently as his own mother tongue. Since you are an English major, I think you might be able to introduce me to such a man."

Spring was over, the southeastern winds had started to blow, the temperature rose quickly to thirty-five-celsius. In 1981, as a fourth-year English major, I was given a one-week summer job at the city's examination centre, where I met several hundred English teachers and professors from across the city.

"Lao Tan, good news, good news! I think I have found a God-sent, middle-aged English prof for you!"

I had dropped by her apartment in excitement.

"Madam, you are truly one young English professor,'" I was retelling Lao Tan about how I'd met Professor Chen.

"So I told him I hope to be a future professor of English. He said he had only just been promoted to become associate professor, having been a lecturer for twenty-five years, from before the Cultural Revolution."

Lao Tan was listening to me attentively.

"How did you find out he is single?" she asked me anxiously.

"Well, later he offered to walk me to the bus stop. He rides an old bicycle himself. I asked him where he lives, he said on the campus of the Geology College. The college will assign him a new apartment soon, he said, but whether he gets a two-bedroom or three-bedroom depends on his marital status. As a single man, he can only get a two-bedroom. So I figured out he is single." I finished my report, "And he asked me if it's all right for him to come and visit me tomorrow evening. So Lao Tan, I'll bring him over. You can decide whether you want to date him or not after that, all right?"

Ten days after Lao Tan met Professor Chen, I was greeted by them both standing at my doorway, smiling radiantly.

"Hu Nü, we want to invite you over for dinner tonight," Professor Chen said, "you are our *hongniang*, who helped us find each other in an ocean of people."

Hongniang literally means a lady in red, referring to the matchmaker in an old Chinese opera. "Well, it's your karma," I said. I was overjoyed to see them dating.

When I got to Lao tan's apartment, Xiao Jin was already there. There was a large vase of fresh flowers on top of the desk in the corner. Professor Chen poured each of us a small glass of red plum wine. I heard Lao Tan humming in the kitchen. In no time she brought out six dishes. In a sunflower summer dress, she looked more energetic than ever. How amazing! Were they engaged?

"We want to take this opportunity to make an important announcement," Professor Chen stood up and said formally as if he were on a university podium addressing a large crowd. "Professor Chen and Dr Tan are happily married today!" He applauded himself, then made a gesture to invite Lao Tan to join him. "Now, may I kiss my bride?" He started kissing her passionately.

Xiao Jin dropped her jaw, I couldn't respond. Standing up clumsily, we raised our glasses. Then gazing at the newlyweds in each other's arms, I commented, "You are taking us for a rocket ride."

They both laughed heartily. "Yes, yes." Professor Chen picked up my metaphor: "Since we are living in a supersonic era, actually in a space age, we should think about going to the moon for our honeymoon soon, am I right, honey? Ha ha haaa . . ." He laughed loudly and I could see Lao Tan was a little embarrassed. "When he is happy, he is like a kid," she explained.

After dinner when I was in the kitchen helping Lao Tan make tea, she told me the reason they got their marriage certificate today was really for handing in their application for a three-bedroom apartment. "He is crazy about me, it makes me feel twenty years younger. His wide interests in the arts broaden our life immensely; now I feel there is a lot more to live for than just waiting for my son to come out of jail."

"You think you know enough of each other?" I asked.

"It is hard to get into the depth of a person, Hu Nü, you know that. Sometimes it takes a lifetime, sometimes a week, before you think you can trust the person," Lao Tan said tactfully.

From the sitting room, Tchaikovsky was drifting from the two speakers. Professor Chen stepped inside the kitchen. Lao Tan dried her hands on a kitchen towel and joined him. He held her waist, gracefully, the two of them swirled across the sitting room floor as she protested gently. "Not so fast, not so fast."

My father told me at the dinner table that Xiao Jin had fainted in her office. I realized it had been several months since Lao Tan moved away, and I had not seen either of my friends.

I rushed over to Xiao Jin's apartment. She was in bed, propped up with two pillows, reading a book.

"So what happened?" I asked.

She sighed. "My relationship with Lao Tin goes nowhere. His wife is suspicious about him; she comes to work with him on weekends." Xiao Jin sounded tired. She was otherwise a strongly built woman with a rounded bone structure and muscular legs and arms. Her dark complexion and short haircut enhanced her boyishness.

"But why did you faint today? I know how strong you were before you got that infectious love disease." I tried to sound playful.

"Hu Nü, I wish I could still joke with you, but you are right, I got this infectious love disease. It's eating me away physically and emotionally. To tell you the truth, I have been selling my blood regularly." Her last sentence came out from her mouth softly, but it hit me like a bullet.

"What? Selling—-selling blood? Are you crazy?" I yelled at her.

"Now listen, it's for a cause. I want to raise one thousand *yuan* for Lao Tin . . . to help put his daughter in that special school for the disabled. It will help eliminate his guilt as a father who is about to walk out of his marriage. And perhaps his wife will let go of him."

Hearing her talk like this, I wished Lao Tin were there at that moment. I could only wish his love for her was as unconditional as hers was for him.

In China, blood banks bought fresh blood regularly from registered sellers. However, since the Chinese considered blood too precious to lose, selling blood was always considered the last straw in a desperate situation.

"Does Lao Tin know this?" I asked.

"No. I just want to save the amount and put it in his hands, and then ask him to fulfil his commitment."

"Woman, woman," I screamed again, "why are you so heroic that you want to die for love?"

That night I lay on a cool bamboo bed next to Xiao Jin's double bed. Lights were off and the balcony door was open. We could see the sky outside and above, bright and cool.

"Have you heard from Lao Tan after she moved away?" I asked Xiao Jin.

"No, have you? Don't you think it's disappointing that after you introduced her to Professor Chen, we lost a friend? Why don't we go visit her tomorrow, have a reunion?" Xiao Jin suggested.

After a while, she added, "If I were a man, you know what I would do?" I was getting sleepy. "If I were a man, Hu Nü, I would chase you to the edge of the earth, across the Milky Way to the Heavenly Palace, or down the East China Sea to the Dragon's Place if I have to, until you marry me." Xiao Jin was talking away in darkness, I was fighting my sleepiness, struggling to keep up with her wild statements. "But, but since we both are women," she sighed, "we can only let men chase us."

"I see," I was getting too sleepy. "I think I am just going to sleep here . . . on this . . . bamboo bed . . . instead of going home." I heard my own voice fading, and I fell asleep.

The next morning, Xiao Jin and I set off for the Geology College. It was a forty-minute bus ride, followed by a twenty-minute walk on a long unpaved dirt road leading to the college gate. There was only one new residence, and someone on the ground floor directed us to a second-floor unit.

"Lao Tan! Lao Tan! Where are you?" We rushed inside her apartment, calling her name like two schoolgirls looking for their playmate.

As soon as we saw Lao Tan, Xiao Jin and I screamed simultaneously, "What happened to your arm?" She was wearing a large sling across her shoulders to support her right arm. We couldn't even give her a hug.

"I fell off a bicycle and broke my arm two months ago," she said. "What a happy surprise to see you two! Oh, I miss you so much. I miss our divorcees' club."

"So do we, but you are no longer a divorcee, so we decided to come here. Otherwise we wouldn't see you any more," Xiao Jin explained. "Where is the professor?"

"He is out jogging," Lao Tan said. "I don't know why he has so much energy and I have none."

I took a good look at Lao Tan. She had changed. "So how long have you been married?"

"Just a year," she answered, "do you think I have aged?"

I couldn't really tell, but I knew she had changed. It was the anxiety in her eyes that had replaced the peace and tranquility in her previous marble-statue appearance. She was nervous, constantly looking at the door, as if expecting someone.

"How is the happily-married-ever-after?" Xiao Jin demanded.

"I'm not sure it's such a great idea to get remarried at my age and with my personality," Lao Tan said, glancing at the door again with that alert look. "I'm glad he is not here; he is crazy."

"What do you mean?" I thought she had used the word to mean passionate.

"He is mentally ill, that's what I mean. He wants attention all the time. After working for eight hours in the hospital, coming home, I want to rest. But he wants me to listen to him reading poetry, his Byron, his Shelley, his Browning, and the list goes on and on, while I am falling asleep. At midnight, he says let's go to a concert." Lao Tan looked at Xiao Jin and me.

"How can you go to a concert at midnight?" I asked, imagining how difficult it would be to get to the bus stop.

"Right here, his own solo concert." Lao Tan laughed helplessly. "He loves opera, its grandness, its sensational music, from Wagner to Mozart to Puccini, he hums the tunes, plays the tape, and sings in languages you don't understand."

"This is so romantic, isn't it?" Xiao Jin responded with awe. I nodded.

"Yes, but it all depends on the time of the day, and whether you have energy and are in the right mood. I used to enjoy a quiet evening by myself after work, Hu Nü, you know that. But now, riding my bike to work and back, forty-five minutes' each way, then grocery shopping on my way home, then cooking and cleaning up in the evening; after that, I would really appreciate a cup of tea, or read the newspaper for half an hour by myself before going to bed. But I have to sit through his concert or reading while I am nodding off. By the time we finally go to bed, he won't sleep. He laughs or cries like a child. This is simply too much for me." I had never heard Lao Tan complain about her husbands before. I knew in reality Professor Chen had to be be ten times worse than her description of him.

"Hello! Hello, I heard we have guests." A familiar voice came in from outside. Professor Chen, in his fashionable red jogging pants, flew in.

"Has my darling shown you our new residence yet?" He pulled us both up from our seats and started giving us a tour.

"This is my office. This is our entertaining room, we have our concerts and readings every other evening. Our dining room. . . though we haven't used it for formal dinners yet." He was dragging us from room to room, whirling across the floor as if in a waltz. I recalled the dinner the previous year to celebrate their marriage, when Professor Chen and Lao Tan danced. "Not so fast, not so fast," she had protested.

That was the last time that I saw Lao Tan. I came to Canada to pursue my postgraduate studies in September, 1984. Before the Chinese New Year in 1987, I received a letter from Lao Tan's son, who was out of jail by then. He thanked me for sending his mother a Christmas card from Canada. It was kept on the night table beside her bed until the last minute of her life. She died in January 1987, three months after she was diagnosed with liver cancer. Aunty Jin dressed his mother and went to the crematorium with him, Lao Tan's son wrote. Professor Chen apparently was in America as a visiting scholar, when he was informed of his wife's terminal illness. But he didn't want to shorten his one-year term by coming home earlier for her funeral.

Holding the letter in my hand, I cried. It had been a long time since I had cried this way. The loss of Lao Tan hurt too much, the pain penetrated my bones, chilled my blood.

> I cry for you in a way I have never cried before
> my tears are yours, are ours, to flow
> cleansing a pathway beyond the horizon
> the sacrifice we should never have to make
> for the worship of the rising sun

In 1989 after cancelling my flight to China because of the events at Tiananmen Square, I received a letter from Xiao Jin thinking she might travel with me, she had aborted her fetus upon receiving the letter about my planned return trip in June. After waiting for Lao Tin for six years in vain, she married a young man ten years her junior. In 1991, she told me they had a baby boy and she named him *Mengmeng*, "always dreaming of seeing you," she wrote.

Ding-Dong Ringing Hope

It was the first day of the new school year, her last year in the university. Hu Nü tried to clear her mind before entering the campus, but she still couldn't forget the last scene in the courtroom. After a delay of three years, the court had finally arranged for her and her husband to meet. An hour earlier that morning, they were sitting on opposite sides of a table facing each other like two statues; a court clerk, sitting on the third side of the table, read the divorce agreement to them in a dry monotonous voice. When the clerk asked Wen whether he agreed to the divorce, the latter said only if he wouldn't carry any financial obligation. Child support and child custody were considered a burden for a divorced person, if he or she wanted to remarry. The stigma of a previous marriage could easily spoil a new relationship.

Hu Nü believed she could bring up her child on her own; she had done it from the beginning since Wen had been abroad. A clear break seemed priceless to her compared to a future agony of waiting for the monthly fifteen-yuan child support payment or having to chase after it. Hu Nü picked up the pen, scratched out the line about child support which had been prepared by the court, and signed the document. Without any delay, Wen did the same. The court clerk stamped the documents, giving them each a copy. After three years' of endless waiting, their eight-year marriage was dissolved in less than five minutes.

Hu Nü felt quite eager as she walked through the corridor of her department, looking for the right classroom. She was a fourth-year English major in this Teachers' College, admitted into the program in the spring of 1978 as a special student, because at twenty-eight she was five years older than the age limit set by the admission guidelines. The special status required a student to have much higher academic records. The first day she entered this university, she embraced the large poplar at the entrance gate, feeling truly at home and grateful for this learning opportunity finally granted to her.

Three years had passed. She was still one of the best students in the department, but the five-year difference in age had created a noticeable gap between her and other students. Most of them had never had a boyfriend or girlfriend, some looked as if they were going through puberty. And to these students, Hu Nü had had more life than they could ever imagine. Not only was she married, having had a child, she also was going through a lawsuit to get her divorce. Personal experience like hers was viewed as the shameful burden of one's past mistakes. Hu Nü had few friends in her department or in the university; most of the students preferred to socialize with their own age group. Some shunned Hu Nü because they thought it was morally wrong for a wife to divorce her husband.

However, realizing she was finally free from the shackles of an unsuccessful marriage, she felt her steps much lighter. Hu Nü saw a fresh notice on the wall, "Grade 77", with an arrow. Walking in that direction, she stopped suddenly. "Whose voice is this?" she asked herself. The thick powerful male voice sounded like a bronze bell, echoing through the hallway with a pronounced rhythm. Following the voice, Hu Nü came to a large classroom full of students and teachers, listening attentively to a tall, grey-haired Western man. Hu Nü sat down quietly in an empty seat in the back row, afraid to make any noise. She had heard the department was going to hire a new foreign expert this term.

"Tragedy. . . is an imitation of an action of high importance, complete and of some amplitude. . . by means of pity and fear effecting its purgation of these emotions." Hu Nü had never heard anything so profound and philosophical. As she tried to repeat the sentence, she had already lost half of the words, but "purgation of these emotions" stayed in her mind and started to create ripples.

His name was James, and he was a Canadian college professor of English who had come to China to teach English during his year of sabbatical leave. In his early sixties, James looked much older to the Chinese, not only because of his grey hair at the ear lobes, but also because he was a pipe smoker, reminding them of country gentlemen they saw in old movies. His deep echoing voice, which they thought was related to his pipe-smoking, could mesmerize several hundred students in a lecture hall. Hu Nü was totally absorbed by Sophocles' famous tragedy *Oedipus Rex*. The riddle of the Sphinx and the downfall of men as an inevitable outcome struck her deeply, especially when read by James. Later she wrote her first analytical essay, using Aristotle's theory to analyze Sophocles' play. The following week, when the essays were handed back to the class, Hu Nü was surprised to read James's comment, "A distinguished essay" on her paper.

Hu Nü liked to read by herself in the morning, especially while walking on the dirt paths behind the university campus, where vegetable farmers were busy digging, planting or harvesting all year round. Since no other students or teachers would walk that far, Hu Nü felt as if she had a secret place to go to when she wanted to disappear under the vast sky. One morning, as she was turning around at the end of her dirt path, she was surprised to see James standing behind her, his shoulders draped in the golden morning sunshine.

"Good morning, I wonder who this cowgirl is," he joked. There were a few teenage boys and girls walking their cows on the dirt paths.

"Good morning, James. I wish I were as young and as innocent as the cowgirls." Hu Nü answered.

"Do you mean you are no longer young and innocent?" James asked playfully.

"No, I'm thirty-one years old already," Hu Nü stated, "no longer young." In China, thirty-one was considered middle aged.

"Oh, what a big surprise! But I have been there already, only thirty some years ago." James smiled as he took out a small container of tobacco from his traveller's bag across his shoulders.

"And you want to hear more surpriseing things about my life?" Hu Nü asked.

"Yes, especially because the first one didn't work," said James, his hands busy filling the pipe.

"I was married, have had a child, and now I am divorced." Hu Nü finished reporting the three stages of her life, mostly failures, and now she was waiting for James's response.

"Am I still standing on my feet? I'm not knocked over by your surprises yet."

Why was James still joking? Hu Nü wondered. Why wasn't he shocked by her life, if he knew how innocent her classmates were?

"I have heard about all this before, only too many times, from both men and women. Hu Nü, no surprises for me." James paused to light his pipe. Then he continued, "But, to tell you the truth, I am a little surprised to hear from your tone that you are burdened by your own life. And you don't know, in fact, you have more experience than others, and you probably won't make as many mistakes in the future as your classmates might."

"You're so kind," Hu Nü said. It seemed that life experiences weren't such a shameful burden to Canadians.

"Good morning, cowgirl!" James greeted Hu Nü almost every morning in the fields, where fresh morning dew touched her toes. She would look forward to seeing him too, in the fresh morning air. They would exchange a few questions and answers about her life in China and his life in Canada. Hu Nü discovered that James was once a journalist, a correspondent in Paris for Canada's national newspaper, the *Globe and Mail*. He was also an active member in the teachers' union in Toronto. Having taught English for twenty-some years to college students, he was disappointed to see the college now undergoing a fundamental change to become a factory. "By the time I go back to Canada, there will be no English Department in my college, it will be called Communications Department. English will be treated simply as a tool to serve the technical world. So if I want to teach English and English literature in the future, I will have to come to China," James said, "and look for cowboys and cowgirls."

"Good morning, cowboy, you're early today." Hu Nü was surprised to see James walking at the edge of the fields before she had got there. The weather had turned cold, narrow dirt paths were covered with a thin layer of frost in the morning. Few cowboys and cowgirls would get up that early to walk their cows; in the fields there were only rows of cabbages left to be harvested; later only wheat would stay in the fields throughout the winter. James wore a down-filled jacket and a scarf around his neck. Hu Nü saw his pipe glowing, she knew he had been there for quite some time.

"I have come here to say goodbye to you, so when you hear it in class today, you won't be too surprised," James said emotionally.

"Why, the term hasn't ended yet," Hu Nü argued.

"Hu Nü, you know before I came here I had some problems with my college at home. Some people wanted to close the English Department and I was the chair of the Department. Now during my sabbatical leave, not only have they done it, they have also replaced me with someone else as the chair of the new Communications Department. If I don't go back to fight this now, the college will never be the same."

Hu Nü tried to follow the Canadian scenario with her Chinese imagination. She thought closing an English Department in an English-speaking country would be like closing the Chinese Department in her university. It sounded unbelievable. "How are you going to fight it? Those who dared to do this must have obtained support from top authorities."

"They did, indeed. But there are also many teachers and students on my side. We're going to get organized and send petitions to the province and collect signatures from other supporters," James said hopefully. "Canada is a democratic country."

Suddenly a gush of wind blew James's white hair, he brushed it aside with his hand, and tucked it behind his ears. Holding his pipe tightly, he sucked a few times as if to draw strength. He looked at her staring at him.

"If a cowgirl wants to become a scholar, where does she go?" Hu Nü asked James a question that had been on her mind for several weeks.

"That's a good question," James said, thinking aloud. "Where would a cowgirl go if she wants to become a scholar? Honestly, I don't know." He looked at Hu Nü, and shook his head.

"Can she go to Canada, for instance, to pursue her master's

degree?" Hu Nü asked.

"Well, you understand, first of all, it is very difficult, I mean graduate school in Canada. Not to mention it is *extremely* expensive for foreign students." "What about a scholarship? or working?" she asked. She had heard in the old days this was how overseas Chinese students supported themselves.

"First, a scholarship is very difficult to get for anyone, not to mention that in most cases international students are not even eligible, meaning they are not qualified to apply. I am not sure international students are allowed to work outside of campus," James said.

"But can we find a way, if the cowgirl is determined to pursue her goal," Hu Nü asked firmly. "Is there a way?"

"In that case, I promise I will try to find out," James said firmly.

A week later, James flew back to Canada to fight his fight.

Half a year later, in the spring of 1982, Hu Nü graduated from her university. Two years had passed since James returned to Canada. Near the end of 1983, Hu Nü received a Christmas card from Canada addressed "to the determined cowgirl in Wuhan." The message said, "There is hope," and it was signed "Ding Dong" with a graphic image of a bell beside it.

A View from the CN Tower

On an early evening of September 1984, a small crowd gathered on the platform of Wuchang Railway Station. Cool fluorescent lights flooded down from the ceilings, imbuing the platform with a misty blue atmosphere. A dark, starry sky loomed behind the half open platform.

The crowd was there to see me off to Beijing, where I would take a flight to Canada the next day.

I was thirty-four years old, an assistant professor at a local university, a mother of a nine-year-old child, and a newly-wed. On the platform stood my parents, my three sisters and two

brothers-in-law, my girlfriends, and my new spouse. Although I had left home many times before, my departure for Canada came at a time when everything else in my life seemed to indicate that I was finally settling down. I had just married an environmental engineer and moved to a three-bedroom apartment near the beautiful East Lake. While my close friends were puzzled by what was happening lately in my life, I knew I couldn't just settle down yet. I heard my fate calling me from a distant unknown land.

The clock above the platform was ticking away. Through the loud speaker came the music of a march, reminding the travellers of their journeys ahead. My mind was preoccupied with the distance that was about to pull me away from my family on the platform.

Xiao Jin was leaning on a platform pillar by herself, away from the crowd. I guessed how she felt; I went up to her. Tears ran down her cheeks; giving a twisted smile, she said, "I'm happy for you, Hu Nü, I have always known that you belonged to a better world." I was disappointed Lao Tan had not come, perhaps she hadn't received my letter in time. Now with the two of us remarried, Xiao Jin was the only person left in a limbo, between a divorce and a bad marriage. Leaving Xiao Jin was as hard as leaving the rest of my family.

Suddenly, my daughter Zen dashed at me from the crowd as if she had just realized that her mother was leaving. In the previous week, I had tried to explain to her why I had to go to Canada and the impending changes in her life and mine. But the child that she was, she didn't want to deal with what was coming until the last minute.

"Mom, when are you coming back?" Zen raised her voice above the noise on the platform, pulling at my hands for an answer. "In a year," I said softly, hoping to make it sound shorter.

"How many days in a year?" she asked innocently. "Three hundred and sixty-five," I answered helplessly. "But time goes fast," I added cheerfully, "be a good girl, respect your new dad, and don't forget to write to me." I brushed away my tears with the back of my hand, so they wouldn't fall on her face. Picking her up from the ground and hugging her tightly to my chest, I wished I didn't have to leave her behind with someone who was almost a stranger.

James and my other sponsor in Canada knew I had a nine-year-old child, but since it was very difficult for them to raise money for me to study in Canada, I understood that it was impossible for me to bring my daughter along. Meanwhile I had a difficult time getting my passport. A friend from the university's Party Committee told me that a divorcee's application for a passport would be automatically rejected. "Because, because you see, as a divorcee, you are not happy, otherwise you wouldn't be divorced. So if you are not happy in China, you probably won't come back after finishing your studies."

"Good logic," I replied, "so you are telling me that I won't get my passport."

"But a divorcee with a child, you see, has a better chance than a divorcee without a child," my friend smiled. "Your daughter will be a hostage left at home, get it?" She blinked her eyes, waiting for me to comprehend the situation. "Still more, it would speed up the whole passport process if you considered getting remarried."

"What? Get remarried?" I burst out. Shocked by my response, she quickly put her hand on my mouth.

"What makes you think I want to get remarried when my life is undergoing a major change?" My words came through her muffling fingers.

"Don't get upset, I am only giving you an insiders' advice, you don't have to take it."

Bing, another girlfriend, had a brother who had got divorced a few months earlier and wanted to find a girlfriend in Wuhan. If the relationship worked, meaning if he were remarried to someone in Wuhan, he could ask to be transferred to the big city from a smaller town in Hunan province. "But, you know very well that I'm on my way to Canada to study for one or two years. I won't be able to settle down with anyone before I have accomplished my own goal," I told Bing.

"Why not just meet my brother first, if you like him, then you can take it from there," Bing suggested. "And I really think you will like him, he likes literature and writes poetry. You two will make a good couple. But that's just my opinion. Whatever happens, you're my friend first. If you do become my sister-in-law, so much the better. If not, let's leave him out of our relationship."

So I agreed to meet her brother for tea.

The day after I had tea with Bing's brother Dawei, I was surprised to find him standing outside my classroom at the university. "I hope you didn't ask anyone for me," I whispered to him as harshly as I could. I simply didn't want people to gossip about me.

"Of course not," he said with a mischievous smile, "but I want to see as much of you as I can while I am in Wuhan." He looked into my eyes, making me blush.

"Why, why is it so urgent?" I was uncomfortable with his directness. Usually, it took at least a few meetings before a man said such things to a woman.

Stretching his hands out, he explained, "You see, neither of us is eighteen years old, and we both are very busy. I don't think we want to waste time on courting rituals and that kind of nonsense, do you?"

"Courting rituals don't have to be nonsense. Are you joking?" I tried to sound serious. I really wanted to tell him that I disagreed with him. The courting rituals of my first marriage were simplified because Wen had to go to Zambia shortly after we met. In fact, there was no courting at all, only a consensus expected from me. And three years later, after he came back from Zambia, we had a divorce. Sometimes I thought the reason we had a divorce was really because we didn't know each other. I would not want to sacrifice the courting rituals this time.

Dawei was about five feet six, not a tall man but a man of action. He sped up the development of our relationship by waiting for me everyday after work, asking me to let him meet my family as soon as it could be arranged, and having his whole family meet me as his girl-friend. After two weeks, which was the duration of his vacation, Dawei asked me to marry him. He promised me that he would raise my daughter as his own, take care of my family, and wait for my return loyally while I went to Canada to pursue my dream.

I tried to accept the mountainous windfall of love, passion, and promises from him. Meanwhile letters from Canada were arriving every week, bringing my dream closer. My final admission to a graduate school, a scholarship offer from an education foundation, a photocopy of a personal check made in my name, and visa application forms from the Canadian Embassy in Beijing—all of a sudden, my dream of going to an English-speaking country to study became a reality but for the fact that I needed a document from the Chinese government—my passport.

"But where is my passport?" I got up everyday with the same question and went to bed without an answer. I started to debate with myself. Should I marry Dawei? That would give the government two reliable hostages—a husband and a child—to whom, as it was believed, I would return upon finishing my studies abroad. But why should I rush into another marriage without the rituals of courtship, even though this time I was the one going abroad?

It was the end of May 1984, there was still no news of my passport from the local government security bureau. I went to the bureau several times and heard the same explanation, "Your university Party committee hasn't signed your release paper yet." Back at the university, I was told my documents had been sent to the local bureau a long time ago.

I gave myself the second week of June as the deadline upon which to decide whether I should marry Dawei and change my marriage status in the application form for a passport. A newly-wed certainly would be seen as a happier person than a divorcee. Maybe the Party committee would let me go to Canada in September after I was remarried.

Two more weeks passed and there was no news of my passport. I decided to draw my lot. I knew there would not be any rational decision in this case, so I should simply obey my fate.

Drawing my lot was a sacred ritual that I had developed but seldom used except for making impossibly difficult decisions. It can only be done under extreme pressure, such as at a few minutes before the clock struck midnight, when a decision had to be made. So on the last night before the deadline expired, I waited until everyone in the family was sound asleep and the apartment dead quiet.

I cleansed my thoughts and calmed myself down before starting this sacred ritual of testing my fate.

I cut a piece of paper into two identical halves and wrote on one piece, "Do not get married," and on the other, "Get married and go to Canada to study." I folded up the two strips of paper in exactly the same way. "I can draw my lot only once," I told myself, "and I shall obey the decision unconditionally." Closing my eyes and taking a deep breath, I shook up the two pieces of paper in the cavity of my closed palms and then threw them on the desk.

"God of Destination and Fate, tell me what to do," I prayed with my eyes closed, "I'll obey your decision." My right hand searched the surface of the desk until it touched a piece of paper. Picking it up solemnly and opening my eyes, I became calm again. Everything was clarified now as I carefully unfolded the paper: "Get married and go to Canada to study." My fate was speaking to me! I was not surprised by the decision. Intuitively, I had always known that I was on my way to Canada.

My husband was standing beside me on the platform. He was to come to Beijing to see me off at the airport. While the loudspeaker was announcing the last three minutes before the train's scheduled departure, I went over to say goodbye to my parents. Mother's eyes were red but there was a faint smile on her face; Father had his hands on Zen's shoulders. I hugged Mother for a long minute. "Take care, Mama." Then I hugged my daughter Zen one more time. "Come back soon, Mom," she urged me. I felt a need to hug Father, but stopped halfway. How could I embarrass him in public! Chinese men were not supposed to show their emotions. I couldn't hug him. Instead, I stretched out both hands, he shook them with his. Suddenly the whistle was blowing and the loudspeakers played the march at the highest volume and my husband pulled me onto the train.

Standing behind the closed door of the train compartment, watching everyone on the platform receding as the clanking wheels picked up speed, I finally believed the story of my destination. After I had obtained my visa from the Canadian Embassy in Beijing and knew for sure that I was on my way to Canada, Mother told me that when I was one year old my paternal grandma had predicted that I would be bound for a distant land.

The evening of September 23, 1984 I landed at Toronto's Pearson International Airport. After a sixteen-hour-flight, I was exhausted. Following the crowd to the luggage area on the ground level, I saw many anxious faces behind the glass partition between the luggage area and the waiting room. Until then my awareness of human skin colour had been limited to Chinese homogeneity, with a few white American and Canadian English teachers as the exceptions; all of a sudden, everything in front of me was dazzlingly different.

I started searching for the only face I knew in this vast country while my eyes paused over every variation in skin pigmentation, hair colour and style, and body build. Suddenly, a tall, strong man with grey hair appeared behind the glass partition. His silver wire-framed glasses were sitting on his big tall nose, and a pipe was sticking out from the corner of his mouth. He was wearing a dark red Chinese padded jacket with eight butterfly buttons at the front. His hand was waving at me up and down behind the glass.

"James! James!" I ran. My hand reached out to his behind the glass wall.

By the time I came out to the waiting room, pulling my luggage behind me, James was waiting for me at the exit. From behind his back, he pulled out a single red rose. Then, stretching out his long arms around my shoulders, he hugged me tightly. "Finally, you're here. Hu Nü, welcome to Canada," he whispered the words into my ears.

"Yes, finally, James, I can't believe it. Thank you for bringing me to Canada," I said.

"My pleasure, my pleasure. Now let's go somewhere to celebrate."

Outside, the ground was covered with a thin layer of frost; the air was chilly. I couldn't stop shivering while waiting for James to bring his car from the garage. My memory was still occupied with the fresh autumn blossoms at Beijing Airport. It was hard to believe that sixteen hours later I was standing on the soil of a cold northern country.

We drove towards downtown Toronto. Lights from the oncoming traffic on the other side of the highway stung my eyes. My ears were drumming like engines and I was still shivering. James was humming as he drove. From time to time, he turned his head towards me with a big smile.

It was a long ride, but finally he stopped and parked the car alongside a street. Street lights cast long shadows on the quiet sidewalks. "What time is it?" I asked. "Why aren't there any people on the street?"

"Ha ha ha, you think this is China, where you see people everywhere. We only have a small population in Canada. And now, never mind other people, we're going up to the highest building in the world to celebrate your arrival." James picked up my hand as cheerfully as a child.

The elevator took us straight up to the dining floor of the CN Tower. A well-dressed waiter politely greeted us and led us to seats beside a glass window that overlooked thousands of tiny lights a long distance below, comprising the city of Toronto. James ordered two drinks right away. After lighting a tealight candle inside a glass bowl, the waiter left quietly.

"At last," James said, squinting. "Are we in a dream?"

I let out a sigh. "So it seems."

I knew, finally, that I was in the mysterious land that I was born to embrace.

Author's Note

Memories of the past are dusty heirlooms packed away in the attic, valuable maybe, but nearly forgotten. The stories in this book have been left in such a condition for a long time. I started my first draft in 1993 with a different title, "My Mother and Her Daughters"; then the writing found its own direction, moving gradually away from Mother's experience to that of the daughters'. Hence, the final title.

Creative memoir is a form of life writing. All the characters and events in the book came from real life experiences and from the dusty attic of my memories. In the process of recreating the past, I made choices. The names of the characters, details of the events, different perspectives of the narrative, and various opinions are among the choices I have made, for which I am solely responsible.

At different stages of writing and editing this manuscript, I have received generous grants from the Toronto Arts Council, the Canada Council, and the Ontario Arts Council. I want to thank the Councils for treasuring these past experiences.

Finally, I wish to thank my publisher, Nurjehan Aziz, who chose the manuscript, and M G Vassanji, who worked tirelessly to polish the piece. My heartfelt gratitude also goes to my dearest friend Virginia Rock, for reading the text, to Peng Ma for his illustrations, which have added a visual perspective to enrich the book, and to Avianna Chao for helping to design the cover.

Lien Chao
November 2001